Eugénie Sellers Strong

Portrait of an Archaeologist

Eugénie Sellers Strong

Portrait of an Archaeologist

Stephen L. Dyson

Duckworth

First published in 2004 by
Gerald Duckworth and Co. Ltd.
90-93 Cowcross Street
London EC1M 6BF
Tel. 020 7490 7300
Fax 020 7490 0080
email: inquiries@duckworth-publishers.co.uk
www.ducknet.co.uk

A CIP catalogue record for this book is available
from the British Library

ISBN 0 7156 3219 1

Typeset by E-Type, Liverpool
Printed in Great Britain by
CPD Ltd, Wales

for Pauline

Contents

List of Illustrations

Acknowledgements

This biography has been brought to completion with the kind help of many people. I owe a special debt to Kate Perry, archivist at Girton College, and to her colleagues. Not only have they organized the massive Strong holdings in a very research-friendly manner, but they were ever helpful in providing assistance, answering questions and creating an atmosphere in which it was pleasant to work. Without their support, and especially that of Kate Perry, this project would have been impossible.

I also owe a great deal to colleagues at the British School at Rome. Successive directors, and especially Richard Hodges and Andrew Wallace-Hadrill, took a great interest in my research and aided my work in every way. Amanda Claridge, then Assistant Director of the British School, was one of the first to impress on me the importance of the Strong material in their possession. Valerie Scott, the BSR librarian, provided me with efficient access to the Strong papers at times when that was not always easy.

Other archives and their staffs were also extremely helpful. Thanks are owed to the Harvard-I Tatti archives, to that of the Devonshire Collection at Chatsworth House, to Colby College special collections, to the Beinecke Library at Yale University, and the Houghton Library of Harvard University. Professor Ian Begg of Trent University generously shared with me information related to the friendship of Gilbert Bagnani and Eugénie Strong. Librarians at the American Academy in Rome and Lockwood Library of the University at Buffalo provided a range of bibliographical assistance.

Research time for this project was made possible by a sabbatical from the University at Buffalo. During my residence in Cambridge, I enjoyed the privileges of a fellowship at the MacDonald Archaeological Institute and residence at Churchill College. Special thanks are owed to Professor Colin Renfrew, director of the MacDonald Archaeological Institute. I have also benefited from conversations with a number of colleagues about my research. I have especially enjoyed discussing Eugénie Strong with Mary Beard, though I am sure that she will disagree with much that I say. Eleanor Birne of Duckworth has not only been an excellent editor but also a good guide through what is for me a new publishing world.

My wife Pauline has helped me in many ways to complete this biography. I dedicate the book to her.

Introduction

I have often been asked why I chose to write a biography of Eugénie Sellers Strong. After all, I am a middle-aged American male writing about a late-Victorian woman with whose social, political and religious views I am not always in sympathy. Perhaps that in itself is part of the challenge. When one comes to admire someone (as I have Eugénie Strong), one is forced to overcome differences of background and viewpoint to understand that person and her world. Eugénie Strong was a complex, intelligent and cultivated individual. She set a brave course for herself as a woman seeking a scholarly career in late nineteenth-century Britain. Empathy should be a quality in a good historian, although it should not overwhelm critical judgment. I have tried to portray Eugénie Strong's limitations as well as her strengths.

A biography of Strong can be justified in terms of women's history, cultural history, religious history and the history of classical scholarship, especially of classical archaeology. Few women of her era exercised her freedom, received her education, achieved her quality of scholarship and held such important and honoured places in her profession. What she accomplished and what she failed to accomplish say much about the place of women in late nineteenth- and early twentieth-century European society.

Eugénie Strong was an intellectual in close contact with the changing literary and artistic movements of both England and the Continent. She was enormously well read and was involved with art, theatre and music throughout her life. Friendships with Edward Burne-Jones, Frederic Leighton, Mrs Pat Campbell, Maurice Baring and Edmund Gosse suggest the range of her non-academic associations. Her cultural experience stretched from the world of the Pre-Raphaelites to that of the Futurists. While she had a strong respect for the great European artistic and literary traditions, she remained into old age open to the ideas of the young.

Religion was central to Eugénie Strong for the last twenty-five years of her life. She had been raised a Catholic, had turned away from the Church in early adulthood, yet in 1917 returned to the fold. She was a person of deep faith who appreciated the history and cultural traditions of the Catholic Church. Her circle of friends included a number of cultivated clerics, among them two important cardinals. She was also a Catholic scholar, lecturing on subjects such as religious writings from early Christianity, St Francis and the art of the baroque. Her life in the Church says a great deal about her faith but also about the appeal that the early twentieth-century Catholic Church had for the educated and the cultured.

First and foremost, Eugénie Strong was a classical archaeologist. Her long life in the profession stretched from the archaeological looters in the tradition of Lord Elgin to the nationalistic archaeologists of Fascist Italy. As a young classical archaeologist she blended two distinct intellectual traditions – those of nineteenth-century Germany and Britain – and won the respect of the best classical archaeologists in Britain, France, Italy and Germany. She made powerful arguments for the importance of Roman art in an era when it was little appreciated in the English-speaking world, and wrote scholarly works that still command respect. Through her publications, and especially through her extensive programme of lectures, she brought the latest archaeological discoveries to a wide lay audience.

For the scholarly biographer one of the most appealing aspects of writing Eugénie's life is the archive of her papers that is preserved in some twenty-eight boxes at Girton College, Cambridge, and the second major collection of her papers at the British School at Rome. For much of her adult life Eugénie Strong was compulsive in her practice of saving autobiographical documents. Letters, appointment books, invitations are all there. Since her life was so long and her circle of friends and acquaintances so wide, these are documents not only of a life, but also of an age. Eugénie talked regularly about publishing her autobiography. Friends mention the preparation of her memoirs as early as 1919 when she was less than sixty, and she made reference to the project up to the time of her death. Unfortunately she produced only a few scattered, if illuminating, fragments.

It is appropriate that Eugénie Strong receive a full biography in the Victorian life, letters and times tradition. Her life spanned a long, fascinating and tragic period in European history. She was born in the golden age of Queen Victoria in a Europe very much at peace. She died at the moment when the titanic struggle of World War II was reaching its height, with some of the most dramatic scenes happening close to her Roman door. Her background and personality brought her into contact with some of the most cultivated and interesting people of each age. Much of her world has now become unfamiliar and the characters on the stage, however important in their day, unfamiliar to contemporary readers; backgrounds and biographies are necessary.

A short biography of Eugénie Strong was published just after World War II.[1] The author was Gladys Scott Thomson, a private historian who wrote on seventeenth- and eighteenth-century England. It is a decent work written by an author who had known Strong in her later years, had access to her papers, and could consult people who had known her. Thompson herself claimed modest goals. She aimed to set out the basic facts and not write a reflective biography or a Victorian 'Life and Letters'. The work was commissioned by Eugénie's sister, Charlotte Leigh Smith, and was in part an effort to correct the picture of Strong as an elderly Fascist sympathizer who elected to stay in Italy during the war. There is a sanitized quality to the work, in which both erotics and political controversy are hidden. It does not capture the charm and complexity of the woman or the significance of her scholarly accomplishments. In the words of one reviewer:

> Yet just as the identity of Justinian's Empress Theodora impinges vividly upon those who see the highly conventionalized Byzantine mosaic, which is her only remaining portrait, so through Miss Scott Thompson's accurate, non-committal piecing together of events and letters and publications, there emerges a character with all the idiosyncracy, the magnificence, the over life-size quality, which the talk and reminiscences of two generations recognized in Mrs Strong.[2]

Ironically, just as the Scott Thomson biography appeared, the more negative view of Eugénie Strong that is still dominant in British classical academia was emerging. One need only ask any former member of the

British School at Rome about her, and one hears about the Mussolini sympathizer, about her ghost haunting the library, and about the violent feud that she had with the former director Thomas Ashby and his wife. Even female scholars buy into a legend that has, ironically, served to keep women marginalized in the academic power structure. Any biography of self-confident, productive women like Eugénie Strong must also be an exploration of the academic forces that conspire to 'keep them in their place'.

Biographical interest in women of Strong's pioneering generation has increased in recent years. In particular, two figures with close associations with Strong, her mentor Jane Harrison and her protégée Gertrude Bell, have received scholarly attention. Harrison has been the subject of two biographies, one of which explores imaginatively, if not always judiciously, the relationship between her and Strong,[3] and Bell has captured recent attention because of the adventurous quality of her life and travels in the Near East. Two recent biographies have chronicled her life, but have not given accurate emphasis to the role that Eugénie Sellers Strong played as a shaping force and role model.[4] To a lesser degree some of the same issues relating to the accomplishments and limited options of a female academic can be raised with another younger friend of Eugénie Strong, the British medieval historian Eileen Power.[5]

Non-academic females of her generation have also attracted increased biographical attention. Two women who played key roles in Eugénie's formative years, Barbara Leigh Smith Bodichon and Mrs Humphry Ward, have been the object of recent studies.[6] So have such diverse friends as Ottoline Morrell, Mary Costelloe Berenson and Mrs Pat Campbell.[7]

To write about Eugénie Strong with sympathy and understanding, an author must deal with gender history, and must have at least a passing acquaintance with topics as diverse as the Pre-Raphaelites, Victorian country-house life, the Dreyfus Affair, and Mussolini's urban initiatives. Eugénie Strong's extraordinary gift for friendship means becoming acquainted with a great range of figures, some still known, others largely forgotten. I am a classical archaeologist and a historian of my discipline. Eugénie Strong's scholarly world is familiar to me. Understanding much of the rest has been a process of self-education with all the limitations that involves. I hope that I have been able to provide a reasonable picture of an extraordinary person and the complicated and exciting eras in which she lived.

1

A Victorian Youth

Eugénie Sellers was born in the heart of London, 'within sound of Bow Bells' as she put it, on 25 March 1860.[1] While across the Atlantic dramatic events were leading slowly and inevitably to the most tragic conflict in American history, Europe was enjoying the peace that had lasted since the defeat of Napoleon forty-five years before. England was poised at the pinnacle of the Victorian era; the vigorous jingoist Lord Palmerston was prime minister and the classicist William Gladstone served as chancellor of the exchequer. In France, Napoleon III was at the height of his glory, and he and his beautiful wife Eugénie, whose name the young girl received, presided over a brilliant court.[2] Both Germany and Italy were, to paraphrase Bismarck, not yet nations but just geographical entities, although in both the process of nation building was well under way. The London *Times* of the Monday after Eugénie's birth highlighted budgetary problems in India, Queen Victoria's recent drawing-room reception and Gladstone's fiscal policy.

Eugénie Sellers was born into a cosmopolitan if rather rootless family. Of her parents she said very little. That silence was strange and perhaps significant, for she fully documented most other aspects of her life. Her father, Frederick William Sellers, was of Yorkshire Quaker lineage. He was a wine merchant, a profession that provided him with opportunities to travel on the Continent. He had many contacts in the Mediterranean and possibly more of a past life than either he or his daughter were willing to discuss in that Victorian milieu. For one thing, it seems William had been married at least once before he met Eugénie's mother. The register of the British chaplain at Oporto in Portugal records the 1851 marriage of a Frederick Sellers to an Anne Child, but also lists an earlier marriage in 1841 between Frederick William Sellers and an Ann Wilcock.[3]

Her mother Anna Oates remains a mysterious character as Eugénie said almost nothing about her in later life. She was the daughter of Charles Oates, of the Oates family of Messina, and had links through them with the major British wine-producing families of Sicily. Through that oenological connection Frederick Sellers must have come to know her. An Oates was vice-consul in Sicily in 1848, and several members of the family were killed in the disastrous Messina earthquake of 1908.[4]

Anna Sellers had a French mother. Her maternal great-grandfather was the Baron du Cluzeau, who owned the Chateau de Cleran in the Perigord region of south-west France.[5] Eugénie saved a picture of that ancestral chateau in her personal postcard collection, and while she talked little about the English side of her family, she was proud of her French ancestors, whose lineage could be traced back to the fifteenth century. They had been strongly anti-revolutionary, a tradition that appealed to the conservative Roman Catholic that Eugénie became in her later years. She spent part of her childhood in the family home in the Dordogne, where she became fluent in French, and remained a Francophile throughout her life.

Eugénie's mother insisted that she be baptized in the baroque church of St Roch near the Tuileries in Paris, and as a child she attended both Anglican and Catholic services. Her most vivid memory of the former was a flirtation with one of the choirboys, and in the end it would be the Catholic side of her spiritual upbringing that would triumph. She renewed her Roman Catholic identity in middle age, and Catholicism became a major, sustaining force in her life.

Eugénie's was a Victorian childhood with all the limitations that implies. In later life she reflected on those early years: 'My earliest childhood was passed in London; England holds my heart's allegiance. Yet my childhood there was drab and cramped … Victorian England, for all its cult of domesticity and large families, understood little of childhood, its strained sensitiveness and obscure feelings, its need for outlet.'[6] Her childhood anxieties were increased by a lack of siblings. A younger sister Charlotte, known affectionately as Charlie, was born eight years after Eugénie. While the two became very close as adults, the difference in their ages did little to break Eugénie's sense of isolation. Years later, she remembered her early childhood sadly: 'My English childhood was solitary; I had no companions of my own age, no outside activities to divert the growth of morbid sensibility. Dualism of parental influence intensified this.' She later articulated the psychological complexity of her situation: 'Passionate love for my parents was, not unnaturally in so confined a milieu, racked with jealousy and fear that they loved one another more than they loved me; at times I would even hate them alternately in my grasping claims upon one or the other. Undoubtedly I afforded apt illustration to the as yet undreamed Freudian theories.'[7] Her tensions and anxieties must have been markedly increased by the death of her mother just before puberty. It is not surprising that she later read with understanding and appreciation that classic of Victorian filial-parental conflict, Edmund Gosse's *Father and Son*.[8]

While London was her principal home in early years, the family travelled extensively on the Continent. Frederick Sellers clearly had the financial means to support such a peripatetic lifestyle. He was a restless soul, one of many contemporaries who wandered Europe in search of identity. Sometimes he took off on his own, leaving Eugénie and her mother lonely and neglected. (It was perhaps appropriate that the Sellers family settled for one extended period in the Spanish city of Valladolid, the home of Don Quixote.) It was an era when living on the Continent was still inexpensive. At the same time, the introduction of the railway and the growth of a middle-class tourist infrastructure had made travel more rapid and convenient, and except for the relatively brief period of the Franco-Prussian War, the final conflicts leading up to Italian unification and some internal conflicts in Spain, Europe was at peace.

Despite the paternal wanderlust, her parents provided Eugénie with a good, if somewhat unconventional, education. Her schooling started at Valladolid, a city of many historical associations and graced with an exuberant baroque architecture, which provided her first exposure to the style that she would later learn to love so much in Rome. She retained warm memories of those Spanish years. 'In Spain, my childhood expanded in colour and light and happiness,' she recalled.[9] She fondly remembered her early schooling under a Jesuit father, who first interested her in Roman history. Another Spanish memory was of her father talking religion with the

Jesuit rectors of her school while she played ball with the boys in the school courtyard. In spite of this early positive exposure to Spain, the culture of the peninsula influenced her less than that of the other major European countries. Even her Catholicism was shaped much more by Italian, French and English traditions than by the beliefs and practices of the Spanish saints.

By the 1870s Europe had become more unsettled. The glitter of the Second Empire of Napoleon III ended with the defeat of the French army at the battle of Sedan. The Emperor and his family fled to England. The uprising of the Commune in Paris and its brutal repression highlighted the deep social and economic tensions in French society. However, Eugénie Sellers' Dordogne, with its charming countryside and medieval monuments, was little touched by those events.

Frederick Sellers, much influenced by the pro-Teutonic writings of Thomas Carlyle, became a great admirer of Germany and its culture and often took his family there. It was still the Germany of beautiful old villages and handsome historical cities with the unspoiled landscapes of the Rhine valley, the Black Forest and the mountains. Germany was the intellectual and cultural leader of Europe, its universities, libraries and museums generally regarded as the world's best. At the same time the new, modern, Bismarckian Germany was emerging, distinguished for its science, industry and, increasingly, its military prowess.

Eugénie's family travels extended to Italy, the place that was to be the centre of so much of her life. They were drawn partly by family ties, but also by the art and culture. Italy in the 1870s was a land in transition. When Eugénie was ten, the armies of the Italian state stormed into Rome, unifying the peninsula and driving Pope Pius IX into self-imposed Vatican exile. The Italian aristocracy, and especially that of Rome, became for three generations divided into two worlds, one the clerical 'blacks' and the other the secular 'whites', between whom there was only limited, highly ritualized, contact.[10]

In 1877, just before his death, Frederick Sellers took Eugénie away from her convent school in France for an extended tour of Italy and Greece. It was an impressionable time in her life, and she always deeply appreciated the fact that 'between the ages of 16 to 18 I was taken to see the most beautiful things in Italy and Greece'.[11] Perhaps Frederick sensed that his end was near, and wanted to impress his ideas and values on his brilliant elder daughter. Many years later Eugénie recalled appreciatively the impact of her father's deeply felt, if rather traditional, aesthetic values: 'My father, who when taking me travelling when quite a girl in days when Ruskin's "Mornings in Florence" were beginning to be circulated in cheap fashion for the edification of old ladies bade me be faithful to the Caracci's and Guido Reni. I remember our standing before the great "Entombment" in Bologna as he spoke.'[12] Indeed John Ruskin's blend of moral and artistic rhetoric never appealed to her. She later rebuked her friend the art critic D. S. MacColl: 'You spoke of Ruskin knowing what was "imaginatively clean and unclean". Are you so sure? I never think it particularly "clean" to have recourse to violins in place of criticism and to throw people into a terror as he did and then force them to accept his views.'[13]

This last trip with her father extended into southern Italy, Sicily and even Greece, regions of the Mediterranean not then normally visited by British tourists. She remembered the journey through Calabria, one of the most isolated and unchanged parts of Italy, and the little boat that took them from the mainland to Sicily, where they stopped in the city of Messina to visit members of her mother's family. The earliest surviving photograph of Eugénie dates from this visit and shows her as an attractive young woman dressed as a southern Italian peasant for a costume ball (plate 2). They then moved on to visit the archaeological sites. Frederick Sellers knew Sicily well from his years as a wine merchant and had a network of contacts among the Anglo-Italian families of the island who provided hospitality in a land with few amenities for tourists. Her father must have been both an informed and an inspiring guide. Years later she remarked that her interest in archaeology had been born during these travels.

During these archaeological explorations she met her first famous archaeological personality, the Frenchman François Lenormont, one of the founders of Greek archaeology in southern Italy. He taught at the Sorbonne and wrote popular books on the subject. A controversial figure in academic circles, he was even accused of forging antiquities.[14] However, his research among the ruins of a still primitive and isolated southern Italy, exploration that contributed to his early death, helped establish the archaeology of Magna Graecia as a serious research field.

Eugénie's pre-university education was totally Continental. It had started with the Jesuits at Valladolid, then, in 1871 after the early death of her mother, she became a day student of the sisters of St Paul at Dourdan in France.[15] Dourdan was then a small town some forty kilometres outside Paris whose major attraction was a ruined thirteenth-century castle. The rigorous regime of a French convent education must have been a difficult experience for someone as independent and self-confident as Eugénie. However, she found many experiences that were appealing in the calm life of the cloister and even claimed that she had considered the religious life. The programme of study was, however, very different from that pursued by English boys or girls with university aspirations. Greek and Latin in particular did not play the central role that they did in British schools. As a result, Eugénie found herself poorly prepared to compete in the conservative, public-school shaped, classical curriculum of Victorian Cambridge.[16]

Independence, even isolation, had characterized Eugénie Sellers' youth. For eight years she had been an only child. Unlike many only children she does not appear to have had close bonds of affection with her parents, and talked little about them in later life. Even their ages and causes of death are unknown. This is strange for the Victorian age, when the memory of deceased parents was carefully cultivated. Her sense of isolation was compounded by the apparent lack of any close family besides her sister.[17] She was left with adequate financial resources to provide her with a university education, but not enough to escape earning her way in the world. The complex experience of these maturing years created the self-sufficient person that Eugénie became.

The nineteen-year-old Eugénie Sellers who matriculated at Cambridge in 1879 was a person of independence and intellect; she had also grown into a woman of rare beauty. Shortly after her death, the art critic D. S. MacColl, one of the few surviving friends who had known the young Eugénie Sellers, wrote to *The Times*:

Your very full obituary notice of Eugénie Strong omits one thing – her beauty. Few now survive from the eighties and nineties who knew it in its splendid prime. Miss Jane Harrison, inviting me to meet her, wrote, 'I think her the most beautiful woman in London', and the claim was not extravagant. The daughter of a Scottish father and French mother had rare passionate force and the beauty could be formidable as well as gracious when the blue eyes blazed and thunder gathered on the brow. I think of her at such moments as a superb Bellona of the Roman art she did so much to elucidate and praise.[18]

Ludwig Curtius, the German archaeologist and long-term friend, described her as one of the greatest beauties of her era, with something of the Pre-Raphaelite.[19] Oscar Wilde, whom she met in the theatrical social world of 1880s London, dubbed her a 'young Diana',[20] and she posed for the distinguished Victorian painters Frederic Lord Leighton and William Holman-Hunt. The famous German conductor Wilhelm Furtwängler, at whose father's house she had been a regular visitor, remembered her as 'eine schone Frau'. One story that circulated was that 'at the beginning of the century she was obliged to lecture from behind a screen, because her beauty was so sublime that it distracted the students'.[21]

Photographs of the young Eugénie Sellers confirm these accolades, and throughout her life she aroused a complex if veiled eroticism in friends and acquaintances. The diplomat Rennell Rodd addressed her as 'Hypatia', evoking the image of the beautiful, pagan intellectual of early Christian Alexandria, and Salomon Reinach reminded her that many of her most important male friends, including Rennell Rodd, Adolf Furtwängler and Bernard Berenson, had been in love with her. Given the number of references in his own letters to her physical attractiveness, Reinach himself clearly belonged in that group.

The adolescent Eugénie Sellers was not interested in the life of a beautiful socialite awaiting a suitable marriage. Nor was she in a good position to play that role. She had limited funds, and her orphan status meant a restricted social network: no mother or other close female relative was there to arrange the appropriate social contacts. In addition, she had spent much of her life outside of England. In an era when very few women went to university, it was a bold step for Eugénie Sellers to seek a Cambridge education.[22]

But she was always bold, and a university education was what she wanted. In 1879 a new chapter in her life began.

2

The Girton Years

However she got from the French convent to Cambridge, the process could not have been easy. At later moments of crisis in her life, her Cambridge tutor and friend John Postgate called on her to again do something as heroic as 'when you threw up everything to go to Cambridge'.[1] We have no sense of what that word 'everything' meant: was it a romantic attachment or just the opportunity to live comfortably but unchallenged in some household in France or Italy? Certainly Girton College patrons were on the lookout for bright, ambitious women, with or without means, who would fulfil the college's mission of promoting women's intellectual and professional development.[2] Eugénie early on attracted the attention of one of the most important of these, the formidable Lady Stanley of Alderly, one of Girton's founders, who displayed an intellectual rigour and sense of principle that frightened even her grandson, the future philosopher Bertrand Russell. He wrote of her:

> She was an eighteenth-century type, rationalistic and unimaginative, keen on enlightenment and contemptuous of Victorian goody-goody priggery. She was one of the principal people concerned in the foundation of Girton College and her portrait hangs in Girton Hall, but her policies were abandoned at her death. 'So long as I live,' she used to say, 'there shall be no chapel at Girton.' The present chapel began to be built the day she died.[3]

Another early friend and mentor to Eugénie was Lady Stanley's daughter, Maude.[4] Maude was devoted to good causes and especially to helping the poor working women of London. Although Eugénie's earliest letter to Maude raised the possibility of her doing social work in Soho, she never became one of those earnest young Victorian women who devoted their lives to 'causes'. However, she was not insensitive to the needs of the less privileged members of society, and lectured at Toynbee Hall, the education centre founded by young Oxbridge students in the impoverished East End of London. Her later devotion to St Francis and St Filippo Neri, the patron saint of the Roman poor, expressed a social conscience that was often hidden behind an elitist façade.

When Eugénie Sellers arrived at Girton, women's education was still very new at Cambridge. As recently as 1869 Henry Sidgwick, a strong advocate for the advanced education of women, had written indignantly to the *Spectator* that 'the present exclusion of women from the higher studies of the University is perfectly indefensible in principle and must sooner or later give way'.[5] The time was ripe for action and others rallied to the cause. By 1875 two women's colleges, Girton and Newnham, were operating at Cambridge.

In choosing Girton, Eugénie had selected the more rigorous and challenging of the two. The leading force in its foundation had been Sarah Emily Davies. In appearance a demure woman, Davies was indeed a person of steel who devoted her life to advancing the cause of women's education, arguing that the aim should be career independence and intellectual self-improvement, not just the cultivation of the refinements that would make them better wives and mothers.[6] By 1869 she was the leader of a group of women and men who organized a women's college at the village of Hitchin, between Cambridge and London, with tutors coming out from Cambridge to provide instruction. While the young women enjoyed considerable independence, Davies felt that they needed better intellectual contact with the university, and in 1873 she moved the college to a site on the Huntington Road on the outskirts of Cambridge. The nearby village of Girton gave its name to the new institution. Today, Girton College, with its red-brick Victorian-Gothic buildings, stands in ample grounds some three miles from the city centre. The setting is still rustic, with rooks nesting in the trees and rabbits hopping on the back lawn. When Sellers arrived in 1879 only a few structures had been completed, but the tone of the place had already been set (plate 3).

The location was indicative of Davies's educational aims. She wanted the students to be fully integrated members of Cambridge University, pursuing the same courses and taking the same examinations as the male undergraduates. In this she disagreed with educators like Henry Sidgwick, a founder of Newnham College, who wanted a slower-paced educational programme that recognized the limitations of women's pre-university training.[7] At the same time Davies felt that her college should be located away from central Cambridge, where the men's colleges were clustered, so that the female students would have fewer distractions and greater freedom.

Since Girton women were expected to take the regular Cambridge examinations, quality instruction had to be provided. Tutoring was conducted partly by female fellows of the college, and partly by young male dons who made their way out to Girton, drawn by the prospect of working with bright, attractive young women like Eugénie Sellers. Years later the classicist John Postgate, in requesting a letter of reference from Eugénie, described it as a 'favour of an old coach who used to walk miles to teach you'.[8] Access to the larger university world was sporadic and controlled. Girton did provide a carriage to take students into town and rented a room in Cambridge where the young women could relax, but while many lecturers admitted women to their classes, Cambridge was still very much a male preserve. It was only in 1882 that the prohibition against college fellows marrying had been lifted. Most of the dons in Eugénie's day were bachelors, and the majority of the students products of the all-male world of English public schools.

Emily Davies had retired as Mistress of Girton in 1875, but she continued to exert great influence. The Mistress during Eugénie's time there was Marianne Francis Bernard. Her mandate was to give institutional continuity to Miss Davies's vision, and the college prospered under her direction. She was described as 'an austere and well mannered woman, she neither asked for more authority nor used it, and so was eminently satisfactory from Davies' perspective. But her distant manner and narrow interpretation of her position alienated many students, who wished either for a warmer, more motherly leader or for a more dynamic feminist.'[9]

Girton had only a small faculty. The community of teaching fellows developed slowly, for Davies had not been greatly interested in the formal instruction at the college itself. Moreover, the pool of qualified women tutors was very small. A contemporary lamented:

> The lack of personal guidance or stimulus, intellectual and moral, from older and wiser women was a serious weakness then in the College: it arose not only from the inevitable paucity of staff, but from what seems to have been a definite aim to leave the students to develop in their own way. Sentimentality was a deadly thing, influence belonged to schooldays, and personal relations at college might lead to these. The value of the tutor in the men's system ... was ignored. I knew what such influence could be from my own experience ... lofty, intellectual, absolutely free from sentimentality, full of power 'to warn, to comfort and command'. There was in Girton no such friend to whom one could go for counsel.[10]

The resident classics lecturer when Sellers was a student was Elizabeth Welsh, a veteran of both the Hitchin and the early Girton years, and one of the first women to study for the Classical Tripos. In 1876 she was appointed Classical Lecturer and in 1883 became Mistress of the College. While she had problems dealing with the formidable and aged Emily Davies, she was an engaging individual, 'a charming, vivacious Irishwoman, who won the students' confidence and handled them with tact'.[11]

Eugénie's Continental education made her an exception among the young Girtonians. Of the twenty-five entering students profiled in the *Girton College Register* for 1879, none had received any pre-university education outside of England. Many, such as Sellers' best friend at Girton Katharine Jex-Blake, were educated at home. Others were graduates of the rapidly developing public and private secondary schools that were helping to transform women's education.

Eugénie always spoke well about her experience at Girton and held a life-long affection for her college. Much of her undergraduate life revolved around the close-bonding experiences so characteristic of life at a women's college and the various organizations that enhanced community at Girton.

One photograph shows her among the members of the Girton College Fire Brigade (plate 4). She shared the late-Romantic literary tastes of her peers. Robert Browning was her favourite author, and while at college she gained her first theatrical experience, appearing in a tableaux vivant of 'The Ring and the Book'.

Eugénie chose to read for the Classical Tripos, the most respected and the most demanding of the degree programmes. As was true of most Victorian classical education, the emphasis was very much on the close reading of Greek and Latin. Little attention was paid to literary or aesthetic interpretation. She commented ruefully about how the dry teaching of Greek at Cambridge had stifled her appreciation of the greater meaning of classical works. Her study of Plato, she lamented, had only stressed Greek particles and ignored the higher realms of philosophy.[12] Even as an undergraduate she appreciated the importance of archaeology for understanding the world of antiquity. Years later a fellow Girtonian recalled how during a study session on Euripides' *Ion*, Eugénie had explained the plan of the Greek theatre, placing the play in its performance context. She was one of few Cambridge undergraduates who had actually visited a Greek theatre.[13]

The emphasis on the detailed mastery of Greek and Latin clearly placed the Girton women at a disadvantage. Early classical language preparation was generally not available to young women, since many educators regarded the female mind unsuited for such studies. Victorian women recalled the frustration of seeing their brothers admitted to the mysteries of Greek and Latin texts, while they themselves were excluded.[14] Eugénie was more poorly prepared than most and she needed to use her impressive mental powers to compensate for her 'little Latin and less Greek'. So deficient were her classical language skills that her Girton teachers at one point expressed serious doubts about her ability to survive in the Classical Tripos. In spite of such deficiencies Eugénie impressed her tutors. John Postgate, later to become fellow and classical lecturer at Trinity College, Cambridge, and a respected student of Latin poetry, held her in high regard, and A. H. Cooke of King's, her tutor for three years, remained her strong supporter.

Fortunately, not all Oxbridge educators continued to support the rigid and narrow classical curriculum. Few doubted the general worth of a classical education for the elite, with teachers such as Benjamin Jowett of Balliol seeing it as central to the shaping of the nineteenth-century Platonic guardians and neo-Roman proconsuls needed to run the British Empire.[15] The problems came with the delivery of that education. Few teachers of Classics at either Oxford or Cambridge lived up to Jowett's ideals. Most Classics tutors had been bright undergraduates who had done well in their examinations, won a college fellowship, and spent the rest of their lives teaching the same set texts in the same way. They were intellectually insular with little experience of the world outside England or even Oxford or Cambridge. By the late 1870s a growing number of British classicists felt that the old Oxbridge system did not meet the educational needs of the country's elite nor allowed Britain to compete in the international scholarly world, especially that of Germany. They set about improving classical education both inside and outside the universities with that energetic spirit typical of the Victorian age. Central to their programme was the creation of institutions that would improve classical professionalism in Britain. Since Greek studies were at the heart of the Victorian classical education, Hellenic concerns came first, and in 1879 the Society for the Promotion of Hellenic Studies was founded. By 1886 a British School was established in Athens, where young university graduates could study the monuments and the excavations first hand.[16]

Change came more slowly to the Classics curriculums of the major universities. Although individual scholars were attempting to move classical research in new directions, the establishment at Oxford and Cambridge resisted many of the initiatives. That was especially true of classical archaeology. As one contemporary wrote: 'While every German university of note had its active and often brilliant school of classical archaeology, the subject was to all intents and purposes ignored in the curriculum and class lists of Oxford and Cambridge.'[17] However, change was slowly coming. In 1879 a paper in classical archaeology was introduced into the second part of the Classical Tripos and in 1882 students were for the first time examined on the subject.

Such curricular innovations demanded a programme of archaeological instruction. The Disney Chair of Archaeology had been established at

Cambridge in 1851, and the chair-holder during Eugénie's years at Girton was Percy Gardner. However, Gardner based himself in London, closer to the great classical collections, and had minimal impact at the university.[18] In 1880 Charles Waldstein was appointed the first Cambridge Lecturer in Classical Archaeology.[19] Waldstein was an odd figure in 1880s Cambridge, for he was American of German-Jewish origins, with graduate degrees from Germany. He was as much a philosopher and moralist as an archaeologist, and a strong advocate of John Ruskin's belief in the redeeming force of art and beauty. Although considered by many as shallow, he enjoyed a long and extremely successful career at Cambridge, where he became Slade Professor and Director of the Fitzwilliam Museum.

Waldstein established his teaching reputation during Eugénie's Cambridge years. He was especially famous for his 'demonstrations', lectures conducted in the museum using original objects or casts as the focus for his presentations. Eugénie herself later became famous for her own dynamic gallery demonstrations, and probably learned her techniques from Waldstein. Although many of her archaeological friends were highly critical of Waldstein, she placed his limitations in perspective and remained friendly with him long after Cambridge.

Sidney Colvin was the most important art history teacher at Cambridge during Eugénie's years. He was both Slade Professor of Art and Director of the Fitzwilliam Museum of Art. Like most of his generation he was self-educated in art history, but early established his reputation as a knowledgeable and perceptive critic. In his early years he was a committed follower of John Ruskin, although he later tired of the old man's dogmatism and rhetorical excesses.[20] As Slade Professor at Cambridge he was expected to engage the general public, and he became a popular lecturer, whose 'Audiences … consisted for the most part of adult residents of the place, the wives and daughters of professors, a lot of junior dons, girls from Newnham and Girton, and a sprinkling of highbrow undergraduates'.[21] Eugénie was certainly among those Girton girls, and she learned much from him about conveying the excitement of art history to a cultivated lay audience. By following his example she became one of the most successful archaeological lecturers on the international scene.

Colvin worked hard to promote the study of Greek archaeology at Cambridge. His biographer remembered that:

Within the category of the formative arts he would have preferred to devote himself to the sculpture and archaeology of ancient Greece, but he had no opportunity of laying a thorough foundation of that kind of knowledge which was not taught in Cambridge in his youth. His lectures on the work of the Germans at Olympia were the nearest that he ever came to this subject. He looked forward to the day when Greek archaeology would find a place in the classical tripos and, in his capacity as Director of the Fitzwilliam Museum, he prepared the way by forming the nucleus of the collection of casts of Greek sculpture.[22]

Eugénie and Colvin became lifelong friends. He did more for her than teach her the art of a stimulating public lecturer. She learned from him the importance of the new German scientific archaeology. Moreover, he was a close friend of Charles Newton, the most respected classical archaeologist of the day, and it seems very likely that Colvin told him about the bright, attractive Girton undergraduate who already had a better knowledge of the Greek and Roman monuments than most of the classics tutors.

Sadly for Eugénie, classical archaeology still had only a secondary role in the Cambridge classics curriculum and success in the final examinations depended on the student's technical mastery of Greek and Latin. By her final year the stakes had been raised, for students at the women's colleges were finally admitted to the honours examinations. Girtonians especially were expected to rise to this new challenge. Eugénie took the first part of the Tripos in 1882, but she only attained a lower level third-class grade. Considering her linguistic abilities, intelligence and general cultural sophistication, that result was a disappointment, but perhaps not surprising given the limitations of her secondary education. Her tutor, Alfred H. Cooke, took pains to assure her that the results did not reflect her ability. Other women students had similar problems: fellow Girton classics student Caroline Amy Hutton also got a third, and Katharine Jex-Blake obtained a first on the first part of the Classical Tripos, but sank to a third in the second.

In spite of the disappointing examination results Eugénie's overall university experience had been a positive one. She had learned much, impressed her tutors, and made a number of lifelong friends. She also established a reputation as an acute observer of the Cambridge undergraduate scene. Shortly after leaving, she was approached about writing a novel on the Girton experience that would complement a series for boys on student life at Oxford.[23] The proposal may also have been intended as a counter to the 1883 novel *A Girton Girl* written by Amelia Edwards. That book's proper Victorian message of the ultimate submission of a spirited female student to the man of her life hardly represented the values promoted by Emily Davies. It is interesting to speculate what type of novel Eugénie would have produced, for it was already clear that she planned to shape her life in a more positive, self-sufficient way.

Eugénie developed two special, life-long friendships through Girton. The first was with Katharine Jex-Blake (plate 5), who came from a cultured clerical family that had promoted and supported the education of both their sons and daughters. She had an important role model in her aunt Sophia, who had become one of the first women doctors in Britain. She and her sister went on to become heads of Oxbridge colleges, Katharine at Girton and Henrietta at Oxford's Lady Margaret Hall. Katharine soon returned to teach Classics at Girton, and in 1916 she was elected Mistress. She became one of the college's more colourful characters, alternately amusing and intimidating to the undergraduates. Her friendship with Eugénie was further strengthened by their collaboration on the edition of Pliny the Elders' chapters on the history of art, and Katharine was instrumental in securing her friend a research fellowship. In later years the two spent many happy summer hours in the cloistered corridors exchanging ideas and talking of friends past and present. Mary Lowndes, the daughter of a Liverpool adjuster, came up to Girton in 1884, the year after Eugénie had departed (plate 6). A Girton connection drew them together, perhaps Agnata Ramsay, a pupil of Eugénie's at her first job at St Leonard's School in Scotland who was then at Girton with Mary. Their friendship rapidly blossomed, and continued as long as Eugénie lived. The Lowndes–Sellers Strong correspondence in the Girton College archives provides a detailed and touching picture of a friendship that extended from the 1880s to the outbreak of World War II, with all the emotional complexity and intensity of many nineteenth-century female friendships.[24] Initially charged with a youthful eroticism, it matured into a supportive relationship that was sustained over great distances and long periods of separation.

The last months at Cambridge were anticlimactic for Eugénie. The examination results had been disappointing, but in a sense were irrelevant; more than half a century was to pass before women were awarded degrees by Cambridge. Now she faced an uncertain future. Only small sums remained from her father's legacy, and she had the responsibility of launching a younger sister into the world. Career possibilities for women were few in the 1890s. Some of her fellow Girtonians became teachers in the expanding British secondary school system, but the pay was low and the future in such positions limited.

Eugénie chose the teaching route for the time being and accepted an appointment at St Leonard's School in St Andrews, Scotland. St Leonard's had been founded in 1877 and had rapidly moved into the forefront of progressive girls' educational institutions. Not unexpectedly, St Leonard's had a solid Girton connection. The first headmistress had been Louisa Lumsden, one of the most dynamic educators produced during the early years of Girton. The second was another Girtonian, Jane Frances Dove.[25] They created a school that emphasized 'honour and duty in lieu of godliness and gentility' and imitated the ethos of male public schools like Rugby and Eton, whose playing fields shaped the later leaders of empire. The early headmistresses had 'opposed the emotionalism that they felt characterized ladies' seminaries, and so they used sports and other team activities to encourage school loyalties. Physical fitness and public duties rather than gentility and academic work were emphasized'.[26]

Eugénie Sellers proved to be an extremely effective teacher. She knew her subject well and had a dynamic, dramatic personality that could make even a late nineteenth-century classics curriculum exciting. That can be seen in the experiences of Agnata Ramsay, whose First Class in the 1887 Cambridge Classics Tripos proved that women could outshine men in the examination competition. Many years later, Agnata's sister remembered Eugénie's early influence: 'My sister Agnata (Mrs Montagu Butler) and I had lessons from her which we much enjoyed. Miss Sellers taught us classics – Virgil's *Aeneid* and Horace's *Epistles*. Her lessons were delightful; she was so bright and vivid, and evidently appreciated herself what we were studying.'[27] The ambience at St Leonard's, however, was hardly appealing for a worldly young woman used to Cambridge and the cities of the Continent. St Andrews University was the major educational institution in a small, isolated Scottish community, and it was in many ways a small and parochial place. However, some members of the faculty were distinguished. Lewis Campbell, the respected Professor of Greek, soon befriended Eugénie, and their friendship endured long beyond her brief stay in Scotland.[28] Even growing differences in their scholarly values failed to dampen it, although he cautioned her against a too-close identification with Germanic scholarship. After reading one of her first forays into serious scholarship he observed wistfully, 'I hope that you will some day emerge from the forest of learning and twilight of constructive criticism and apply your rare gift of aesthetic intuitions to the monuments themselves.'[29]

Her friend Vernon Lee had observed early on that St Andrews was a very bleak place for someone who did not play golf, and Eugénie soon discovered that to be the case. She also found that her efforts to encourage contacts between St Leonard's and the university were thwarted by colleagues who feared that the young women would be corrupted by associating with the university's students and faculty. The atmosphere soon proved too restrictive and isolated for Eugénie and after only a year she departed for the larger, freer world of London. However, Eugénie had learned never to cut herself off totally from any phase of her life. She maintained friendships with the faculty at St Andrews, and shortly after the publication of her first book the university awarded her an honorary degree.

3

A Young Woman's London

A range of interests and ambitions drew Eugénie to London. She wanted to star in the amateur theatricals that were becoming a central activity for certain London circles, and was keen to make her way in cultured London society and to learn more about classical archaeology. However, making a living was her first concern.

It was a brave but not uncommon move for a young woman to make at that time. The London of the early 1890s provided increasing freedom and opportunities for young, unattached females. Only a few years before no unmarried woman could walk alone down Piccadilly, and only in the 1870s were they allowed to receive guests on their own. By the 1880s, an increasing range of respectable occupations and avocations were opening to women, but it was a world not without its risks, even for a self-confident cosmopolitan like Eugénie. A friend, Blanche Airlie, cautioned: 'The development of women's work is so rapid that something ought to be done for them at once. If not we shall have a great number in the towns dangerously free and unprotected.'[1]

Eugénie had to earn a living. The expenses of a Girton education had exhausted much of her patrimony, and she had to think about providing not only for herself but also for her younger sister Charlotte, who lacked her drive and self-sufficiency. She arrived in the city hoping to obtain private tutoring, which she succeeded in finding. She and Charlotte took a small flat at 13 Cornwall Residence, near Regents Park, which they shared with a fellow Girton alumna, Hertha Marks. It was a pleasant area and one respectable for young ladies. Hertha had studied maths and science at Girton, and she and Eugénie formed a comprehensive science and humanities tutoring team.[2] They advertised that they could prepare students for

London University matriculation and tutor in classical and modern languages and mathematics for the Cambridge Higher Local Examinations. Eugénie supplemented her tutorial income with piecework, such as reading French examinations for the Civil Service.

The friendship and close working association with Hertha Marks brought Eugénie into more regular contact with the artist, feminist and political activist – and another driving force in the foundation of Girton – Barbara Leigh Smith Bodichon.[3] She adored Hertha and was quickly drawn to Eugénie, attracted by her brilliance and ambition. Eugénie was invited to her country home at Scalands Gate in Sussex, and came to know and appreciate this creative, complex woman in her declining years. She also brought along her sister Charlotte, who attracted the attention of Ben, Barbara's middle-aged bachelor brother. Their marriage was to play a very important part in Eugénie's life.

The London tutoring enterprise proved very successful. While Hertha soon left to pursue a pioneering career as a woman of science, Eugénie continued her private tuition. She was a natural teacher and inspired her young charges. Her Girton papers preserve enthusiastic testimonials from both parents and students. One father wrote of his daughter's experience, 'I do not think any other tutor male or female can replace the stimulus and delight which she derives from her work with you.'[4] The enthusiasm of one young charge was captured in the short note: 'Miss Sellers, you are such a duck.'[5]

Her tutoring provided important social and cultural contacts. Prime among these was the friendship that she developed with the Ward family.[6] Humphry Ward, a former Oxford don, was then the art critic of *The Times*. His wife Mary, the daughter of Thomas Arnold and sister of Matthew Arnold, was to become a very successful novelist. However, they were then newly arrived in London and were polishing their image and vigorously expanding their social network. Eugénie was hired to instruct both mother and children in classical languages. One of those children, Janet Trevelyan, reminisced years later to Eugénie: 'I have been going very deep into old times lately, in writing the first part of my mother's life and find so many mentions of you and how you came to Borough and to Russell Square and were always and everywhere our goddess.'[7] The Wards also appreciated her intelligence, vivacity and sophistication and soon included her in their social gatherings. At such soirées Eugénie met some of the most influential people in the London artistic, cultural and political scene. A tutorial session might be followed by a dinner party, and an instructional retreat at the Wards' country house could lead to a garden-party encounter with Henry James. The English poet and diarist William Allingham recalled such a country tea in 1888 where the guests included 'Mrs Humphry Ward, Mr Ward, Miss Sellars [*sic*] (tall and beautiful), and Mr Henry James'.[8] One wonders what the Master, always a connoisseur of bright, self-confident and attractive young women, thought of Eugénie Sellers.

The demands of such a multifaceted life extracted its physical and psychological toll. Being a private tutor was financially successful and socially useful, but also exhausting. Years later Eugénie recalled the tiring round of omnibus rides in dreadful London weather. The physical grind and the uncertainty of her long-term future contributed to periodic breakdowns. By the summer of 1887 she had reached such a state of nervous exhaustion that she was forced to take a spa vacation at St Moritz.

One of the reasons Eugénie had left St Andrews and moved to London had been her ambition to take part in classical theatricals. Her performance in the tableau of Browning's *Ring and the Book* at Girton showed that she had the personality and presence suited to the stage. The production of plays and tableaux based on classical themes was then a fashionable part of the London cultural and social scene. Most of the elite had read the classics at public school and university and by the 1880s student groups at both Oxford and Cambridge had begun performing Attic tragedies.[9]

But the London push for classical theatricals had another agenda. Intellectuals felt that the classics as the cornerstone of English education were threatened and means had to be found to reach a wider audience if Greek and Latin studies were to maintain their centrality. Innovative dramatic productions based on Greek literary themes could attract a general, educated public and stimulate more serious study. In 1886, *Helena in Troas*, a pastiche of Greek tragic themes written by Anglo-Irish doctor and folklorist John Todhunter, had great success in London.[10] Oscar Wilde praised the production, observing that 'The performance was not intended to be an absolute reproduction of the Greek stage ... it was simply the presentation in Greek form of a poem conceived in the Greek spirit and the secret of its beauty was the perfect correspondence of form and matter, the delicate equilibrium of spirit and sense.'[11] The play combined good theatrics with sound scholarship. The staging was designed by the architect and stage designer E. W. Godwin, lover of the famous Victorian actress Ellen Terry and father of her son Gordon Craig, who became a controversial theatrical designer and a good friend of Eugénie.[12] To ensure archaeological accuracy Godwin consulted Alexander Murray of the British Museum. Appropriately, the profits realized from the production went to assist the fledgling British School of Archaeology in Athens.

A vital figure in the promotion of these theatricals was George Warr of King's College, London. Warr was one of those classicists who felt strongly that the discipline had to expand its audience and experiment with new media if it was going to maintain its privileged place in the British school and university curricula. He had also been active in promoting women's higher education, and in 1877 assisted at the foundation of the Ladies' Department of King's College in Kensington. Proceeds from his tableaux helped finance 'Lectures for Ladies' at King's College.[13]

Soon after her arrival in London, Eugénie played the part of Helen in George Warr's 1883 masque, *The Tale of Troy*, in which episodes from the *Iliad* were paired with those from the *Odyssey*. Another emerging classicist, Jane Harrison, played Penelope.[14] Eugénie was also selected to play the starring role in the tableau *Aphrodite's Pledge Redeemed*, whose sets were designed by Frederic Leighton. The presentations involved the reading of classically inspired text, while the actors and actresses assumed appropriate poses against elegant stage sets.

Sellers' good looks and confident stage presence made a striking impression. The elderly Gladstone, who had a classical-erotic fixation on Helen of Troy perhaps related to his interest in reforming prostitutes, was enthralled by the young Girton beauty. He refused to attend a later performance of *The Tale of Troy* with Mrs Maud Beerbohm Tree, the wife of the famous London producer, as the alternative Helen, for he had come to regard Eugénie as 'his first and only love'.[15] Years later Maud Beerbohm Tree recalled 'that beautiful Miss Sellars [*sic*]' and the general atmosphere, 'when we all loved to be the willing slaves of all the great artists of the day: Leighton and Watts and Millais, Tadema, Poynter and Burne Jones'.[16]

Something of the aim and atmosphere of the productions was captured in Warr's 1887 book *Echoes of Hellas*, an elegant, large-format volume that included the texts of the plays and numerous drawings by Walter Crane. Crane, who had been dubbed the 'Hellenic William Morris', was regarded as one of the best book illustrators of his day. He worked in a Pre-Raphaelite, Arts and Craft style, but he was also a great devotee of Greek art and had copies of the Elgin marbles in his studio. His illustrations in *Echoes of Hellas* aimed, with their black and red colouration, to reproduce the style and atmosphere of Attic vase paintings.[17] A Crane drawing of the 'Aphrodite's Pledge Redeemed' tableau, one of the more erotic of the presentations, depicts Eugénie as Helen at the moment her veil is drawn away, revealing to Paris her thinly-clad beauty.

Because of the social and cultural prominence of the participants, these tableaux were well reported in the London press. Generally the reception was positive; the cause was good, and the sponsors were respected and powerful figures on the artistic and intellectual scene. However, not everyone joined in the praise. One of the performers, Elinor Ritchie Paul, had a jaundiced view of the whole business, dismissing it as 'a very amateur affair and rather laughed at as giving society ladies an opportunity for dressing up and displaying their beauty as they did in groups'.[18] Certain cynical critics shared her reservations. Shortly after attending *Tale of Troy*, the satirist H. D. Traill published in the *Fortnightly Review* a comical piece entitled 'South Kensington Hellenism: A Dialogue', in which the Greek philosopher Plato and the English neo-classical poet Walter Savage Landor discoursed on the sad state of Greek studies in contemporary England. They especially lamented theatrical performances whose 'Hellenism is a sham product, redolent of that modern and modish suburb in which its festival was held'.[19] Landor was scandalized that, contrary to classical convention, 'the female parts in these Homeric tableaux were performed by women, the wives and daughters of the actors'. To Plato's remark that 'The chief beauty of Homer is undraped simplicity', he replied:

31

So it was of the Homeric damsels, I am told, at the late representation. I can understand the Hellenic enthusiasm of young and pretty women, and their devotion to a cause in which a graceful figure may be so effectively and liberally displayed. Upon them, no doubt, the performance has exercised a most improving effect. The drama, however, is meant to educate, not those who act in it, but those who witness it.[20]

George Warr was not amused by this savage wit.[21]

Eugénie never returned to the stage after those early London performances; it would not have suited the dignity of an emerging serious scholar. However, the tableaux had served their purpose in getting her known in London, and although her acting career was brief she retained a lifelong interest in both ancient and modern theatre. While at the British School in Athens she plunged into controversies relating to the archaeology of the Greek theatre, and she and later her husband were both regulars at the London theatre. She became a friend of the famous actress Mrs Patrick Campbell, and received special invitations to her opening nights.[22] She also became very interested in dance, performance art and theatrical design and presentation. One of her close friends in later years was the dance scholar Beryl de Zoete, who she met when de Zoete worked on a translation for an art history series that Eugénie was editing.[23] De Zoete became fascinated with the dance of East Asia, doing pioneering ethnographic research on the subject, and Eugénie read her Balinese dance publications with interest and appreciation.

More performance artist was another intimate, Diane Watts, who took her modern dance presentations to both the American and British stages. Eugénie's American friend Esther Rowland was impressed by her physical grace, but not by the aesthetic philosophy that inspired her routine.[24] Still, Watts could attract distinguished audiences: George Bernard Shaw attended one of her performances at the Knightsbridge Hotel.

Another close theatrical friend was Gordon Craig, the son of Ellen Terry and Edward Godwin. Craig was an actor, but was more interested in costume and stage design. The artist William Rothenstein profiled him: 'Craig's gifts were so varied to allow of his acting and nothing more;

perhaps, too, his genius stood in the way of his talents. Ideas poured from his brain, but ideas were not easily coined into guineas.'[25] Craig later settled in Italy, where he continued his theatrical experimentation. Bernard Berenson despised him as 'that strange freak' who had 'mad schemes about the renovation of the theatre and the elimination of all actors from the stage'.[26] Eugénie was more tolerant, for Craig was the type of creative eccentric she found so appealing.

However strange the classical tableaux may seem in retrospect, they helped launch Eugénie Sellers on her archaeological career. The archaeologist Charles Newton of the British Museum was much involved in those dramas, and always had an eye for bright, attractive young women with an interest in antiquities. Sidney Colvin may also have mentioned Eugénie to him. On 11 May 1883 Eugénie was invited to a 'subrehearsal' dinner at Newton's house. The guests included Mr and Mrs Beerbohm, Jane Harrison, Cecil Smith of the British Museum, George Warr and Mrs Sitwell.[27] The invitation was clearly designed to introduce the beautiful young 'Helen' to both Newton's worlds, but that theatrical season in London was not Eugénie's first contact with Charles Newton: just before she had gone to Girton, she had attended one of his lectures in the Elgin Marbles room. She later claimed that his discourse had made her appreciate the true beauty of Greek art.[28]

In 1883 Charles Thomas Newton was at the height of his archaeological career.[29] He had been Keeper of Greek and Roman Antiquities at the British Museum since 1861 and represented a link between the world of imperial looter-collectors such as Lord Elgin and Henry Layard and the newly emerging archaeological professionalism that he did so much to advance. The classicist Richard Jebb characterized him as: 'the recognized head of classical archaeology in this country; the active supporter of all enterprises, whether originating at home or abroad, which could extend the knowledge of antiquity, or which promised to advance an object always so near to his heart, the addition of new treasures to our national collection'.[30]

Newton had studied at Christ Church, Oxford, where he became a good friend of John Ruskin. Ruskin appreciated 'his intense and curious way of looking at things' and his jovial iconoclasm and they remained close for years.[31] Newton joined the British Museum in 1840. Although he had no formal education in classical archaeology, such professional deficiencies were not unusual in that era. He set about learning on the job, working first on coins and then on Greek vases. The Italian-born director of the museum, Antonio Panizzi, appreciated his abilities and scholarly dedication and advanced his career.

Newton cultivated friendships among the now aging circle of Romantic writers and artists. In 1860 he married Ann Mary Severn, daughter of John Severn, the painter friend of John Keats. The marriage ended with her tragic death six years later, but Newton maintained his links with her parental circle.[32] In 1852 he was appointed British Vice-Consul on the island of Mytilene, the post clearly intended as a platform for archaeological collecting. For the next seven years, aided by his connections at the British Foreign Office and at the embassy in Constantinople, he exported to England sculptures such as the fourth-century reliefs from the tomb of Mausolus of Halicarnassus. These represented the most important additions to the British Museum's classical collection since the purchase of the Elgin Marbles.

However, Newton was more than just a raider. He vigorously promoted a scientific classical archaeology. In 1850, he delivered a paper entitled 'On the Study of Archaeology' to the Oxford Art Society, articulating an impressively broad view of what he regarded as the proper concerns of modern archaeology.[33] It included not only the antiquarian study of artefacts, but also research in such related fields as oral poetry, peasant customs and folk artefacts. In an era when German scholarship was becoming dominant and British classical archaeology tended to be associated with amateur aesthetes, Newton felt the need to demonstrate high standards of scholarship. As well as his post at the British Museum, he worked hard to establish the Society for Hellenic Studies and the British School in Athens and to promote classical archaeology in the universities. In 1880, he was appointed Yates Professor of Archaeology at University College, London, and became known as a conscientious if not overly popular lecturer.

Newton had a complex and sometimes contradictory personality. For

Sidney Colvin he was 'Staunch and even tender in kindness toward those he cared for and had learned to trust, he was of a reserved and rather austere habit in ordinary intercourse, and by experience and training had acquired a degree of caution and mistrustfulness with strangers which might easily have been mistaken for cynicism'.[34] Someone who won that trust and experienced that kindness was Eugénie Sellers. Years after their first meeting he wrote to her: 'Merimée used to say when they reproached him for supporting Napoleon III so strongly "Je ne suis pas imperialiste, Je suis Eugéniste". He was an old friend of the empress. I am also an Eugéniste, if you will permit me to say so.'[35] Eugénie's husband Arthur described a meeting with Newton not long before the latter's death: 'He spoke of you and if you had heard him, I think you would never again speak of your own work as if it in itself were not worth the doing. At any rate, Sir Charles is of a different opinion and holds generally that the "sweet girl graduate" (I venture to borrow his own phrase) will render services to science, which we may expect of men in vain.'[36]

By the time Eugénie became friendly with Newton, he had emerged from the period of grief that followed his wife's death and had become a familiar figure in London. He regularly attended scholarly meetings and was open to such new initiatives as George Warr's contemporary adaptations of themes from classical dramas.

For Eugénie the Newton years came to represent not only one of the defining moments in her own life but also the high point in the history of the British Museum's Greek and Roman department. She had little regard for his curatorial successors. In a letter written years later to Bernard Berenson she savagely profiled the classical keepers who followed Newton: 'The Greek and Roman collections have been in the hands of nonentities, ever since the death of the great Sir Charles Newton ... After him came a peppery little Scotsman Murray, whom no one remembers, followed by the elegant, fashionable and early knighted Cecil Smith who never did anything, followed again by A. H. Smith "fat" or "dull" as he used to be called at Winchester.'[37]

These judgments had acquired a special sting by 1939. Eugénie had long been interested in a curatorial position at the British Museum and had better archaeological qualifications than any of Newton's successors. However, the British Museum establishment was not going to appoint a woman to such an important position. Her hostility to the museum was further intensified by the role that A. H. Smith played in her dismissal from the British School at Rome.

The British Museum of Newton's era was indeed an institution that changed slowly. Amateurism was still dominant among the curatorial staff. Percy Gardner, who went on to a distinguished career in British classical archaeology, recalled how he arrived at the museum in 1871 with no archaeological background.[38] The position provided much-needed security, and was learnt on the job. The same system prevailed when Arthur Hamilton Smith was appointed in 1885.[39] It is not surprising that Eugénie, who was to receive a German archaeological education from scholars of the stature of Adolf Furtwängler, would come to look on the British Museum crowd with ill-concealed contempt.

However, some improvements were being made. Most important was a new exhibition of the Elgin Marbles that had opened in 1865. Artists and connoisseurs could now look at them with fresh eyes, and the new display helped stimulate a classical revival among London artists such as Walter Crane and Frederic Leighton, who displayed casts of the marbles in their studies.[40] The cult of the Elgin Marbles in aesthetic circles reached sufficient intensity to be parodied by the cartoonists of *Punch*.[41] In 1878 the natural history collections were transferred to a new museum and that allowed the expansion of the classical galleries. By 1884 Newton's mausoleum sculptures had a setting worthy of their importance.

Hours spent in the British Museum galleries made Eugénie Sellers into one of the best museum archaeologists of her generation. Her knowledge of ancient art and her abilities and experience as a teacher soon provided her with new opportunities. Newton was a firm believer in what today would be called 'public outreach'. Neighbouring Bloomsbury provided the museum with an audience of cultured individuals, mainly if not exclusively female, who enjoyed learning about Greek art. Newton encouraged the bright young women who worked with him to satisfy this curiosity with public lectures. The presentations took two forms: one was the formal lecture, increasingly illustrated with lantern slides; the other was the 'demonstration', a more informal exercise conducted in the galleries that used original sculptures or casts from the museum's extensive collection as illustrative examples.

Eugénie had, in the lectures of Sidney Colvin and the demonstrations of Charles Waldstein, experienced excellent examples of both genres, and she rapidly became a very successful lecturer, combining a deep knowledge of and enthusiasm for her subject with superb communicative skills. Long after she had left London she returned regularly to speak at the British Museum and attracted large and appreciative audiences. A friend praised her 1909 British Museum lectures: 'Lucky those leisured ones to whom you lecture and for whom, as another Hypatia, you bring renewed life and meaning to the graven image, a fragment thereof that has found an abiding place in the gray region of Bloomsbury.'[42] Eugénie extended her speaking engagements beyond the British Museum. In the early 1890s she lectured frequently for the London University Extension Programme, presenting new discoveries in classical archaeology to diverse audiences in the London suburbs. She also lectured at Toynbee Hall.

She developed two special female friendships during those British Museum years. One was with her fellow Cambridge classicist Jane Harrison, who Charles Newton had brought into his circle of archaeological protégés.[43] She was a complex, brilliant, passionate and intellectually adventurous woman. Her father, a timber merchant from Yorkshire, encouraged her educational ambitions, and at the relatively advanced age of twenty-four she took up a scholarship at Newnham College, Cambridge. Upon the completion of her studies in 1879, she taught for a year in Oxford and then moved to London. There she pursued studies in Greek archaeology with Newton, lectured at the British Museum, and, like Eugénie, became involved in theatricals. Eugénie came to know her through Newton and Warr. Harrison was ten years older, but they had a number of things in common, including their Yorkshire roots, the early loss of a mother, disappointing results in their university examinations (Harrison had obtained a second) and a passionate interest in archaeology and classical dramatics. They even shared a certain Pre-Raphaelite style. Harrison provided a role model of how a young woman could succeed in the intellectual and cultural world of London. Years later, when their friendship had long been broken, Eugénie still appreciated the important role that Jane had played in her early development: 'I made acquaintance with another personality, who in a manner very different from Sir Charles Newton fanned my desire to study archaeology. For here preceding me was a woman actually making for herself a career on the lines, more or less, that I desired to pursue.'[44] She also acknowledged the important role that Harrison had played in shaping her intellectual and aesthetic vision. In 1886 she observed in a letter to Violet Paget: 'I was a terrible materialist – pictures and statues seemed to me pleasant and things to look at, and that was about all. It is to Miss Harrison's teaching solely at first that I owe having even thought that their mission might be quite other than to amuse me. I indeed owe such a mighty debt to Miss Harrison, not to say that she has been one of my kindest friends in more material ways.'[45]

Harrison and Sellers shared the tensions and triumphs of the London lecturing circuit. Jane had a dramatic style of lecturing, characterized as a 'set or show oration in which she would attempt to overwhelm her audience through fervor and brilliance'.[46] It was in its own way very effective, and Eugénie helped promote her lectures to the London cultural elite. She also served as intermediary between Jane and such prickly figures as their mutual friend Violet Paget.

Harrison was also rapidly establishing herself as an imaginative and productive scholar. Early works such as *Myths of the Odyssey in Art and Literature* (1882) and *Introductory Studies in Greek Art* (1885) employed an aesthetic, idealistic approach to Greek art that reflected both English and German influences. Important to the young Harrison was Ruskin's vision of the improving mission of art. In the preface to *Myths of the Odyssey* she wrote: 'I believe the educational value of a study of archaeology to consist far more in the discipline of taste and feeling it affords, than in the gift of definite information it has to offer.'[47] In the preface to her *Introductory Studies in Greek Art* she laid out more fully her ideological premises, asserting that:

38

I have desired to give such readers certain criteria by which to discern good and bad, a sure anchor for their taste amid the fluctuations of modern fashion. I shall be satisfied if, by the help of the wisdom of Plato, I can show any of the citizens of our state why, eschewing the dry bones of symbolism and still more warily shunning the rank, unwholesome pastures of modern realism, they may nurture their souls on the fair sights and pure visions of Ideal art.[48]

Harrison connected the growing popularity of post-classical Greek art to what she regarded as a crisis of values in contemporary art. She polemicized:

It is also easy to see why these Pergamene marbles are popular among us. Ours is an age that delights and excels in realism, that seeks above all things sensationalism. The Greek passed un-warned through idealism to mimetic realism, but we have their story, glorious at first, at last sad before us. Shall history mean nothing, or can our artists learn in time to avoid the 'image of the visible'.

Harrison identified with an art-history tradition, stretching back to Winckelmann, that saw Greek art progressing to its high point in the age of Pheidias and then declining through the Hellenistic period to reach its nadir under Rome. As Harrison concluded, 'It needed the influence of Rome, all her vulgarity, her showy coarseness to sink Greek art to its lowest depth.'[49] This early Harrison was a very different thinker from the more mature scholar, famous for exploring the dark and primitive underpinnings of classical civilization.

At first Eugénie was captivated by Harrison's brilliance, knowledge and ability to articulate important scholarly and aesthetic issues. However, tensions soon developed that would destroy their friendship. Eugénie especially resented Harrison's personal denigrations:

I was to her view and understanding totally unfit and unsuited for such a career and so high a calling as her own, inept for scholarship, incapable of lecturing. Discouragement did not daunt me, but it did react upon my feelings towards her. For that and other more personal reasons, the lack of generosity if not of insight shown by such discouragement helped to open my eyes to flaws in that overemotional character, stressed to the point of hysteria and instability.[50]

Despite their many apparent similarities, there were also major differences in background and personality. Harrison had experienced nothing like Eugénie's cosmopolitan upbringing. Observing the worldly Eugénie operating in the salons and drawing rooms of London and at the dinner parties of Charles Newton, the socially and erotically insecure Harrison felt increasingly jealous of her bright and beautiful young protégée. She focused her hostility on what she saw as Sellers' social pretensions and the 'unscrupulous way she used people just to get on'.[51] Eugénie experienced more of Harrison's difficult personality when she tried to mediate in conflicts between Harrison and Violet Paget, and then with Newton. Ultimately these personal and professional tensions destroyed their friendship, although it has even been suggested that a failed erotic relationship lay behind the break. After the early 1890s they had little communication, even though they had many mutual friends and both spent extended periods of time at Cambridge. This was one of the very rare instances when Eugénie Sellers totally abandoned a friendship.[52]

More enduring was the friendship that Eugénie established with Violet Paget, the art critic and cultural historian who wrote under the pen name of Vernon Lee.[53] Paget, like Sellers, had grown up on the Continent. By the 1880s her family had settled in Florence, where they were major figures in the expatriate community. With the publication in 1880 of *Studies of the Eighteenth Century in Italy*, Violet had established her reputation as a highly imaginative cultural historian. By the early 1880s she was spending part of each year in London, moving easily in various cultural and artistic circles. The experience stimulated her to turn to fiction, and she parodied the fashionable world of artists and aesthetes in her 1884 novel, *Miss Brown*.

Eugénie may have come to know Violet through Newton, the Humphrey Wards, or the family of the painter Lawrence Alma Tadema. However it began, it proved to be a long friendship. The Violet Paget of those early days was a plain-looking woman with a slightly horsey face and round, wire-rimmed glasses, captured in an early portrait by John Singer Sargent.[54] A contemporary observed: 'Vernon Lee ... Mrs Austin calls the ugliest woman she ever saw, but I don't think so at all. It is such an expressive face and she looks young in spite of her spectacles.'[55] Eugénie became a regular visitor at Il Palmerino, the Paget family villa on the outskirts of Florence. They shared friends like the legal historian Frederick Pollock, the writer Maurice Baring and the art historian Bernard Berenson.

Eugénie knew well the world of *Miss Brown*. Her artistic and theatrical interests brought her into those circles delightfully satirized by both Vernon Lee and the *Punch* cartoonist George Du Maurier. Years later the Italian art historian Mario Praz cited a Du Maurier cartoon to evoke the persona of the young Eugénie Sellers.[56] In one, a vacuous young man is about to escort a thin, dark young woman into dinner. In response to his invitation she asks, 'Are you intense?'. Many a young man must have found Eugénie Sellers 'intense'.

Among the most interesting friendships that Eugénie developed during these early London years was with the Pre-Raphaelite and neoclassical painters and their families. Mario Praz, in his memoir of Eugénie, recalled how 'she posed as one of the classical beauties of Leighton and was in all respects similar to one of the types of beautiful aesthetes drawn by George du Maurier for Punch'.[57] Four of those painters, all at the height of their fame, came to play central roles in her London life: Frederic Leighton, Lawrence Alma-Tadema, Edward Burne-Jones and William Holman Hunt.

Leighton, who in 1885 painted a portrait of the young Eugénie Sellers, was then the most distinguished artist in Britain.[58] Educated mainly on the Continent he had a deep appreciation for the European artistic traditions. After a visit to Greece in 1867 he became a strong promoter of Hellenic classicism and, in the words of one scholar, 'the last bearer of the torch of classicism; a torch that had been lit in ancient Greece, tended in ancient Rome, and rediscovered and lit once again by the artists of the Italian Renaissance'.[59] Representative of his neoclassical style was the 1888 painting *The Captive Andromache*. The scene of Hector's enslaved widow drawing water at the fountain could have been painted from a Eugénie Sellers tableau.

Leighton was elected president of the Royal Academy in 1878. He built an elegant bachelor's house in Holland Park, where he entertained the cream of London society. Not everyone appreciated his carefully crafted persona or his artistic creations. Vernon Lee remarked cynically: 'Sir Frederic is a mixture of the Olympian Jove and a head waiter, a superb decorator and a superb piece of decoration, who paints poor pictures of the correctist idealism, of orange, tawny naked women against indigo skies.'[60]

Lawrence Alma-Tadema was an equally important neoclassical painter. Born and raised in Holland, he did not make his first visit to England until he was twenty-six.[61] His paintings displayed a superb mastery of accurate archaeological detail, which derived in part from an extended visit to Rome and Pompeii that he made in 1863, and in part from his study of contemporary archaeological discoveries. He gathered an enormous collection of archaeological photographs to assist him in making his paintings as historical accurate as possible.

Alma-Tadema established permanent residence in England in 1870 and soon became very successful. His was not the Rome of heroic deeds found in earlier nineteenth-century historical painting, but a Rome that combined depictions of daily life, such as a visit to the women's baths, with scenes of imperial decadence. Part of the great popularity of his paintings rested on the play between the Victorian and the classical worlds, what the American painter Whistler mischievously called 'Five O'Clock Tea Antiquity'.[62] They toyed with a 'respectable eroticism', providing Victorians with historical scenes filled with naked young females.

While modernist critics like Roger Fry later derided the paintings of Alma-Tadema for their excessive polish and their general lowbrow appeal, his works demanded a sophisticated knowledge of Roman history and archaeology, and his success reflected a growing interest in ancient history and classical archaeology among the educated middle class.[63] Many of the people who went to view and even to buy his paintings were the same people who attended Eugénie Sellers' lectures at the British Museum.

Alma-Tadema's elegant house at 17 Grove End Road in St John's Wood, in which fellow artists had pooled their talents to decorate the rooms, became a gathering place for London cultured society.[64] Eugénie Sellers was one of the 'London beauties' invited to the classical costume ball held to celebrate its opening. Authenticity as well as elegance was expected from the young classical archaeologist, and Eugénie spent time at the British Museum studying the depiction of female dress on Attic vases.[65] At the ball she must have appeared to be a Walter Crane drawing come to life.

Lawrence Alma-Tadema had a large, lively family, and Eugénie became very friendly with both him and his wife, Anna. Their children admired her spirit and independence, regarding her as an important role model for the young women of their generation. Her friendship with the Alma-Tademas extended well beyond those early London years, and she was to enlist the painter's assistance in several of her later causes.

Edward Burne-Jones, the third of Eugénie Sellers' artistic friends, was more distinctly Pre-Raphaelite than either Leighton or Alma-Tadema. His style had been shaped by Dante Gabriel Rossetti and by decades of collaboration with William Morris.[66] He looked to medieval romance and early Renaissance art for inspiration, and his drawings, paintings, stained glass and tapestries had a dreamy aesthetic quality that continued the traditions of the Pre-Raphaelites. During the 1880s, when Sellers came to know him, he was painting such works as *The Sleep of Arthur in Avalon*, whose tall, willowy figures, bright colours and dreamlike atmosphere very much personify that aesthetic movement.

Burne-Jones appreciated attractive young women, and their portraits often appear in his artwork. There is no specific reference to the inclusion of Eugénie in any of his paintings, but it is very likely that she served as one of his models. As with the Alma-Tademas, she came to know the family well. She became especially close to his daughter Margaret, corresponding with her on topics such as the inherent vulgarity of contemporary Britain. Margaret married the brilliant young classicist John William MacKail, further reinforcing her connection with Eugénie's world.[67] They remained in contact, although they were not nearly as close as in their young years.

In 1888, William Holman Hunt wrote to Eugénie asking to paint her portrait, although it is not known whether the commission was completed. Hunt was one of the original Pre-Raphaelite brotherhood and worked in that tradition throughout his long life. He was known especially for his religious paintings.[68] While Eugénie did not have the close family association with Holman Hunt that she enjoyed with the Alma-Tademas and the Burne-Joneses, the two remained in contact until his death.

Time spent with these painters gave Eugénie a deep appreciation of the processes of artistic creativity. It also reinforced her identity with the neoclassical tradition in the arts. Leighton and Alma-Tadema's paintings, together with performances in the classical tableaux and the hours of observing the Elgin Marbles and the Attic vases at the British Museum, provided her with a complex impression of the physical realities of antiquity and its meaning for her contemporary world. They also made her more sensitive to the world of women in Greek and Roman society, a subject that the British male classical elite hardly considered.

While she tutored, lectured to the Bloomsbury ladies and the London University classes, and adorned the artistic circles of St John's Wood, Eugénie sought to find focus in her life and formulate the big, imaginative project that would harness and direct her considerable energies. In spite of her growing involvement with archaeology, she had not lost interest in secondary education. Indeed, she began gathering support among her friends for the establishment of an experimental school for young women, whose curriculum would be centred on the visual arts. The project reflected the lingering influence of Jane Harrison, who had stressed to her the educational potential of art and archaeology.[69] The school would be a counter to the male-dominated, philology-centred world of secondary education. The project attracted considerable interest and had the possibility of solid financial support. Eugénie, with her combination of archaeological knowledge, sense of contemporary artistic dynamics and proven pedagogical skills, seemed the ideal person to bring such a project to fruition. It would have been a bold undertaking in the tradition of the Girton women who had made St Leonard's such a success.

However, the project proved in the end too bold, especially for someone whose life and career goals were so uncertain, and Eugénie abandoned the scheme and left for the Continent. But she always felt ambivalent about that road not taken. Years later her friend Florence Bell sent her an article on the

Victorian educator Thomas Arnold. It revived her 'significant regrets for the educational schemes of my youth which now I shall never be able to carry out', although on reflection she realized that the abandonment of the project was 'better for my own happiness as I doubt whether women's education can ever be placed on a really high level for the simple fact that teaching can never be made into a really attractive profession for superior women'.[70] If she had gone ahead with the scheme, Victorian England could well have had another exciting experiment in women's education, although it would not have had its first female classical archaeologist.

The decision to move to the Continent was a carefully considered one. Eugénie had been thinking hard about her future goals. She wanted to be a classical archaeologist in the best contemporary 'scientific' mode. She could realize that ambition only through prolonged, systematic study with the great German masters.

4

A Mediterranean Interlude

Hours spent in the British Museum and in conversation with Charles Newton had intensified Eugénie Sellers' fascination with Greek archaeology. Her initial forays into the field had been those of a self-educated amateur, but as her knowledge increased and her intellectual sophistication grew, she became increasingly unsatisfied with the paradigms that dominated Greek archaeology in Britain. The Parthenon sculptures were still seen as embodying ultimate beauty,[1] a belief that had its roots in the Romantic views of ancient Greece and had been strengthened by the combination of idealism and homoerotic aestheticism preached by writers such as Walter Pater.[2] As one contemporary critic caustically remarked, 'At the very moment that Nietzsche was revealing to Germany the fierce, Dionysiac side of the Greek soul, the English were marching boldly backwards towards Winckelmann and Goethe.'[3]

Eugénie had initially been sympathetic to the aesthetic interpretation of Greek art; it was what her teachers at Cambridge had preached. However, under Newton's tutelage she came to appreciate the value of the more rigorous German scholarship. Vague and vacuous statements about beauty and soul were no longer sufficient. The Germans thought it necessary both to master literary sources and to study all the surviving works in detail. This evidence was then integrated into a stylistic history of Greek sculpture and used to reconstruct, through the study of Greek originals and Roman copies, major works created by a Pheidias or a Praxiteles. Such scholarship was impossible without the casts, the photographic archives and the catalogues of the great museum collections, and the specialized libraries that formed the foundation of German scholarship. Most of all one needed the rigorous research environment provided by the archaeological seminars of the great German universities.

Eugénie realized that she must experience this new world of archaeological scholarship if she was to become more than an intelligent, well-informed amateur. First, however, she needed more direct knowledge of the archaeological monuments of Greece and Rome. The problem was how to achieve those goals. There was no opportunity for graduate study in England; most of the dons at Oxford and Cambridge ignored or despised German scholarship. She had learned what she could from Newton, and the rest of the classical archaeologists in London had little to teach her. However, financial constraints and her obligations to her sister Charlotte held her in England. Furthermore, no marriage prospects were on the horizon. These tensions and frustrations began to take their physical and psychological toll, and letters from friends and relatives make increasing reference to health problems and to her 'nervous personality'.

One obstacle to a new life was removed with the marriage of Charlotte to Benjamin Leigh Smith. Ben was fifty-nine, but he had an eye for younger women, and the beautiful nineteen-year-old had caught his fancy.[4] They married in the summer of 1887, much to the indignation of the Leigh Smith family, who were concerned about the difference in their ages and the fact that Charlotte was a Roman Catholic.

Charlotte soon became pregnant and by the summer of 1888 Eugénie was an aunt. Philip Leigh Smith eventually went on to a diplomatic career and was to play an important part in Eugénie's later life. A second child soon followed, but the marriage was not a success, and Ben was hardly mentioned in Eugénie's voluminous correspondence with her sister. There was even talk that 'Charlie' and Ben would separate.[5] When their mutual friend Mary Lowndes received notice of Ben's death in 1913, she wrote, 'I saw in the paper the notice of your sister's husband's death and wonder if that affects her plans – but hardly, I suppose.'[6]

Charlie found solace from her domestic trials in religion, becoming active in promoting Catholic settlement homes for the poor of London. Faith, good works and the responsibilities of child-rearing sustained her in this difficult marriage, which did at least provide her with financial security and freed Eugénie from responsibility for her.

Eugénie could now strike out on her own. In 1888 she set out on a trip to Italy and Greece. Her Italian sojourn included an extended stay in

Florence, where she got to know the family of Violet Paget. She then returned to Greece for the first time since the formative trip with her father.

She sought a thorough, professional introduction to the Greek sites, and joined an archaeological tour led by Wilhelm Dörpfeld, one of the most important classical archaeologists of his generation.[7] He was already a veteran of several important excavations, including those of Heinrich Schliemann at Tiryns and Troy, where he had played an important role in introducing Schliemann to the best German archaeological field methods.[8] He had recently been appointed director of the prestigious German Archaeological Institute in Athens.

Dörpfeld's archaeological tours had become famous and attracted serious students of Greek archaeology. Eugénie did not leave a record of the 1888 itinerary, but it was probably similar to later trips led by Dörpfeld, when he spent considerable time at sites in and around Athens. However, he also included a tour of the Peloponnese, where the Germans had conducted their pioneering excavations at Olympia. Travel in Greece was improving, as indicated by the publication in 1884 of an expanded edition of Murray's *Handbook for Travellers in Greece*, written by Amy Francis Yule. The fact that a woman had prepared the standard guidebook for English tourists in Greece shows that touring that country was no longer a male preserve. However, communications were still poor, accommodation primitive and banditry not totally eradicated.

The Girton archives preserve a photo of twenty-eight-year-old Eugénie Sellers at Olympia, riding beside a handsome young man identified as Dörpfeld (plate 7). She was clearly very attracted to Dörpfeld; in her collection of photographs of special friends, she treasured another picture of him dressed in traditional Greek costume. They renewed their acquaintance two years later in Athens when Sellers was a student at the British School and Dörpfeld director of the German Archaeological Institute. Dörpfeld probably introduced her to the circle of Heinrich Schliemann.

The 1888 trip whetted Eugénie's appetite for Greece, and she began planning for a more extended stay. In 1890 she became the first woman to be accepted for study at the British School in Athens, which had been founded only four years before by the distinguished classicist Richard Jebb. He had argued that English classicists lagged far behind their German,

French and even American counterparts in providing students with first-hand study of the Greek monuments.[9] The lack of a British school in Athens was particularly embarrassing since England was at the height of its imperial glory and a classical education was seen as central to the preparation of the imperial elite. Public appeals finally bore fruit and enough money was raised to open a small institution in Athens. In 1884 the Greek government provided land for the British on the slope of Mount Lykabettos next to the American School of Classical Studies. F. C. Penrose, a respected if aged architect, was appointed the first director.[10]

1890 was only the second full year of operations for the school. It was a male-dominated, clubby place on the outskirts of the small provincial city that was late nineteenth-century Athens. Ernest Gardner, a young Cambridge graduate, was now the director, but he was no more open to advancing the cause of women in British archaeology. Eugénie could not live at the school nor take part in its excavations. She stayed with her friend Mary Lowndes at a pension, and since it was closer to the centre of Athens, she found it easier to explore the city and its monuments, use the libraries and come to know the archaeologists resident there. She soon established a reputation as a vigorous explorer of the museums and monuments. Years later Lewis Farnell, then a distinguished student of Greek religion, remembered visiting the Acropolis by moonlight with Eugénie.[11]

As was her habit throughout her life, Eugénie developed a wide circle of new friends during her year in Athens. Among the classicists at the British School was a young Oxford graduate named Henry Stuart-Jones, who became her lifelong friend.[12] He later became a central figure in the early development of the British School at Rome and helped launch Eugénie on her career in Roman art. Another important friendship that deepened during that year in Athens was with the young diplomat James Rennell Rodd. Years later he recalled:

> It was there [Athens] also that I first met a great friend of after years, Mrs Arthur Strong, then Miss Eugénie Sellers, who was at that time blind to all that was not Greek. If her subsequent activities at the British

School at Rome have induced a certain transfer of allegiance and have even stimulated exploration of the artistic values of the baroque I can only testify to my admiration of her work in every phase.[13]

Rennell Rodd was a rising young member of the British foreign service assigned to the Athens embassy. He was also one of the late nineteenth-century 'aesthetes', a follower of the American painter James McNeill Whistler and a friend of Oscar Wilde. With his interest in the classics and his passion for the arts, Rennell Rodd represented the best of the cultivated British diplomatic tradition.

Eugénie's official research project during her Athens year was the study of Greek vases. It led to one of her first publications, a careful iconographic analysis of a group of white ground lekythoi (Greek funerary pottery) from the island of Eretria. This research was the culmination of an interest in Greek painted pottery that supposedly started with the search for authentic costume details for Alma-Tadema's Hellenic ball.[14]

This was a period in which both scholars and artists were discovering the archaeological and artistic potential of Greek ceramics. German scholars had made great strides in classifying and dating Greek pottery, Charles Newton had emphasized the important information on Greek art, social life and mythology that was to be obtained from it, and Jane Harrison had drawn heavily on the iconography of the vases for her research on Athenian ritual and religion.[15] At the same time aesthetes like Aubrey Beardsley and Walter Crane were inspired by the refined linear artistry of the Attic vase painters. Jesse Stewart, Jane Harrison's friend and biographer, claimed that 'the aesthetic movement made appreciation of Greek vase painting possible'.[16] An important link between the world of the aesthete and the scholar in this field was to come a few years later in the figure of John Beazley. He was the son of an Arts and Crafts interior decorator and an aesthete in his youth. However, he devoted his academic career to the detailed technical study of drawing on Greek vases and produced a catalogue of potters and painters that still forms the framework for Greek ceramic studies today.[17]

*

If Eugénie had a restricted and rather marginal position at the British School, things were different in the wider international society of Athens. She had a Continental sophistication that set her apart from her rather raw male contemporaries. Her French was fluent, she knew some Italian and German, and she exercised her social and cultural skills well among the various communities of diplomats and scholars. The most famous archaeological figure in Athens at that time was Heinrich Schliemann. He returned to Athens in the autumn of 1890 after what was to be his last season of excavation at Troy. It is easy to imagine the beautiful and worldly Eugénie Sellers joining the famous soirées held at his elegant house-museum.[18]

During that year Eugénie pulled off a major scholarly coup, when she was invited to prepare an English translation of Carl Schuchhardt's *Schliemann's Excavations: An Archaeological and Historical Study.* Wilhelm Dörpfeld or Charles Newton, who was one of Schliemann's major supporters in England, probably provided the introduction to both Schliemann and Schuchhardt. The book was an effort to make Schliemann's excavations known to a wider, educated public.[19] Eugénie not only translated Schuchhardt's 1889 German text, but also added a short account by Schliemann himself of the most recent Troy discoveries, an evaluation of the excavations by eight archaeologists who had visited the site at the invitation of Schliemann and Dörpfeld, and a short account of some recent finds by Dörpfeld. She also included a short notice on the death of Schliemann, and a checklist of objects in the British Museum that related to the recent Troy finds. The work was ready for the printer in the early spring of 1891.

The death of Schliemann in December 1890 made the publication timely, and the book was a great success. It also helped establish Eugénie's scholarly credentials and showcased her abilities as a translator. While she did not devote herself to the newly emerging field of Aegean prehistoric archaeology, she retained an interest in the subject, becoming a friend of Arthur Evans, the excavator of the Minoan palace at Knossos, who kept her up to date on the latest discoveries. Years later the American art-historian Bernard Berenson turned to her when he needed recent bibliography on Mycenaean archaeology.[20]

Another subject that stirred scholarly controversy at the time was the relationship between Greek theatre structure and ancient performance. Eugénie had starred in London productions that attempted to make Greek drama more relevant to contemporary audiences, and this revived interest in the physical settings for ancient drama, which in turn led to research on the architectural history of the Greek theatre. Several major theatre excavations were underway when Eugénie was in Greece: Dörpfeld was studying the remains of the theatre of Dionysos in Athens, the British had begun excavating a theatre at ancient Megalopolis, and the Americans were exploring the remains of the theatres at Eretria and Phlius.[21] Strong scholarly personalities and ambiguous archaeological evidence led to fierce debates on the reconstruction of ancient Greek theatre buildings, one of the most vehement pitting the young Ernest Gardner of the British School against the formidable Dörpfeld.[22] With the strong interest in Greek drama among the classically educated elites, the arguments spilled over from the learned journals into the literate press.

Eugénie plunged enthusiastically into these archaeological battles. She had visited the British excavations at Megalopolis with Dörpfeld and had heard lectures on the American theatre excavations at the American School in Athens. She knew about the realities of theatrical performance from her London experience. She published several pieces on the latest theatre discoveries and corresponded on the topic with such eminent classicists as Gilbert Murray and Richard C. Jebb.[23]

The arguments became heated, and relations between scholars tense. Sellers tended to support Dörpfeld's positions over those of Gardner. In one letter to the *Athenaeum* she described Gardner's arguments as displaying 'amusing perversity', and dismissed his current attitude as being 'as ungenerous as it is futile'.[24] She displayed spirit, but a dangerous lack of tact. Gardner was after all the director of the British School in Athens and a person who could damage her scholarly career. It was no wonder that Lewis Campbell, her old St Andrews mentor, urged restraint.[25] Memories of the hard feelings lingered long after the debates were forgotten. Years later William Loring, one of her contemporaries at the BSA, remembered apologetically that: 'I was not much use to you in

Athens – perhaps rather the reverse, but those "theatre" matters are things of the past.'[26]

Eugénie had no reason to hurry back to England, so she followed her Athens year with an extended stay in Rome. She had travelled in Italy many times, but this was the first time that she had chosen to stay in Rome for more than a few weeks. It was the true beginning of her lifelong love affair with the city. Eugénie and Mary Lowndes moved into the Palazzo Tittona on the Quirinale hill, not far from the official residence of the King of Italy, and spent the year there together. The palazzo was slightly removed from the bustle of the central city, but provided easy access to the monuments and museums. They spent their days visiting the archaeological sites and the museums, and socializing with both the Italians and expatriate communities.

Rome itself had changed drastically from the sleepy, pleasant city she had known in the 1870s. The Quirinale quarter where she lived was increasingly dotted with newly built government buildings. The nobility had sold most of their villa gardens on the outskirts of the city to developers, and their elegant parks had been replaced by new residential quarters. Secular rituals, which Eugénie described as 'the press of royalty or their representatives', had replaced the leisurely processions of popes and cardinals through the city.[27]

The Pope still lived in self-imposed isolation in the Vatican, and a tense stand-off existed between Church and state. The antagonisms between the secular 'white' and clerical 'black' nobility continued in Italian high society. Direct contact between the two groups was limited, although some neutral meeting grounds were created.

One such place that Eugénie frequented was the salon of the American journalist William J. Stillman and his artist wife Marie Spartali. Stillman was the London *Times* correspondent in Rome, and combined a serious interest in archaeology with a profound knowledge of Italian politics and politicians. Years before he had been American consul in the city. Through Marie, a Pre-Raphaelite painter, he was also closely connected to London artistic circles.[28] Both artistic and archaeological interests drew Eugénie to the Stillmans, and they remained friends for years. Long afterwards she recalled those Roman evenings:

With Roman society divided as it was into White and Blacks, supporters of the Government or of the Pope, I was not much concerned. The hospitable house of the Anglo-American Stillman, which I did frequent, was neutral ground. I recall an occasion of the meeting there of two old friends, whose divergent positions had kept apart for years and still kept apart in Roman life. Here they could talk and recall old days to their hearts' content.[29]

Eugénie continued her scholarly activities. She frequented the superb library of the German Archaeological Institute, then located on the Campidoglio behind Michelangelo's great piazza. She remembered well the slight irony of her position: 'I was something of a *luxus naturae* to them, educated as I had been at Cambridge when their own women were still rigorously excluded from the universities. My eagerness to learn was a sufficient open sesame. They gave me every facility for study and much personal help.'[30]

The archaeological scene was changing rapidly. The intense development of the city that followed its designation as the Italian capital led to many new archaeological discoveries, and new museums were established to house the finds. Eugénie spent much time mastering this new material and establishing friendships with the new generation of Italian archaeologists. Occasionally she and Mary would cycle to the sites on the outskirts of the city where the old, magic world of the Roman campagna still remained largely unchanged.

Study of the older collections housed in the palaces of the Roman nobility still remained central to an apprentice archaeologist like Eugénie, even though the conflicts of Church and state occasionally intruded there, with the papal nobility often closing their collections to those they regarded as too supportive of the state. The German archaeologists, whose government was frequently locked in conflict with the papacy, were particular targets of this noble hostility. Eugénie, as a cosmopolitan young Englishwoman and baptized Catholic, received a warmer welcome, and occasionally helped her excluded friends to receive the same. One such episode involved the collection of the Villa Albani. Johannes Winckelmann, the man regarded as the founder of German classical archaeology, had been the librarian there. In that capacity he helped develop one of the best collections of classical sculpture in Rome. However, the current owners were of the 'black' party, and German scholars were unwelcome. Eugénie remembered with amusement an occasion when colleagues from the German Archaeological Institute crowded in on her special permission to visit the villa, and for a few moments they swarmed over the sculptures that were so difficult for them to study.

One of the most important friendships that Eugénie established that year was with Desiderio and Maria Pasolini. Desiderio Pasolini belonged to a cultured noble family from Ravenna, who as liberal Catholics served both Pope Pius IX and the Italian government. A contemporary described Desiderio as 'an interesting and charming eccentric, a senator, a scholar and distinguished historian, a statesman and philosopher; he looked like a Perugino bishop'.[31] Maria was the cultured daughter of a Milanese industrial family. As an early collector of photographs she took particular interest in preserving images of buildings threatened by development in the new Rome. In addition, she hosted one of the most important salons in the city.[32] Rennell Rodd, a regular at her gatherings, remembered their dynamics: 'Intellectual society found a meeting-ground in the apartment in Palazzo Odescalchi of the historian Count Pietro Desiderio Pasolini, where the countess, enthusiastic, intelligent and moderately rebellious to conventions, assembled as her guests the most interesting personalities in the world of politics, economics and letters.'[33] Eugénie's old friend the novelist Mary Ward had similar memories: 'Contessa Pasolini was equal to them all, and her talk, rapid, fearless, picturesque, full of knowledge, yet without a hint of pedantry, gave a note of unity to a scene that could hardly have been more varied.'[34] Both Pasolinis quickly incorporated the bright and charming Eugénie Sellers into their circle, and they remained friends into old age.

More important as an archaeological role model for the young Eugénie was Ersilia Caetani Lovatelli. She lived in a Renaissance palace in the centre of Rome, where she received 'all who had some claim to distinction'.[35] Rennell Rodd remembered those receptions as well: 'In the Palazzo Lovatelli, whose mistress, a sister of the Duke of Sermoneta ... was one of the finest classical scholars in Italy, you would be sure to find any foreign literary celebrities who were visiting the city.'[36]

Contessa Ersilia Caetani Lovatelli belonged to one of the great Roman aristocratic families and had received an excellent education. She became a friend of Giovanni Battista De Rossi, a pioneer in the field of Christian archaeology, and he inspired her to study antiquity. She produced a wide range of publications on Roman topography, social history and religion, and became one of the most respected scholars of her generation.[37] Eugénie had few such role models; Ersilia Lovatelli, with her blend of scholarly distinction and social sophistication, showed that women could be successful in a world dominated and shaped by men. The friendship that was formed between them during that first year in Rome continued until Lovatelli's death in 1925.

Eugénie travelled frequently to Florence to visit Vernon Lee, who had become a pillar of that city's self-contained and eccentric foreign community. She shared her villa with her companion, Clementina 'Kit' Anstruther-Thomson, in one of the more open lesbian relationships of the era. Kit was an art student with a strong interest in criticism and visual theory.[38] Vernon's own interest in ancient art had been sparked by Eugénie's lectures on Greek sculpture at the British Museum, and she retained a great respect for her as an art historian. Years later she referred a student to Eugénie, noting: 'I am teaching her all I can in the way of aesthetics along my lines. But I want her also to get some notion of Kunstforschung in your sense.'[39]

In the preface of her 1896 book, *Renaissance Fancies and Studies*, she made a special point of thanking Eugénie for her advice and assistance.

At that time the expatriate American art connoisseur Bernard Berenson was establishing himself in Florence. Berenson and Vernon Lee had a long, complex and often stormy relationship.[40] Berenson had read her early writings with some appreciation when he was an undergraduate, and had set out to cultivate her friendship when he arrived in Italy. Initially Lee found the young man interesting, and made him part of her salon set. However, when the ambitious and egotistical Berenson established his own reputation as a technical art critic, their relationship soured. He was always suspicious of potential rivals, and he became convinced that Vernon and Kit were pirating his ideas in their publications. In the end he accused them of outright plagiarism, and an enormous fight ensued. The Lee–Berenson friendship was only renewed after Kit's death in 1922.[41]

It was probably Vernon Lee who introduced Eugénie to Berenson. Both were regular visitors at her villa, Il Palmerino, and their paths continued to cross, mingling with other expatriate intellectuals, for example, at an 1895 Florentine soirée.[42] By 1896, 'the temperamental and beautiful' Eugénie was touring the galleries and private collections of Rome with Berenson and Mary Costelloe, his then mistress and future wife. The American Harry Brewster, writing to his friend the composer Ethel Smythe, described the art-appreciation dynamics: 'Miss Sellers, whom I like very much, Mrs Costelloe, a cultivated American young widow [*sic*] afflicted with the mania for knowing who has painted what, and rewriting the picture galleries (which could be done in three words 'requiescant in pace') and the young man, Berenson, whose words they drink in'.[43] Strong intellectual, social and erotic attractions drew Berenson and Eugénie to one another. They were both talented and ambitious individuals making their way in an often hostile world. Berenson was a bright Jewish boy from Boston who had attracted the attention of the powerful American cultural patron Charles Eliot Norton, who helped him through Harvard. He was just making his presence felt on the European art and cultural scene, and displayed that combination of intellect, elegance and self-confident sexuality that attracted her. Their complex and occasionally stormy friendship endured until the outbreak of World War II.

Eugénie established an even more intense friendship with Mary Costelloe. Mary came from a Philadelphia Quaker family who encouraged her intellectual and cultural development.[44] In 1885 she married Frank Costelloe, a British barrister, and moved to London. Mary and Eugénie probably met through her brother Logan Pearsall Smith, who was a friend of Eugénie. They soon became close, sharing their most intimate thoughts and feelings, although Eugénie's frankness occasionally strained their relationship. Mary noted in her diary for 9 July 1896:

Miss Sellers came up to spend the night. She was full of kindly lecturing, and she has a fine outspokenness, so that she really gave me what is so rare, a perfectly friendly adverse criticism of Bernard and myself. She thinks that to take people up and to drop them with such indignation as we do is undignified ... Bernard has the reputation of being a man, who cannot bear other men, as he is furiously jealous of their reputation.[45]

Two other Florentine friends of Eugénie embodied the eccentric diversity of that city's English and American communities. One was the American diplomat Lewis Einstein, who divided his life between the cultured world of Florence, where his villa was famous for its good table and good conversation, and a rather undistinguished career as an American diplomat. He was distinctive in 'his polished diction, his historical anecdotes and cosmopolitan urbanity', but was also as 'ponderous in manner as in physique'.[46] His diplomatic posts included Paris and Peking, but also isolated dead ends like Costa Rica. His heart remained in Florence, where he returned periodically.

More permanently attached to Florence was another American friend, Charles Loeser. He came from a rich New York Jewish family, and always had the means to live a cultivated, independent life.[47] At Harvard he fell under the spell of Charles Eliot Norton's aestheticism, with its glorification of Renaissance Italy. He settled in Florence, where he devoted his energies and resources to collecting art and to the improvement of his villa. He and Bernard Berenson had much in common, but Berenson became increasingly caustic about Loeser's limitations as an art critic.[48] However, Loeser in contrast to Berenson retained genuine if naïve affection for Florence's golden age. As the philosopher George Santayana observed, Loeser 'loved the Italian Renaissance and was not, as it were, displaying it'.[49]

During these years Eugénie formed another friendship that was to be central to her life, that with the French archaeologist and savant Salomon Reinach, who belonged to a distinguished Jewish family of Swiss origins. Unlike Berenson the Reinachs affirmed their Jewish heritage. His brother Theodore, also a classicist, wrote a history of the Jews, and another brother, Joseph, was an active defender of Dreyfus. Salomon, although a free thinker on matters of religion, was one of the founders of the Jewish Colonial

Association and was highly critical of Berenson for his failure to come to the defence of Dreyfus.[50]

The Reinachs were a family of considerable financial means, and deep, diverse culture. Salomon had studied at the University of Paris and at the French School in Athens. He conducted his early archaeological research in French North Africa. Much of his career was spent at the prehistoric and Gallo-Roman archaeological museum at Saint-Germain-en-Lay, near Paris, where he was director from 1902 to 1932. He edited *Revue archeologique*, the premier French archaeological journal, for nearly thirty years.

Reinach's archaeological and art-historical interests were wide ranging, and his list of publications vast. The years spent at Saint-Germain-en-Lay made him a recognized expert on Celtic and Gallo-Roman archaeology, and Eugénie's appreciation of the art and archaeology of the western Roman provinces, unusual in a classical archaeologist of her generation, was due in no small measure to her friendship with him. They also shared an interest in ancient religion. He was one of the first French scholars to use the comparative anthropological researches of Robertson Smith and James Frazer, and was the author of such works as *Orpheus: histoire generale des religions* and five volumes of *Cultes, mythes et religions*.

Reinach was also art history professor at the École du Louvre, where he lectured on Renaissance painting. That position drew him into the complex and often treacherous world of late nineteenth-century art connoisseurs. He respected the ability of the young Berenson to employ detailed stylistic analysis in the attribution of Renaissance paintings to specific artists and schools. However, Reinach was more sympathetic to the traditional, document-based approach to art history. As one who was by nature a conciliator, he tried to keep lines of communication open to all factions.

Reinach led a very full, cosmopolitan lifestyle. One contemporary remembered:

His home, in a suburb of Paris, was a beautiful house, full of beautiful objects and containing an art library of the most comprehensive character. There he gathered about him students of all countries. His conversation was most stimulating and ranged over a very wide area of human interest. He was the reverse of a pedant. He lived in contact, not merely with a group of scholars, but with intelligent persons of all kinds and qualities.[51]

He was not without his limitations. He was involved in too many projects and did not pursue subjects in sufficient depth; his mastery of information was much better than his aesthetic insight. His publications tended to be manuals and compilations rather than imaginative new contributions to art history, and his tastes were rather conservative at that moment when French art was being revolutionized. He observed of Monet's paintings that 'he never saw such an abominable display of insanity or charlatanism'.[52]

As Eugénie wandered through the monuments and museums of Rome and exchanged ideas in the *fin de siècle* salons, she increasingly articulated a clearer vision of what her scholarly future might be. The Greek and Italian experience had confirmed her commitment to classical archaeology. Interactions with intellectuals like Bernard Berenson and Salomon Reinach had strengthened her scholarly self-confidence. Observing the urbane and talented Ersilia Lovatelli she realized that a woman could have a successful career as an independent scholar.

5

The German Years

Eugénie had already recognized the centrality of German archaeological scholarship, but realized that in doing so she was challenging the views of most of her countrymen. A typical British reaction to German research was expressed in a review of one of Adolf Furtwängler's books on Greek sculpture: 'In our own country in particular his name has become almost a household word in certain circles, thanks in great measure to the energy with which his views have been propounded in lectures and otherwise by those learned ladies who, for a number of years, have been wont to hie from Cambridge and Oxford to complete their archaeological studies in Berlin.'[1]

The German research that most interested Eugénie focused on Greek sculpture. One school, whose roots went back to Heinrich von Brunn, concentrated on what the ancient authors had to say about art and artists. Those scholars sought to reconstruct Greek artistic personalities and create the documentary framework for the study of Greek and Roman art.[2]

The ancient sculpture that has survived is mainly Roman copies of Greek originals. Thousands of these are to be seen in the great European collections. Scholarship on this material goes back to the eighteenth century and the pioneering research of Winckelmann, who had glorified the artistic world of fifth century BC Greece and, in both his scholarly research and his artistic ideology, laid the foundations of the Germanic classical archaeological tradition.[3]

Eugénie had to come to grips with the Winckelmann legacy, although in her later years she expressed ambivalence about his views on ancient art. The German archaeologist Ludwig Curtius, himself a great admirer of Winckelmann, remembered her reservations.[4] However, Curtius had not known the young Eugénie who had matured in the generation of the aesthetes and moved in the circles of Leighton and Burne-Jones. Significantly, Walter Pater's personal copy of Winckelmann was one of her most prized possessions.[5] She admired the German savant's knowledge of the great Roman collections and his ability to synthesize the fragmentary evidence into a credible art-historical framework. Her reservations were less about Winckelmann's judgments and more about his legacy. She was especially bothered by a sterile British aestheticism, which she felt stifled innovative thinking about Greek art. As her own interests shifted toward the Hellenistic and Roman periods, she came to reject Winckelmann's negative judgments on later classical art.[6]

Eugénie Sellers was ready for the challenge of the German scholarly world. At the British Museum she had mastered a collection of original Greek sculpture greater than any in Germany. Her travels with Dörpfeld and her year in Athens had made her familiar with the Hellenic monuments, and she had come to know the museums of Europe well. Her command of languages both ancient and modern, her knowledge of the ways of the Continent, and her personal and financial independence allowed her to undertake an extended period of study in Germany.

The decision was also an existential one, a personal statement of independence and self-sufficiency and of her desire to escape from the limitations of her London life. Laurence Alma-Tadema praised her action, writing supportively, 'I think you are so right to take your life into your own hands and lift it out of this quagmire.'[7]

Following the German student custom, she moved from one university community to another, working with particular mentors. By late 1892 she was in Berlin, then the greatest university and museum centre in Europe, the intellectual and cultural showpiece of the emerging German state, with great scholars such as Theodor Mommsen still active. Eugénie was on the whole well received, although some senior academics found the self-confident, even brash, young British woman less than totally appealing. Her friend Alice Sophia Green reassured her: 'I am very glad to hear that the professors have been so satisfactory. Mommsen belongs to another age and his approval or disapproval of women's work won't make any more difference to the rest of them than it does to you.'[8] In the end even Mommsen yielded to her intellect and charm.

It was in Berlin that Eugénie came to know Adolf Furtwängler, the brightest star of his archaeological generation. The son of a Gymnasium director, he had studied at Freiburg, Leipzig and Munich. His major professor had been Heinrich Brunn, and from him he had learned the art of combining literary and archaeological evidence.[9] Furtwängler was awarded a travelling scholarship, which he spent in Italy and Greece, participating in the early excavations at Olympia, the training ground for the new generation of German archaeologists. He then returned to a curatorship at the Berlin Museum. There he laid the foundations of his formidable reputation with his research on Greek vases and gems and on the history of Greek sculpture. His mind ranged widely, and he could appreciate the relevance of modern works like Darwin's *The Expression of Emotion in Animals and Man* to the study of Greek art.

In 1894 Furtwängler was called to the professorship of classical archaeology at Munich, a chair created for his old teacher Brunn. There his students included such famous classical archaeologists as Ludwig Curtius, Georg Lippold and Ernst Buschor. An American, J. E. Church, who studied with Furtwängler in 1899, provided a vivid picture of him in his prime:

He was a man of striking individuality. In external appearance he was a German edition of Mark Twain – tall, lithe, with bushy hair and nervous. To a stranger he might appear austere, and his nervous expectancy tended to make the stammering foreigner stammer worse in his search for words. He had a keen sense of the ludicrous, though he held himself in check whenever his merry laugh would deeply cut the perpetrator of some stupidity ... He was admired by his students, and his lectures were as numerously attended at the close of the semester as were the lectures of some professors at the beginning. He, too, was fond of his students, of the Americans, as well, and to women he gave a generous welcome, even freely admitting them to examination for the doctorate before such admission was formally given by the university.[10]

Not all contemporaries were so impressed. While a French scholar described Furtwängler as the Napoleon of classical archaeology, some of his German contemporaries thought of him as an Attila.[11]

In Munich Furtwängler also became director of the Glyptothek, the archaeological museum founded by King Ludwig I of Bavaria to house the Aegina sculptures. Furtwängler assembled a first-class library, expanded the cast collection and published a new catalogue. Open to technical innovations, he created extensive photographic and lantern-slide archives. He wrote of the potential of photography for archaeology: 'Anyone who understands how to observe the monuments, and who is willing with indefatigable ardour, to test afresh and compare all forms, may nowadays, by means of photography, which helps to fix the individual objects, obtain a picture of Greek art far more richly coloured than the pale and meagre image we have hitherto possessed.'[12]

Eugénie followed Furtwängler from Berlin to Munich in 1893. He clearly found her combination of archaeological knowledge, artistic insight, intelligence, good looks and sophisticated charm very appealing (plate 8). She in turn was sympathetic to Furtwängler's scholarly goals and admired his energy, organizational ability and mastery of archaeological evidence.

She sought to propagandize his methods and accomplishments in the English-speaking world. To that end she prepared for the publisher William Heinemann an English translation of his 1893 *Die Meisterwerke griechischer Plastik* (*Masterpieces of Greek Sculpture*). It was an elegant edition with good illustrations.[13] Eugénie used her editor's preface to praise Furtwängler and to express her own views on Greek sculpture. The book appeared at a time when discoveries of original Greek sculptures at sites like Olympia and Athens were undermining scholarly interest in the study of Roman copies. She supported Furtwängler's position that many originals discovered in Greece had escaped looting by the Roman conquerors because they were considered inferior works. The most valued had been carried off to Rome, where the copies that had survived were produced. Thus the study of those Roman copies still had to form the basis of any serious history of Greek sculpture.

Eugénie came to know the Furtwängler family very well and often visited their home in suburban Schwabing. Furtwängler's wife Adelheid ('Addy') came from a family with strong musical and scientific interests and was an amateur painter. Eugénie later recalled with affection their cultured lifestyle: 'The Furtwängler household preserved much of the old German soul; its informality, absorption in study, faithfulness to old customs, above all love of music.' That intense musical environment fostered one of the great conductors of this century, their son Wilhelm Furtwängler.[14]

Her other academic mentor during the Munich years was the classical philologist Ludwig Traube (plate 9).[15] As she plunged into her study of Pliny the Elder's writings on ancient art, Traube provided her with the philological balance to Furtwängler's archaeological expertise. Sellers' diaries record frequent meetings to read Greek and Latin, and in the background one can feel their deepening friendship and a growing erotic attraction. Mary Costelloe sensed her growing attachment:

I should never dream of classifying your feelings in any hackneyed category. There are such infinite nuances in the emotions of self-conscious, not-too-young people that it is absurd to set them down under school girl heads. Some people never 'fall in love' in that idiotic way – which nevertheless has its claim; but they are no less capable of very deep and enduring affection and such that I am sure that you must feel for that exquisitely cultivated and sympathetic man.[16]

Traube was the son of a well-to-do Berlin Jewish doctor. He received an excellent education and in his early years travelled extensively. However, he also had numerous physical and psychological problems. Most debilitating was his agoraphobia, which made it difficult for him to leave home even to fulfil basic university duties. In spite of such limitations Traube had great appeal for his students. They enjoyed his convivial personality and appreciated his great learning.

Friends hoped that Eugénie might help him lead a happier, more productive life, but the invalid Traube and the dynamic, independent Eugénie Sellers were not destined for each other. Nevertheless, their friendship continued unabated through the years. Eugénie kept a picture of Traube with her throughout her life and friends updated her on his activities and especially his growing health problems. She grieved deeply when he died.

Years later Eugénie admitted that the time spent in Munich had been the happiest of her life.[17] A foreigner could still live very cheaply there, and Munich was a city where both Germans and foreigners felt comfortable. Although it had a population of half a million, there were few factories. In the words of a pre-World War I guidebook, 'works of art and beer are the only products which Munich supports in any considerable quantity'.[18] Its universities, libraries and museums drew many English and American students, and its large artistic community ensured a lively cultural scene. There were concerts and skating in the English Gardens.

Mary Lowndes shared much of the Munich experience with Eugénie. They lived in a romantic if somewhat damp apartment by a mill pond in the rustic suburb of Schwaberei, the artistic centre of Munich. One contemporary observed, 'anyone who walked about there without palette, or without canvas, at without at least a portfolio, immediately attracted attention. Just like a "stranger" in a village.'[19] While Eugénie worked on Pliny, Mary pursued her own historical researches.

The project that commanded Eugénie's scholarly attention during the German years was the preparation of a translation with commentary of the sections of Pliny the Elder's *Natural History* related to ancient art. It was a collaborative effort, with fellow Girtonian Katharine Jex-Blake translating the Latin text and Eugénie providing archaeological and philological commentary. The elder Pliny was a first-century Roman official best known for his efforts to rescue the refugees from the AD 79 eruption of Vesuvius. He was an energetic polymath who ransacked the Greek and Roman writers for his wide-ranging *Natural History*, which provides the most complete body of information on the art and artists of the Greek and Roman world.[20] Eugénie undertook the difficult task of writing an introduction and commentary that would give context and meaning to Pliny's scattered observations on art, many of which had been excerpted from Greek commentaries. That body of literature was enormous in antiquity, but has almost all been lost. Most authors are known by their names, the titles of their works and a few fragments. Reconstructing what they thought and wrote is a massive challenge.[21] Philological and historical analysis of the ancient texts represented only the first stage of her research. The fragmentary information provided on the ancient artists and their creations had to be integrated with the vast corpus of unsigned works of art that survived from antiquity. Sculptures that had been grouped together on the basis of style had then to be assigned to artists whose careers and accomplishments were known from the texts. The combined body of texts and monuments provided the foundations for a new 'scientific' history of ancient art.

The Pliny project required an impressive combination of literary and archaeological knowledge. Eugénie always regarded the final book as one of her major works of scholarship. The soundness of her judgment has been demonstrated by the fact that the work was reprinted in the 1970s. Father Raymond Schoder, in his preface to the new edition, observed: 'Sellers' introduction and commentary brilliantly utilized the complex researches of 19th century German scholars on Pliny, presenting the results in a clear and specific analysis of the background to Pliny's treatise on art and in very intelligent notes below the text.'[22] If anything the work has assumed greater importance in recent years, for scholars have gained a greater appreciation of the originality of Pliny the Elder's intellectual and cultural agenda. As Father Schoder also noted: 'No one surely would be more pleased than Eugénie Sellers herself to see Pliny now more esteemed for his true scholarship and fundamental originality.'[23]

The writing of the book produced a dispute over scholarly turf that provides insight into both the forceful character of Sellers and German academic politics of the day. Eugénie had become aware of the parallel research of a young German archaeologist named Heinrich Urlichs. The two communicated on the project, and Urlichs shared with her some of his notes. The collaboration became so extensive that Urlichs claimed the right to be listed as an author on the title page, a claim driven in great part by his personal career anxieties – his father was a distinguished classicist, and he wished to prove his filial worth. He also needed a major publication to justify a research stipend granted him by the Bavarian educational ministry. If he failed he faced the prospect of being dispatched to some backwater pedagogical post. He was outraged when Eugénie refused his request and attacked her in correspondence and in print. She continued to reject his claims. They finally reached a face-saving compromise. Urlich's 'additional notes contributed' were acknowledged on the title page, but he did not receive full author status. In her preface, Sellers explained this final compromise:

> One group of contributions has been made to this book calling for special notice. When my work was already advancing towards completion, I learnt that Dr H. L. Urlichs was himself engaged upon an edition of the same parts of Pliny. With ready generosity, however, Dr Urlichs offered me at once for my own book a number of his notes which he agreed should be printed in square brackets and marked with his initials H.L.U. Subsequently, however, Dr Urlichs informed me, to my regret and surprise, that the present edition would block the way for his own; accordingly, since he had given us notes, whose value is undeniable, we acceded to his request that his name should be placed as a third on our title-page.[24]

In later years she felt that she had been rather harsh with Urlichs, and acknowledged that she had acted out of momentary anger. Urlichs was not destined to scholarly obscurity, however: Furtwängler asked him to co-author and edit a general book on Greek and Roman sculpture.[25]

The Elder Pliny's Chapters on the History of Art was well received. A. G. Bather in the *Classical Review* was especially laudatory about Eugénie's preface:

> The study of the sources of Pliny's information, though no new one in Germany, has never been seriously taken up by English scholars, so that students of the subject have had to have recourse to numerous scattered German monographs, several of them difficult to obtain. We are doubly indebted therefore to Miss Sellers for collecting with admirable patience and completeness the results arrived at by these scholars and for putting them before us in a clear and concise form ... though we may not be as firm believers as Miss Sellers herself in the German methods and the deductions derived from them, it is essential that any archaeologist should know and be able to judge of the fruits

of the most methodical analysis which any writer has perhaps ever undergone.[26]

The most revealing review appeared in the *Guardian* for 24 February 1897. It was by S. Arthur Strong, the man who was already courting Eugénie and who would soon become her husband. The circumstances of its publication provide a good insight into the closely knit, slightly corrupt world of contemporary English journals. Newspapers and periodicals made widespread use of anonymous reviews. Reviewers closely associated with authors could praise their work without any partisanship being revealed. On the other hand the shield of anonymity allowed impressive displays of academic nastiness. Control of the review process was of major concern to authors. Not only did Eugénie have her book reviewed by the man she would soon marry, but the two arranged for friendly reviewers in other publications.

Arthur Strong's review was wide ranging, yet slightly pretentious. Needless to say, it was also highly positive. As was typical for reviewers in Victorian intellectual publications, Strong not only discussed the book, but also used the occasion to advance his own views on a variety of topics. His often barbed comments reflected his views on the current state of art-historical research. He acknowledged the limits of scholarship based on the mechanistic compilation of facts without aesthetic insight; at the same time he despised aesthetes like Berenson who based their art historical judgments on 'a refined eye and an exquisite sense of taste'. His last sentence read: 'To those who have learned wisdom under the long discipline of restraint, knowledge will now come quickly, and of this synthesis posterity will reap the fruit, provided only that they do not forget love.' It was a coded message from one scholarly lover to another. By the time the book was published, Arthur and Eugénie were engaged.

The publication of the book marked an important turning point in Eugénie Sellers' life. Her most immediate need was to recover from the exhaustion of what she described as 'a long scientific orgy'. However, she also had to plan her future. Her principal reason for the long residence in Munich was fulfilled, and she entertained visions of her future that ranged from the life of a rural intellectual to that of a scholarly socialite. Her relationship with Mary Lowndes remained close, and they intended to continue their life together. One plan was to acquire a house in the village of Haslemere, some forty miles south-west of London. That would allow them to continue to enjoy the rustic life while having regular access to the capital. They had even found a suitable cottage not far from the country house of Mary Costelloe's family, and Mary's brother, Logan Pearsall Smith, had already begun planning the interior decoration.[27]

At the other extreme Eugénie still dreamed of moving in the socially and culturally elite worlds of England and the Continent. During her years in Munich she had regularly returned to London, where she had maintained her many friendships among the capital's intellectuals and artists. However, she was too old and too educated to continue to play the role of the London beauty, and she lacked the financial resources to set herself up as a hostess, entertaining in the grand manner. One friend told her bluntly: 'You want to live an elegant life, surrounded by "picturische" people – you forget that for that much money and social position are needed, and that for better or worse you have chosen the life of a Gelehrte.'[28]

Academic prospects remained as bleak as ever. Teaching positions were few, and her turn from classical philology to classical archaeology ended any real possibility of teaching classics at the women's colleges. Jane Harrison, older, more experienced and much better published than Eugénie, still did not have a permanent position. A return to secondary education held no appeal.

Museum opportunities were even more limited. Even though she possessed as good a knowledge of classical art and archaeology as any male scholar in England, had a level of German professional archaeological training still very rare among British museum curators, and had just published an important, well-received book, her chances for a position at the British Museum were virtually nil. That remained a tightly knit male club that was not about to welcome a glamorous female with a German archaeological education.

She was also confused about the future direction of her own scholarship. On the one hand she wanted 'to get beyond archaeology, beyond the mere cataloging of monuments'. She talked of writing a history of art criticism among the ancient Greeks as a follow-up to her Pliny. At the same time her developing friendships with Berenson and with Arthur Strong had given her a sense of inferiority about her own powers of aesthetic analysis, and she lamented that 'I shall never be good at the purely aesthetic side of art, for I have not the intuition.'[29]

One other option remained open, and that was marriage. At thirty-six, Eugénie was well beyond the normal Victorian age for marriage. However, she was still handsome and had a persistent, long-suffering suitor. Much to the surprise of her friends, she decided to take a husband.

6

Courtship and Marriage

Friends had long admired the intelligence and charm of Eugénie Sellers. Mary Costelloe relayed to her the praises of a mutual friend: 'you were the most to be envied woman in existence – independent with brains and having won a position everyone respects, beautiful, healthy, with friends who adore you and work you like.'[1] However, Mary was very conscious of the negative side of Eugénie, what she referred to as the effect of 'the wicked fairy who wasn't invited to your christening, stole in and laid the curse on you that these things should not make you content'.[2] That discontent manifested itself in a variety of forms, including a restlessness that provoked periodic health crises that deeply concerned close friends.

One thing that is striking in Eugénie's extensive youthful correspondence is the lack of references to serious romantic attachments. Certainly an erotic attraction developed between her and Traube, but it came to nothing. Eugénie, like so many women, was sexually drawn to Bernard Berenson, and they may well have had brief affairs. However, she was too dynamic and independent to enter into a long-term romantic relationship with the domineering 'BB'. The one documented courtship before Arthur Strong was unilateral and absurd. In October of 1894, Bertrand Russell wrote to his fiancée Alys Smith, 'I am much interested about Logan and Miss Sellers.' He was referring to a rumoured romance between Eugénie and Logan Pearsall Smith, Alys's and Mary Costelloe's brother. The romantic overtures 'consisted on Logan's part of his putting on his best clothes, picking some flowers and wandering about waiting'.[3] Logan was described by a contemporary as an individual who couldn't 'find a wife or a career to suit him'. He was a confirmed bachelor and somewhat misogynistic.[4]

Eugénie had several intense female friendships. Mary Beard has suggested a strong romantic and even sexual relationship with Jane Harrison.[5] She was also a lifelong friend of the openly lesbian Vernon Lee. Certainly Mary Lowndes was a continuous presence throughout those years, and was to react to Eugénie's marriage more like an abandoned lover than a dispossessed friend. However, the language of Victorian female friendship was an intense one, and hard for a modern scholar to interpret. In the interchange of epistolary emotion it is not easy to distinguish the Platonic from the sexual. Hesitations about marriage may have derived in part from her sexual inclinations. However, they may also have reflected her desire to establish her reputation as a scholar, a goal that early marriage and child-bearing would have made impossible.

Nevertheless, in 1897 Eugénie did marry. Her new husband was Sandford Arthur Strong, a scholar of oriental languages and literatures and a historian of art. He was a handsome man and like her an energetic, innovative intellectual with strong Continental connections. It is probable that they were introduced by mutual friends at the University of London, where Arthur taught, or through the many artistic and cultural circles they both frequented. By 1892 they were corresponding regularly.

They shared many tastes and interests, especially in the arts. In London, Eugénie and Arthur toured the latest art exhibitions and attended concerts. Eugénie soon developed a deep respect for Arthur's brilliance and learning. However, they had very different personalities. Eugénie was poised, socially self-confident and open to new ideas. Arthur was much more insecure, and that insecurity often manifested itself in his haughty, distant manner. Conflicts marred their long and frequently stormy courtship and were the bases of many tensions during their marriage. Eugénie early acknowledged Arthur's limitations to Mary Costelloe:

> He is a man who had not the patience to wait and struggle in obscurity, since our England has little encouragement to give to scholars at the beginning ... Poor man, I was cruel to call him a snob ... what he really does when in the presence of people whom he feels might ignore him is to pile up proofs of his ignorance ... One day he spoke cruelly ... bullied me about having left England and I retorted that ... he had not the courage to struggle for his profession.[6]

Central to their disagreements was Eugénie's need for a personal freedom that extended beyond the accepted role of a Victorian wife, and her determination to continue her scholarly career. Arthur was at heart a very conservative Victorian male. Mary Costelloe warned: 'But goodness, if a man realizes that your kind of woman is a "paradox", if he likes that kind, he ought to pay the price and treat her as such instead of trying to break her will and bullying her into compliance, which after all could not last and would not satisfy him while it did.'[7]

Arthur Strong was repeatedly forced to address her concerns. As early as 1892 he wrote: 'What would make me feel sore would be the thought that I had even in the slightest degree robbed you of your complete (and most precious) freedom of thought and speech. For true help means doing the best one can to remove obstacles for another's chosen path in life.'[8] A few months later he had to apologize for some ill-received remarks: 'Of course, I cannot tell how much women have suffered in the way you speak of, but I had seen enough to know that they might and probably did suffer, when I resolved that if ever the privilege came to me of offering help and support to a woman, her freedom to feel and do as she chose and to be what she chose should not suffer.'[9]

More than once the courtship appeared to have reached a dead end. At one point Sellers broke their engagement and ran off to tour Italy with Bernard Berenson. Her friendship with the American art historian certainly represented a major source of tension with Arthur. Berenson and Arthur Strong's paths had already crossed in the scholarly art circles of London and Florence. They disagreed professionally and disliked each other personally. The bright young Bostonian was always very prickly and defensive when dealing with art historians whom he regarded as serious rivals, and Strong was at his worst with bright, worldly competitors, especially those who had the social self-confidence that he lacked.

They disagreed violently about the proper approach to the study of art history. Berenson had become an apostle of technical connoisseurship, where small points of style were used to attribute paintings to artists and schools. He saw this approach as providing the foundations for a truly scientific art history. He was also employing his mastery of that method to lay the foundation of a very profitable consulting business that catered to the growing world of American art collectors.[10] He balanced this technical approach with a vague aestheticism that derived from the English cultural historian Walter Pater and his own Harvard teacher Charles Eliot Norton, talking of such concepts as 'tactile value'. However, he was less interested in the archival research and detailed Germanic historical scholarship that provided information for the reconstruction of the economic, social and cultural ambiance in which great art was created.

Arthur Strong argued for the centrality of such documentary research and the development of art history as a solid branch of scientific cultural history. He regarded the Berenson approach as much too limiting and too superficial. Strong's model for good research remained Joseph Archer Crowe and Giovanni Battista Cavalcaselle's classic *History of Painting in Italy*. Crowe was an English journalist who had developed both a deep love for art and considerable expertise in art history. Cavalcaselle was an Italian art historian whom the events of the abortive uprisings of 1848 turned into a political exile. The Englishman and the Italian embarked on a lifelong collaboration that made them among the most highly regarded experts on Italian painting during the mid-nineteenth century.[11]

Strong's reputation as a well-respected supporter of Crowe and Cavalcaselle led to an invitation to revise and update their classic text. His co-editor was to be Robert Langton Douglas, an Anglican cleric turned art historian who had published extensively on Renaissance painting and Italian urban history.[12] The project had the potential of not only enhancing Strong's scholarly reputation but also earning him some much-needed income. However, Arthur's commitment to a variety of other projects and his natural procrastination slowed the revisions, and only the first revised volume had appeared before his death.

The hostility between Arthur Strong and Berenson was also deeply personal. Arthur found the American's carefully crafted persona and his early success extremely galling. Berenson was a rising star in the international art world, while he found himself struggling to find a position suitable to his talents and ambitions. At the same time, Berenson was both contemptuous and jealous of rivals. He realized that Strong, with his wide-ranging intellect and mastery of technical scholarship, would be a formidable foe and remained very suspicious of him.

The politics of Renaissance art history during the late nineteenth century were venomous. The American expatriate Charles Loeser, who knew that world and its principal figures extremely well, warned Eugénie: 'I hope that you will succeed for the future in keeping Arthur's hands off "Italian art". With his great earnestness, his great sense of righteousness, its contact must sour the milk of human kindness within him and all one's worse troubles are the consequence of that.'[13] Berenson's resentments and paranoia were fuelled by the English system of anonymous book reviewing, where one could easily imagine a personal enemy lurking behind a hostile evaluation. When a poisonous review of one of Berenson's books appeared in the *Manchester Guardian*, the Berenson camp attributed the review to Arthur Strong, a charge that was heatedly denied.[14] The charges and counter-charges began to undermine even Mary Berenson and Eugénie's long-standing friendship. Eugénie accused Mary of 'attempting to bully and blackmail all of the world into siding with Berenson'. Mary retorted that a recent remark by Eugénie 'was a scarcely veiled sneer at the life we are living here ... it ended, I remember, with an expression of the deep commiseration "you and your husband felt for what you considered the intellectual tragedy" of my brother's [Logan Pearsall Smith's] life and an attack on his "third-rate" friends.'[15]

Further fueling these tensions was the fact that Berenson was of Jewish origins, even though he tended to deny his Jewish roots in the interest of assimilation and professional and personal advancement.[16] A very unappealing quality of Arthur Strong was his late nineteenth-century conservative British anti-Semitism. As one close acquaintance acknowledged in an obituary, 'To him as to Charles Lamb a Hebrew was nowhere congenial.'[17] He felt that Jews could never be fully integrated into English society, and became vehemently anti-Dreyfus as the fate of the victimized French officer divided society on both sides of the Channel. His friend Maurice Baring remembered Arthur's forceful comments on the case.[18]

Arthur's views on Dreyfus were certainly influenced by his brother Rowland, a long-time resident in the French capital and at that time Paris correspondent for *Pall Mall*, the London *Observer* and the *New York Times*. Rowland had more than a reporter's involvement in the case and participated in some of the more sordid events surrounding Commandant Ferdinand Walsin-Esterhazy, the man who had actually committed the espionage for which Dreyfus was condemned.[19]

Strong's stand on Dreyfus reflected his deep conservatism on all social and political matters. To a French friend he once remarked, 'Je suis un instransigeant.' He wrote for the politically conservative French journal *Action Française*. On his death a highly laudatory obituary was published there.[20] However, his general views about Jews did not necessarily extend to individuals. One friend noted that 'his political hatred of the Jew in general was in singular contrast to his tolerance for individual Jews. On two memorable occasions, when scholarly and not political interests were at stake, he was found to cast his influence (and it proved decisive) in favour of Jewish *savants* against an action which he held to savour of persecution.'[21]

Eugénie's attitudes could not have been more different. One does not find in her extensive correspondence any of the anti-Semitism so characteristic of Arthur. From youth to old age she had many Jewish friends: she and Hertha Marks had been close during the Girton and early London days; Salomon Reinach was, after Adolf Furtwängler, her most important scholarly mentor; she was devoted to the Mond family and to Henrietta Hertz; Ludwig Pollck was an intellectual companion of her Rome years. All were important figures in the contemporary European Jewish community.

Other social and cultural attitudes separated Eugénie and Arthur. In her London years Eugénie had been involved in educational initiatives aimed at popular education; Arthur, in contrast, regularly railed against the democratization of the universities. In the words of one obituary:

All the mutual aid societies of the day, the University Extension and other schemes for spreading knowledge won from him scant sympathy ... He saw with peculiar concern the new University of London busying itself with the task of educating the nation, holding not this, but the nurture of that higher scholarship which can never be the portion of the multitude, to be the chief function of the university.[22]

In spite of his prejudices and rigidities, Strong impressed most who knew him with his brilliance and the range as well as depth of his knowledge. Maurice Baring, one of the most sophisticated and well-read intellectuals of his day, remembered their first meetings: 'I made Arthur Strong's acquaintance at Edmund Gosse's House, and he was from that moment kind to me. In appearance he was like pictures of Erasmus ... the perfect incarnation of a scholar. He knew and understood everything, but forgave little. And the smoke from the flame of his learning and his intellect sometimes got into people's eyes.'[23] Salomon Reinach was equally impressed:

An extensive learning such as I never met excepting in François Lenormant and in Sayce, a genuine enthusiasm for science, a straightness of reasoning which leaves no room to the vague ... an equal knowledge of the primary sources of science and of the huge bibliography pertaining to its various provinces – such are the high and exceptional qualities which appear in you and which induced such a giant as Renan to speak to me about you in the highest terms.[24]

Arthur Strong identified with the rational, learned and slightly cynical world of the later eighteenth century. He loved the works of Joshua Reynolds, Jonathan Swift and Dr Johnson. He preferred the music of Mozart to that of Wagner. However, he also had his Romantic, emotional side. He admired the poetry of Byron and Shelley and was a close friend of Algernon Swinburne. Even more surprisingly, he was drawn to the art of the baroque genius Bernini, and unexpected in one with so little empathy for those outside the social and cultural elite was his deep appreciation of Dickens.

Arthur's complex persona was the product of an unusual family and education and a long period of professional insecurity. His father was a civil servant, while his mother, Anna Lawson, was a learned student of the Hebrew language and literature. His older brother Thomas had a successful student career at Christ Church, Oxford, then entered the Church and rose to be Bishop of Ripon and then Oxford.[25] Thomas's academic and ecclesiastical successes clearly haunted Arthur. There was also another brother, the journalist Rowland Strong, and a spinster sister, Mary.

81

Arthur started his secondary education at St Paul's School in London. However, he hated the place, left, and went to work at Lloyds Bank in London. After some remedial education at King's College, London, he entered St John's College, Cambridge. He overlapped with Eugénie at Cambridge for one year, but they appear never to have met. He studied for the classical tripos, but also developed a strong interest in Middle Eastern languages and literature. His talents in the latter field were sufficiently impressive for him to be sent to Oxford to study with such distinguished scholars as the Indo-Europeanist Max Müller and the Assyriologist A. H. Sayce. He studied both Indian and Semitic languages, worked as librarian and sub-keeper of the India Institute, and catalogued Müller's personal library. His Oxford mentors in turn sent him to Germany and France for more advanced work, culminating in a period of study with the great Parisian savants Ernest Renan and James Darmesteter.

Arthur's mastery of a great range of eastern languages especially impressed his contemporaries. He was fluent in Arabic, Akkadian, Hebrew, Persian, Sanskrit and even Chinese. The lecturer in Rabbinics at Cambridge praised his mastery of the Hebrew language and literature.[26] Moreover, his interests were not limited to narrow philological issues, for he had a good grasp of the literary and philosophical aspects of the texts he studied. Gertrude Bell was later to recall fondly the insights he had provided into the *Upanishads*.[27]

In Paris he became friendly with the historian of religion Ernest Renan, the author of a controversial 1863 biography of Jesus. The Renan that Strong befriended was a suave, somewhat cynical scholar known for his elegant style, his sardonic, amused view of the world, and his supposed lack of intellectual commitment.[28] Some Englishmen, such as the classicist Andrew Lang, savaged his writings; others admired him greatly.[29] Eugénie's friend Violet Markham recalled hearing him lecture at the College de France and claimed to have read every line that he had written.[30]

While Renan was certainly a successful public intellectual in the late nine-teenth-century French tradition, he had also had a long and distinguished career as a linguist, archaeologist and historian of religion. He clearly saw in Arthur Strong something of himself as a young scholar, and admired both his intellectual sophistication and his mastery of a complex scholarly world. A mutual respect and affection developed between the two very different men, and the Frenchman extended to Strong the rare honour of a personal tour of his native Brittany, to whose Celtic heritage Renan had an almost mystical attachment.

The time in Paris marked an important moment of transition in Arthur Strong's life. After long years of study he had to pursue a career. That was not an easy prospect. In spite of England's imperial involvement in the lands east of Suez, the professional study of oriental languages and cultures was poorly supported. As one of Arthur's friends lamented: 'In England, unless a man holds one of the few available posts in the universities, the Museum, or the India Office, he cannot "live of the doctrine" as an orientalist.'[31]

Not all prospects were bleak, for several prominent university teachers in the field were approaching retirement. However, Arthur had managed to offend many in the British academic establishment with undiplomatic statements, such as his characterization of Cambridge dons as 'baptized idlers'. Those dons were not about to make Arthur Strong a colleague: in spite of strong endorsements from an impressive array of scholars he was rebuffed when applying for positions at Oxford and at Cambridge.

He fared no better with the imperial bureaucracy. His extensive knowledge of the languages, literature and culture of the Indian subcontinent did not impress the Indian Colonial Office. In desperation he even considered applying for a position as tutor to the children of the royal family of Siam.[32] A more different figure than the legendary Anna is hard to imagine.

The increased bitterness and frustration that resulted from these thwarted ambitions did little to improve Arthur's rather hesitant, but also intellectually arrogant, personality. A contemporary described him as 'fanatical, overeager, supercilious'.[33] He also suffered from chronic ill-health. Clearly his energies were beginning to be sapped by the serious ailments that would tragically shorten his life. As a Victorian raised in that age of energy and productivity he was increasingly haunted by his inability to pull off the 'great work' of scholarship that would assure his immortality.

Arthur's luck changed in 1895 with his appointment as Professor of Arabic at University College, London. The position did not pay well, but it provided academic status and a structured outlet for his energies. He could teach Arabic and other languages to bright students like Gertrude Bell, soon to become an intrepid pioneer in Iraqi archaeology and British Middle-Eastern intelligence.

An even greater break came when a friend, the art historian Sidney Colvin, introduced him to the Duke of Devonshire. The Duke needed a librarian to care for his large and valuable collection of books, manuscripts and works of art. He was impressed by Strong and offered him the position. This appointment was followed by a second as librarian at Welbeck, the country house of the Duke of Portland; and finally by a third as librarian to the House of Lords.

The Lords librarianship was in many ways the most challenging and satisfying of his new positions. He was expected to provide a range of information and assistance to his noble patrons, activities that brought him into contact with some of the leading political figures of the day. Arthur had his own political ambitions, including a desire to put his conservative ideology into practice. He had considerable sympathy for Benjamin Disraeli's Young England Movement and hoped to play a leading role in the revitalization of the emerging generation of British aristocracy. He also shared some imperial dreams of the day and fantasized that 'his ideal occupation would be to govern orientals'.[34]

Surviving photos, busts and drawings show a young man with a thin, handsome face. Strong was a shy person who was often awkward and aloof with people he did not know well. One acquaintance described him as a 'man of many friends, but few intimates'.[35] One of his close friends, the Spanish-American philosopher George Santayana, provided a perceptive portrait of Arthur at the time of his marriage: 'With Arthur Strong's mind I felt a decided sympathy. He was very learned in important but remote matters, such as Arabic literature. His central but modest position in the great world gave him a satirical insight into affairs, and he summed up his inner solitude in pungent maxims.'[36]

While Eugénie and Arthur shared intellectual and cultural interests, they were clearly very different personalities. He had none of her openness or social skills. He was better at cutting people than making friends. Ironically, he resembled another man who was to play a very important role in Eugénie's later life, the archaeologist Thomas Ashby.

Eugénie Sellers and Arthur Strong married on 11 December 1897. The low-key civil ceremony was held at Kensington Registry Office with the minimum number of witnesses and attendants.[37] Even a few weeks before the wedding close friends did not know the exact date.

Reaction to the alliance was mixed. Eugénie's old friend Laurence Alma-Tadema greeted the news enthusiastically: 'The fearfully widespread spinsterhood of women with brains in this country is disastrous in the extreme. I am happy to think that a woman of your standing should give proof that mental superiority does not rob us of womanhood.'[38] Adolf Furtwängler, ever the ambitious academic, saw it as an ideal union of high society and scholarship that would provide scholars like himself access to the great homes of England. The shrewd and worldly Salomon Reinach was more ambivalent about what the marriage meant for Eugénie, and especially for her future as a scholar.[39]

Some female friends lamented the loss of their independent sister to matrimony. Mary Lowndes put on a good face, but was clearly devastated. She had looked forward to the continuation of their years together. Vernon Lee was unhappy, and even Mary Costelloe reacted negatively: 'I am really quite miserable about your marriage you know. I feel especially afraid it will separate you from all of us Bohemians.'[40]

Reinach's concern that Eugénie would be drawn into the social whirl and cease to be a serious scholar initially seemed justified. Accounts of ball gowns and dinner parties replaced scholarly references in her letters. The side of Eugénie's persona that wanted to move in the swish circles of high society was finding fulfilment in the social rounds of London and the country houses.

She soon realized that the transition from the independent life of an unmarried scholar to that of a married woman in late Victorian high society was not going to be easy. Her diaries document a frenetic round of luncheons, teas and dinners, of receiving calls and being called upon. Those complicated rituals left little time for scholarship, and the calls of conscience of the *Gelehrte* soon made her uneasy. In a letter to Mary Berenson, Eugénie responded with weary resignation about her new existence. 'About my life, what can I tell you.' She blamed the rituals of London society for her failure to be productive. She wanted to do scholarly work, but 'how can one if one is "at home" at 10:30'.[41] Her subdued mood was captured by George Santayana in his description of the recently married Eugénie:

Mrs Strong was a large woman, with bold pseudo-classic features like a late Roman statue of Niobe; and when I saw her in their house in London, she looked like a figure by Burne-Jones that had walked out of the canvas: great heavy eyes, a big nose, a short upper lip, and full, richly curving lips, over a conspicuous round chin. But the most characteristic thing about her was the neck, long, columnar and extremely convex in the throat, as if she habitually leaned forward and upwards at once. She was also, at the time, preraphaelite in dress. I remember her one day at luncheon in green cotton brocade, with a broad lace collar, like a bib drooping over it. She was silent, and let her husband talk. Perhaps her thoughts were far way from him and from me.[42]

Santayana's description of Eugénie matches well a photograph of her that appears to have been a wedding portrait (plate 10).

Tensions caused by her loss of independence and changes in her lifestyle were compounded by the couple's limited financial resources. Arthur received a very small family allowance of £10 per annum and earned a very modest salary from his various teaching and librarian positions. Eugénie also had a small income. From these they had to meet the expenses of life in high society and of two scholarly careers. Eugénie had more experience than Arthur in living within a tight budget, and his lavish expenditure on items such as books soon became a source of serious conflict.

For the next twelve years Eugénie, as both wife and widow, was to divide her time between the Duke of Devonshire's country estate at Chatsworth and a modest abode in London. Their first London residence was at 36 Grosvenor Street, not far from Hyde Park. They maintained a small household with only one maid. While Arthur made frequent excursions to Chatsworth and Welbeck to fulfil his curatorial responsibilities, Eugénie generally remained in the city. While much of their social activity centred on the great galas that clients of a noble family were expected to attend, they also regularly entertained at home. Eugénie's diaries and letters of her early married years document a circle of close friends drawn from their political, artistic and scholarly worlds. The range of these close associations and their long duration say much about the appeal that the young couple had for some of the most respected intellectual, cultural and social figures in late Victorian London.

The return to London saw the renewal of her friendship with Mary Ponsonby. In her youth Mary had been a lady-in-waiting to Queen Victoria, and her husband Henry had served as the Queen's private secretary.[43] She supported the foundation of Girton College, where she came to know Eugénie. Now, as one of the grand dames of the British establishment, she helped Eugénie make her way in London and Court society. Eugénie sought her guidance for she was, in the words of one friend, 'perhaps the wisest and wittiest woman of her time'.[44] She provided support in moments of crisis and followed the career of her protégée with interest and admiration. When Eugénie was awarded a Girton faculty fellowship in 1910, Mary congratulated her 'on being recognized as the most distinguished English woman of the day'.

Most distinguished among their intellectual friends was Sir Frederick Pollock, one of the most learned and cultured jurists of his day.[45] He had read classics at Cambridge, where he was elected to the Apostles, the university's elite student intellectual association. Pollock was not only a legal scholar of international distinction, but a cultured humanist with wide-ranging interests. One close friend, the American jurist Oliver Wendell Holmes, exclaimed, 'You do so many things that I never know whether to expect a drama, a law book, a symphony or a system of philosophy.'[46] Pollock continued his undergraduate interest in the classics, but also wrote on other topics like the philosophy of Spinoza. Some people found Pollock remote, but clearly he warmed to both the Strongs, and his friendship with Eugénie continued long after Arthur's death.

Another close acquaintance was W. E. H. Lecky, a highly productive and influential late-Victorian historian. He wrote extensively on both English and Irish history, with a special interest in the history of ideas and the

87

history of morality.[47] His cultivated world is captured in an entry in Eugénie's daybook that described an evening with the Leckys: 'After dinner sat in W. Lecky's study ... over his mantel ... [was the] only contemporary picture of an auto-da-fe on occasion of Philip II ... Talked of pagans transformed into Christian symbols. Lecky mentioned mosaic of Orpheus playing to animals in Laon.'[48]

Much more worldly and ambitious was Edmund Gosse, who emerged during the 1870s as a promising young poet and critic in the circle of Swinburne and the Pre-Raphaelites.[49] He married Alma-Tadema's sister-in-law, and it is likely that Eugénie Sellers first met him in the Alma-Tadema household. By 1887 he was sending her autographed copies of his books. Her marriage strengthened their friendship, for Gosse was also very close to Arthur. He succeeded him as Librarian of the House of Lords, where his polished social persona, his love of gossip and his sometimes glib and careless scholarship contrasted dramatically with his austere and intense predecessor.[50]

Edmund Gosse and Eugénie lost touch in the years after Arthur's death. Then, in 1925, Maurice Baring sent her a copy of Gosse's recently published autobiographical memoir, *Father and Son*. He described Gosse as 'very shaky' and advised her to 'read it quickly and write to him before it is too late'.[51] She found the book very moving, especially because the sections describing his youth recalled her own rather bleak childhood. She wrote him one final letter, praising the book and recalling his many kindnesses to her and her late husband.

The family that Eugénie and Arthur were probably closest to was that of Hugh and Florence Bell. Hugh Bell was a second-generation Northumbrian industrialist whose large fortune allowed him to indulge in a variety of political and culture interests. His second wife Florence was a successful playwright.[52] However, it was their daughter Gertrude who was to provide the closest link with the Strongs.

Gertrude Bell had a brilliant undergraduate career at Oxford, winning a first-class degree in history. She became increasingly interested in the history and cultures of the Near East, and began to study Arabic and eastern literature with Arthur. Eugénie saw a great deal of Gertrude in London and came to appreciate her many talents and her serious academic commitment. She encouraged her to write on Near Eastern architecture and provided her with introductions to distinguished scholars such as Salomon Reinach. Reinach provided a picture of the young Gertrude Bell much influenced by Eugénie Strong: 'Miss Gertrude Bell came before and introduced herself … I found her quite charming. We spoke a great deal about you. She loves you and admires you. Your influence on her appears even in her vocabulary.'[53] In an era when there were few independent, scholarly women in England to serve as models for aspiring academics, it is not surprising that Gertrude looked to Eugénie, who, although only eight years older, had already established an international reputation as a classical archaeologist.

Gertrude and Eugénie remained close for many years. In 1910 Gertrude spent a prolonged period of time with Eugénie in Rome, where she developed a serious romantic attachment to Richard Delbrück, the director of the German Archaeological Institute. Indeed her father thought that she might settle there. However, personal and professional interests drew Gertrude to the Near East. In 1913 she wrote to Eugénie, 'I feel as if I should never recover my soul except in the orient, if then.'[54] The lure of the exotic was reinforced by the romantic. She was increasingly attracted both intellectually and emotionally to the Austrian art historian Josef Strygowski, a dynamic, appealing man whose archaeological theories reinforced her own views on the importance of understanding the development of Near Eastern cultures.[55]

Gertrude Bell went on to a distinguished career as explorer, archaeologist and intelligence operative in early twentieth-century Iraq. She and Eugénie saw less of each other, although their correspondence continued. During World War I, Gertrude wrote movingly to Eugénie of her visit to the abandoned German excavation site at Babylon, where she had been so hospitably received as a young scholar. As late as 1923, Gertrude hoped to meet her in Rome. Her death from a drug overdose in 1926 brought a mysterious and tragic end to an exceptional career, and Eugénie mourned her deeply.

A very different female friend was Ottoline Morrell.[56] She was the sister of the Duke of Portland, in whose stately home Arthur served as librarian. The bright young Ottoline met Arthur through her brother, and soon found this intense intellectual a refreshing contrast to the hunting, sporting types that generally hung around Welbeck. Arthur sensed that the innocent, ill-educated young woman had intellectual potential and engaged her in serious discussions and set her to reading serious literature. He laid the foundation that allowed her to move in fashionable intellectual and cultural circles in later years. She married Philip Morrell, a minor politician, and became an important figure in the salon and country set. She was also for an extended period of time the mistress of Bertrand Russell. She came to know Eugénie and respected her brilliance and scholarly seriousness; Eugénie for her part found Ottoline appealing, but had no illusions as to her intellectual depth.

The Strongs regularly attended gallery shows and openings and socialized with old artist friends like William Holman Hunt, Edward Poynter, Lawrence Alma-Tadema and Marie Spartali Stillman. Arthur was especially close to the French artist and portraitist Alphonse Legros, who was from 1876 Slade Professor of Fine Arts at University College, London.[57] Legros provided the most striking image of Eugénie from those years, a sketch made shortly after her marriage (plate 11). He rendered her handsome, strongly sculpted face well and captured her powerful, mature personality. This was a newly self-confident Eugénie Strong, who was entering one of the most productive periods of her life.

7

The Chatsworth Years

Arthur and Eugénie's diverse and exciting London world represented only part of their complex existence, for Chatsworth House was the focus of much of their scholarly activity and social life. The country seat of the dukes of Devonshire is located in the rolling countryside that borders the Peak District of central England. The size and grandeur of the house and grounds are impressive even when compared to the other great stately homes of England. A contemporary of Eugénie captured its qualities well: 'Chatsworth is a very impressive place. The magnificence of the house, the pomp of its surroundings, the treasures that it contains, the recollections it revives of much that is best in English public life during many dark and devious years of national history, all combine to the production of a very notable effect.'[1]

The house is set in Chatsworth Park, which was designed by two of England's greatest landscape architects, Capability Brown and Joseph Paxton. The park extends over 1,200 acres and is surrounded by 12,000 acres of farmland, woods and moorland. The owners, the Cavendishes, have over the centuries played important political, cultural and scientific roles in English life. The original Tudor structure was built by Bess of Hardwick, the first of a series of strong women to live at Chatsworth House.[2] The confidence that the Tudor monarchs had in the family was demonstrated by the fact that Mary, Queen of Scots, was imprisoned there. The present structure was started in the later seventeenth century, and expanded and embellished in the eighteenth and nineteenth. The second Duke of Devonshire was a great collector of paintings, drawings, prints, coins and gems. The fourth Duke married Lady Charlolte Boyle, heiress to the third Earl of Burlington, the man who had done so much to promote the Palladian neoclassical style in England.[3]

Most colourful of the lineage was the fifth Duke, who married the beautiful Lady Georgiana Spencer and took as his mistress Lady Elizabeth Foster. The three lived in a relatively harmonious *ménage à trois*.[4] It is not surprising that after being raised in such an unorthodox household the sixth Duke remained a bachelor. He was, however, a great builder and collector, assiduously adding to the library holdings. It was he who hired Joseph Paxton to redesign the grounds. Unfortunately, his building and collecting propensities sent the family deeply into debt.[5]

The Cavendish who was so central to the lives of both Strongs was Spencer Compton Cavendish, Marquis of Hartington, who became the eighth Duke of Devonshire in 1891.[6] He was a leading political figure in the Liberal governments of the Gladstone era. Contemporaries regarded him as not overly clever, but thoroughly honest and decent. He was a good friend of the Prince of Wales, who regularly attended shooting parties at Chatsworth.

While the Duke appeared more interested in horses and bridge than matters of the mind, he did have 'one side of his nature which was continuously suppressed and hidden under his cold and unsympathetic manner, and that is the artistic and aesthetic side'.[7] He had a deep love for music and poetry and was very supportive of both the Chatsworth art collection and library. However, he had inherited an estate deeply in debt. Through prudent financial management he had restored it to fiscal health, but there was little money left for new purchases.

Arthur Strong became involved with all aspects of the Chatsworth collection. He pressed forward with the preparation of a scholarly catalogue, and in spite of the budgetary restrictions he made important new acquisitions for the library. He also discovered some unrecognized treasures in the existing art collection. The best example of his aesthetic detective work was a bronze head of Apollo that his predecessors had dismissed as a Roman copy. Arthur felt he was dealing with a Greek original and invited Adolf Furtwängler to Chatsworth to study the piece. The German scholar affirmed that the head was indeed a rare early classical Greek original. Now known as the Chatsworth Head, it has become part of the classical collection of the British Museum.[8]

7. The Chatsworth Years

In spite of the energy Arthur put into the Chatsworth librarianship, his record of completed projects and publications remained disappointing. Some of that was due to persistent ill-health, but more damaging was his indecisiveness and his propensity to become involved in too many activities. His faults and especially his procrastinations became a central topic of the letters exchanged between Eugénie and her sister-in-law, Mary Strong. Marital tensions originating in Arthur's scholarly failures were exacerbated by quarrels about money and family, especially over Arthur's financial support of his brother Rowland.

While Arthur was floundering, Eugénie was redirecting and focusing her scholarly energies. The personality of the *Gelehrte* moved to the fore. Her research on Pliny had expanded her interests beyond classical Greece to the world of Hellenistic and Roman art. Greco-Roman art, especially as represented by the Roman copies of Greek originals in the great European museums and private collections, became the focus of new academic interest. Repeated visits to Rome deepened her knowledge of its major collections, and she increasingly became a recognized expert in the field of museum archaeology. In 1899 she was asked to review Wolfgang Helbig's *Guide to the Classical Collections in Rome*.[9]

Helbig was one of the most colourful and controversial scholars in late nineteenth-century Rome, serving for many years as the second secretary of the German Archaeological Institute there. Passed over for the position of first secretary, he became a private scholar, active as an antiquities dealer and possibly as a forger.[10] He was also a leading figure in the Roman expatriate community. At his villa on the Janiculum hill he hosted a salon where cultural and scholarly luminaries gathered.

Eugénie furthered her new reputation as an expert on ancient Rome when the publisher Duckworth commissioned her to prepare an English edition of Walther Amelung and Heinrich Hotlzinger's guidebook to the monuments and sites of Rome. *The Museums and Ruins of Rome* was part of a series entitled 'The Modern Cicerone' aimed at the educated, amateur tourist. Amelung succeeded Helbig as the leading expert on Roman museums, and the book was an important addition to sophisticated tourist literature.[11] The guide opened with a short history of Greek art that placed the collections in their historical and cultural contexts. The introduction also included a recommendation to visit the newly installed cast museum at the University of Rome, where the tourist could obtain a comprehensive understanding of the historical development of Greek art.

Eugénie remained interested in the great European classical collections throughout her long life. She continued to lecture in the sculpture galleries of London and Rome and to publish catalogues of the ancient art preserved in British stately homes, and in 1903 organized a major exhibition of classical art in British private collections. Her reputation as a museum archaeologist was to play an important role in her appointment as Assistant Director of the British School at Rome in 1909.

Eugénie was taking other aspects of her scholarship in radical new directions. Her work on Pliny the Elder led her to rethink a central paradigm of archaeological scholarship, dominant since the days of Winckelmann, which held that ancient art reached its peak during the classical period of the fifth century BC and then declined through the excesses of the Hellenistic era to tired imitation in Rome.[12] Eugénie felt that this idealization of 'classical perfection' prevented an appreciation of the impressive creativity of both the Hellenistic and Roman artists, and she once again chose to advance her views through the translation of a seminal work of German scholarship. In 1900 she published *Roman Art: Some of Its Principles and Their Application to Early Christian Painting*, a translation of a work by the Austrian art historian Franz Wickhoff. *Roman Art* was the introductory section of a much larger book entitled *Die Weiner Genesis* that Wickhoff and the philologist Wilhelm Ritter von Hartel had published in 1895. In was included the first photographic illustrations of a sixth-century Christian manuscript in Vienna that represented an important transition from Roman to medieval art.[13]

Wickhoff set himself an ambitious art-historical agenda. He agreed with Eugénie that archaeologists had focused too much on the classic Greek art and had neglected important stylistic developments in the Roman period. At the same time students of early Christian art had been overly concerned with iconography and had not paid proper attention to stylistic developments in late antiquity. Wickhoff intended to challenge Winckelmann's association of Roman art with decadence and decline and to emphasize the important artistic innovations that took place during the centuries of the Empire. In his concluding assessment of Rome's cultural achievement he asserted that:

> A new Western and Roman art has risen before our eyes. Developed in orderly succession from the traditional art practices of the Italic peoples, it introduced with illusionism into the antique a final principle which is at work to the present day. With the establishment of this principle the development of art, that had begun in Egypt and passed through so many different phases among the peoples of the Mediterranean basin, is complete and closed.[14]

Wickhoff's *Wiener Genesis* has been called the first modern book on Roman art, a work that liberated the ancient-art historian from Winckelmann and represented 'victory of the psychological-historical conception of art over absolute aesthetics'.[15]

Franz Wickhoff came to Roman art from the perspective of a medievalist. He had a vast knowledge of Western art and stressed the importance of combining aesthetic analysis with documentary scholarship.[16] He loved seventeenth-century artists like Velázquez, Rembrandt and Frans Hals and embraced contemporary Impressionism. Those artists in particular led him to appreciate the Romans as pioneers of visual illusionism. He stressed the importance of Italic and Etruscan roots in shaping early Roman art and was conscious of the insight that Roman popular art could provide for understanding non-elite traditions that continued to operate under the High Empire.[17]

Wickhoff was a citizen of Vienna, the capital of a multi-ethnic, multi-cultural empire not unlike ancient Rome. His city carried a complex historical burden but was also an active cultural centre where artists and intellectuals were locked in heated debates over contemporary culture. This was the Vienna of the Secession Movement. Wickhoff was in the forefront of those defending avant-garde artists like Gustav Klimt.[18]

Eugénie knew that British scholars would not take kindly to Wickhoff's interpretations and especially to his attacks on the creative primacy of Greek art. She was correct. Characteristic was the review by Percy Gardner, the leading British classical archaeologist of the day.[19] Gardner had very little formal training in archaeology, but that did not prevent him from becoming an Oxford professor. He was a Helleno-Romantic, and that cultural bias was made manifest in the review. Gardner acknowledged that 'the section in books on ancient art dealing with Rome is usually as meagre as would be a chapter on snakes in a description, not perhaps of Ireland, but of England. "The Roman had little taste for art and borrowed everything from the Greeks" – this is the ordinary verdict'.[20]

Yet he held to that view himself. The neoclassicist Gardner could not accept Wickhoff's view that 'illusionist art (in ancient Rome) is far more attractive than the sober balanced art of Hellas'. He regarded Hellenistic art as a product of Greece's 'second childhood' and therefore something the Romans, who had 'less acute perceptions in art than the Greeks', more easily accepted. Gardner's reaction confirmed Eugénie's views on the insular pretentiousness of English classical archaeology.

Franz Wickhoff was not alone in rethinking the nature and importance of Roman art. In 1901 another Viennese scholar, Alois Riegl, published a study entitled *Die Spätromische Kunstindustrie nach den Funden in Österreich-Ungarn (The Late-Roman Craft Production represented by Finds in Austria and Hungary)*. Riegl, like Wickhoff, had not only mastered the Greek and Roman material but had a solid grounding in post-classical art.[21] He also had a keen interest in arts and crafts. For more than a decade he was textile curator at the Österreichischen Museum für angewandte Kunst, Vienna's version of the Victoria and Albert.

The stimulus for *Kunstindustrie* came from a research project on artwork of the late antique and early medieval periods in Austro-Hungarian collections.[22] He expanded that into a major study of the changes in artistic and artisan production that characterized the transition from antiquity to the Middle Ages. Riegl considered a great variety of monuments and objects, ranging from architecture and sculpture to jewellery and the decorative arts. Central to Riegl's interpretation was the concept of *Kunstwollen*, the idea that the artistic expressions of an age were closely interrelated with other cultural manifestations and they combined to form its characteristic *mentalité*.

In the same year that Riegl published his *Spätromische Kunstindustrie*, Josef Strzygowski produced his even more controversial *Orient oder Rom*. Strzygowski was educated at Vienna, Berlin and Munich and later taught at Graz and Vienna.[23] As the title of the book indicated Strzygowski saw the key tension in later antique culture not between Greece and Rome but between Rome and its Hellenized oriental provinces, and even the eastern cultures beyond its control. As an example, early Christian art for Strzygowski developed 'from a Hellenistic tradition fertilized in late antiquity by the influence of resurgent oriental concept and forms in the eastern provinces of the Empire'.[24]

Strzygowski's use of the term 'East' was vague and his geographical parameters fuzzy. He was a strong believer in national, even racial identities, and like many Germanic scholars considered the Mediterranean peoples decadent. His generic East had its locus outside of the classical Mediterranean from where artistic innovations had spread north and west to influence the Germanic peoples and establish the real foundations of Western art. Not surprisingly given such intellectual positions, Strzygowski found it easier than many scholars to accommodate himself to the Nazi regime in Austria.[25]

Strzygowski impressed contemporaries with his knowledge, insight and force of personality. He played an important role in interesting Gertrude Bell in the archaeology of the Roman and Byzantine East. Bernard Berenson, on the other hand, found his rejection of the creativity of the visual arts of the western Mediterranean appalling. Kenneth Clark recalled that, for Berenson, 'Josef Strzygowski became a subject of vituperation second only to Mussolini.'[26]

Both Wickhoff and Riegl died relatively young, and Eugénie was not close to either. She knew Strzygowski much better and had mixed reactions to him as a scholar and a person. She observed of one work that 'Strzygowski in English is quite readable and the book is full of brilliant suggestions, though the man knows too much and does not sift his information.'[27] She found it impossible to accept his picture of Rome as a decadent aftermath of Hellenic civilization, bypassed by the cultural forces that shaped later Western art. For her, Romanità was the very foundation of Western civilization. However, she appreciated his originality and promoted his scholarship, arranging meetings with colleagues when he visited England.[28]

Immersion in this Austrian scholarship reinforced Eugénie's emerging view that the creative power of Roman art had been seriously underestimated. Few in England agreed, but one exception was her friend from Athens days Henry Stuart Jones. In 1905 he published a detailed and sympathetic review of the scholarship of Wickhoff, Riegl and Strzygowski in the *Quarterly Review*. He also wrote regularly on the latest archaeological discoveries in Rome and knew the collections of that city extremely well.[29]

Both he and Eugénie realized that a major obstacle to the appreciation of Roman art in England was the lack of a general introduction to the subject. Eugénie began to contemplate writing such a work, and friends urged her on. It was Duckworth Publishers that provided Eugénie with the opportunity. In early 1902 George Duckworth had approached Arthur Strong to serve as general editor for a new, forty-volume *Library of Art*. The series was to be a pioneering venture that employed the latest printing technology to increase the number of photographic illustrations. Arthur was to determine appropriate subjects and recruit authors. For his services he was to receive the princely sum of £200 per year, a welcome addition to the paltry family income, but with his other commitments, declining health and general indecisiveness, Arthur did little to advance the project.[30] Eugénie assumed increasing responsibilities and took over after his death. With her extensive contacts in the world of art history, organizational skills and forceful personality, she was an ideal editor. She worked closely with Duckworth to recruit authors and move manuscripts towards completion.

Her correspondence with contributors, real and potential, reveals all of the vanities and frailties that any editor comes to know. She tried to persuade Martin Hume, a distinguished historian of early modern Spain, to write a volume on Spanish art. Hume was a private scholar who had to live by his pen, but he found Duckworth's royalties much too low.[31] Admonitions about late manuscripts were matched by excuses from delinquent contributors. The laments of one female author so irritated Eugénie that, in spite of her normal support for women intellectuals, she scribbled in the margin of one letter, 'Never will I invite *female* contributors.'[32]

Eugénie did better than most of her authors, for in 1907 *Roman Sculpture from Augustus to Constantine* appeared. The book ran to four hundred pages and was for its time well illustrated. It was also a striking scholarly achievement. While it is now outdated and has long been out of print, it remained for decades the only serious study of Roman sculpture in English. Only recently has it been replaced by Diana Kleiner's *Roman Sculpture*.[33] The scholarly challenges that Eugénie had faced were daunting. Many of the most famous Roman monuments were inadequately studied and poorly published. The reliefs of the Augustan Ara Pacis, the most important surviving example of Roman sculpture, lay buried beneath the Campus Martius or were scattered in various European museums. High-quality monographs on particular monuments were rare, and photographic collections on Roman art lagged behind those on Greek art.

Eugénie's interpretation of the development of Roman sculpture was sophisticated and imaginative. Since she started her survey with Augustus, she could not explore in detail what she regarded as the Etruscan and Italic foundations of Roman art. She acknowledged the great importance of Greek art for Rome but argued that it was one of several cultural traditions that shaped Roman art. She was equally sceptical about Strzygowski's *lux ex oriente* claims.

Within Roman sculpture her interests were impressively broad. She shared Riegl's appreciation of the so-called minor arts, and her years of study with Furtwängler had impressed upon her the importance of small objects such as gems for an understanding of the development of both Greek and Roman art. In addition, her friendship with Salomon Reinach and her extensive travels in Britain, France and Germany had made her realize the importance of provincial art for understanding the full achievement of Roman visual culture.

Eugénie appreciated more than most classical archaeologists the importance of the Roman contribution to later Western art. She stressed 'the special place it occupies at the special moment when the antique passes from the services of the Pagan State to that of Christianity'.[34] Especially important for her was the role Roman art played in preserving the figural tradition in Christian art and preventing Christianity from becoming a religion that, like Islam, prohibited divine representations. She regularly reminded her readers of the respect artists like Michelangelo and Bernini had for Roman sculpture.

A hardened veteran of publication politics, Eugénie manoeuvred behind the scenes to ensure sympathetic reviews. Furtwängler thanked her for her 'schöne, dicke Buch' and promised to arrange for reviews in Germany.[35] Other friends proved equally accommodating. Her efforts were rewarded, for the book was well received both in the professional journals and by a wider circle of scholars and cultured readers. A. M. Daniel in the *Classical Review* noted that 'the student can study and appraise in Mrs Strong's volume more conveniently than elsewhere both the monuments themselves and the conflicting views to which they have given rise'.[36] An American reviewer, Alice Walton, was generally positive but cautioned that 'as is not unusual in proving a thesis, she is over-solicitous to persuade her readers, and by undue enthusiasm may defeat her own ends'.[37]

Friends were fulsome in their praise. The art historian Robert Langton Douglas observed: 'English women have done a good deal to deserve German contempt of their books on art history. But now we have a book written by an English woman that we can point to with pride; for Teutonic man has done nothing better in its own line.'[38] Charles Loeser praised her because 'in place of a stodgy book of *Kunstgeschichte* you have written a book on a much forgotten subject: *Die Kunst der Geschichte*'.[39] Perhaps most appreciated would have been the good-humoured if ironic comments of the numismatist G. F. Hill: 'If you think that you have not convinced me in the least by your book, it only shows that you have never realized the depth of my depravity before I read it. If I ever succeed in teaching anybody as much by only one of my books as I have learned from yours I shall be very happy.'[40]

Eugénie's growing scholarly focus on Roman sculpture did not mean that she had lost interest in Greek art. Indeed, as she was writing *Roman Sculpture*, she was organizing an exhibition of Greek art held in British private collections for the Burlington Fine Arts Club in London. The club was one of the leading arts institutions in early twentieth-century London. In the words of a contemporary guidebook, the Burlington hosted 'interesting exhibitions' with 'admission on introduction'. Their shows were distinguished by the quality of the objects and the scholarly rigour of the presentation.[41] Needless to say, a show on Greek art drawn from the collections of the leading noble families was bound to be a major cultural and social event.

The exhibition was to open in the summer of 1903. The objects were gathered from an impressive range of private English collections, and Eugénie was responsible for obtaining permission to exhibit them. It was an enterprise that tested her network of social contacts and her powers of persuasion and diplomacy. She had to attract the best objects and dissuade some eager donors from displaying mediocre pieces. One adviser, Alfred Higgins, cautioned:

I think that there is little doubt that the exhibition will be a success, if you yourself are not too amicable. It requires a very hard hearted person to get together a very fine show. The dull second rate things kill the fine ones and the only way is to sacrifice ruthlessly the indifferent things which are generally accepted in the early stages of an exhibition for fear of not getting enough stuff to fill the gallery.[42]

Eugénie gathered pieces from long-established collections, but also highlighted emerging collectors. As she explained in the catalogue: 'By the side of our great country houses, whose taste is naturally that of the days of the "grand tour" and where therefore a good deal of discretion must be exercised to select objects which shall suit modern taste or serious modern archaeological science, we must not forget more recently formed collections.'[43] That philosophy fitted well with the Burlington, an organization that appealed to rich middle-class collectors. Indeed, the collection best represented in the exhibition was that of Lewes House, the gay commune established by E. P. Warren, a Boston expatriate, Berenson patron, and a longtime purchasing agent for classical art for the Boston Museum of Fine Arts.[44]

The exhibition was a great success. The rising young Hellenist Gilbert Murray wrote to thank Eugénie for her 'benefactions to all lovers of Greece in organizing the exhibition'.[45] At the closing the sponsors issued a statement of thanks: 'The Committee desires to record their sense of obligation to Mrs Strong LLD without whose knowledge and energy the loan exhibition of Greek Art could not have been brought together nor the difficulties of its installation surmounted.'[46]

The exhibition was accompanied by the publication of Eugénie's elegant, well-illustrated catalogue. Like other Burlington catalogues it became a prized possession for scholars and connoisseurs. While the exhibition was a glorification of Hellenic values, she used the preface to argue for a serious rethinking of the British attitudes toward Greek art:

> For something like three-quarters of a century we in England have been accustomed to take the marbles of the Parthenon as our standard in all our judgement of antique art. Except for a small section of students in the Universities, the great discoveries of recent years – even those carried on by British explorers – have been practically fruitless of new artistic or aesthetic ideas in our estimation of Greek art at least. If ideas are hard to implant in the mind of the general public, they are equally hard to uproot. For us, Greek art is still synonymous with 'beauty'. It is an art of which we wilfully ignore the beginnings and despise the 'decadence'.[47]

Such a vigorous attack on classical sacred cows did not win her friends in the small, tight-knit British classical archaeological establishment.

One pleasant if poignant event connected with the show was the last visit of Adolf Furtwängler to England and the final meeting of the two old archaeological friends. He was brought in as a consultant for the exhibit, and his wife Addy, who had never seen London, travelled with him. For her and Eugénie it was the renewal of a friendship that went back to Munich days. The passage of time had brought Addy many changes. Her children, who had been young when the beautiful Eugénie Sellers visited their house in Schwabing, were now adults. As for herself, Addy warned Eugénie that 'I am now grey haired and no young woman any more and you must not be too sorry for me when you see me.'[48] Addy had never met Eugénie's husband, and she looked forward to coming to know the man who had won her old friend's heart. Unfortunately, the Furtwänglers' visit coincided with another health crisis. Addy could only look on helplessly as Eugénie nursed her husband while making the final preparations for the exhibition.

Arthur had clearly not been well for some time: a 1902 photo of him shows a gaunt, pale visage. However, by late January of 1903 he had improved sufficiently for the Strongs to take an extended trip to Florence, Rome and Paris. By mid-February, however, his health had deteriorated to the point that his life was in danger. Anxious inquiries and unsolicited health advice arrived from friends, ranging from praise of the curative effects of ass's milk to the name of a Harley Street physician who specialized in acute aneamia, the apparent cause of Arthur's weakening condition.

Arthur rallied, and by the summer the crisis appeared to have passed. A prolonged stay at Brighton provided curative sea air, and he and Eugénie talked of another trip to the Continent in the new year. As 1903 ended, Eugénie Strong felt a considerable sense of accomplishment, relief and hope for the future. The Burlington show had been a great success, and the worst of Arthur's health problems seemed to have passed.

But Arthur was more ill than his friends and family realized. On 18 January 1904 he died suddenly. Eugénie found his body and fled in hysterics to a neighbour. He was buried in London's Brompton Cemetery amid the upper bourgeoisie, retired generals, colonial administrators and the lesser nobility that lie in that High Victorian Valhalla.[49] Their empire is now gone, and the cemetery where they rest is now largely overgrown and abandoned. Vegetation obscures his grave.

Arthur received the eulogies and obituaries appropriate for a man who moved in elite scholarly and cultural circles.[50] Edmund Gosse launched a subscription drive for a bust to be placed in University College. It was sculpted by Countess Feodora Gleichen, a pupil of Alphonse Legros, and unveiled with due ceremony on 6 July 1905.[51] The list of subscribers and attendees was a cross-section of Arthur's worlds. There were cultured intellectuals like Maurice Baring, Edmund Gosse and Frederick Pollock. Sidney Colvin, Humphry Ward, Eyre Crowe and R. Langton Douglas represented art history and art criticism. His former pupil Gertrude Bell attended, as did

Lawrence Alma-Tadema. The House of Lords was also well represented.[52] However, nearly eighteen months after Arthur's death, Eugénie still did not feel emotionally strong enough to be present.

Lord Reay spoke for the University of London, while Lord Burghclere gave the formal eulogy, stressing once again Arthur's resemblance to Erasmus. He also acknowledged Strong's limitations, especially his failure to publish. He characterized Arthur as 'a striking latter-day example of that old-world student who preferred the arduous pursuit of learning to any facile manufacture of its outcome. He worked as if time had no bounds, as though he had an eternity before him.'[53]

Arthur's extensive personal library was donated to University College. Eugénie prepared a posthumous edition of his publications which captured the depth of his knowledge and the range of his interests. Lord Balcarres wrote a preface filled with praise for Arthur, but failed to mention his scholarly wife.[54]

Arthur's sudden and unexpected death devastated Eugénie. Not only did she suffer a deep personal loss, but had once again to chart a new course for her life. She had been active as a scholar, but had been pursuing her academic projects as the wife of the librarian of the Duke of Devonshire. Now, with no position and relatively little income, she faced a bleak future, and it was not surprising that her health collapsed under the strain. The causes were partly physical and partly psychological. Good news did arrive when the Duke and Duchess assured her that she could assume Arthur's position as librarian, and she was especially touched by a visit to her sick bed by the Duchess conveying the news. The salary was £200 a year.[55]

Still, the wounds were slow to heal. To recover her mental balance Eugénie departed for Greece and Crete in the spring of 1905. She was accompanied by Henrietta Hertz, an old friend who proved an excellent companion at that moment of crisis. She was the type of cosmopolitan intellectual whom Eugénie loved. The English aesthete Oscar Browning described Hertz and her life in Rome:

Another most attractive hostess was Miss Hattie Hertz, English by nationality, but German by birth, education, and perhaps too much by sentiment. She lived in the Zuccari Palace, the end of which divides the Via Sistina from the Via Gregoriana ... Her later years were spent in forming a choice library of all works connected with the minute topography and antiquities of Italian cities.[56]

Eugénie's friendship with Henrietta was closely tied to that with Sir Alfred and Violet Florence, Lady Mond. Alfred Moritz Mond, later Lord Melchett, belonged to a German-Jewish family that had migrated to England in 1862.[57] His father Ludwig had been a very successful chemist who had built one of the great industrial empires of the day. He had also been a man of artistic sensitivity and wide cultural interests. His wife Frida was devoted to literature, philosophy and music, and to provide her with intellectual companionship in England, Ludwig invited Henrietta Hertz, her school friend from Cologne days, to come to live with them. Their London home, The Poplars in St John's Wood, became a centre for musical and artistic gatherings, and there Ludwig began gathering his fine collection of Italian paintings.[58]

Alfred graduated from St John's College, Cambridge, studied law in London, and soon followed his father into the family business. He established a reputation as an effective, enlightened industrialist who promoted labour peace. He was also active in politics. Towards the end of his life he became very involved in Zionism and the resettlement of Jews in Palestine.[59]

For thirty years the family wintered in Rome. In 1889, when Alfred Mond was twenty-one, his father purchased the sixteenth-century Palazzo Zuccari at the top of the Spanish Steps. The name derived from the artist Federico Zuccari, who had built it as a residence and studio. Later both Joshua Reynolds and Johannes Winckelmann had lived there. The Monds and Henrietta made the palace into a cultural centre, entertaining scholars and artists in its elegant rooms. Eventually the Monds presented the palazzo to Henrietta. She created within its walls the magnificent art-history library that still bears her name.[60]

Alfred Mond fell in love with Rome, its art and monuments. He identified especially with the architect-emperor, Hadrian. His biographer describes how, in later life, he turned back to the first freedom of his early twenties, when his whole being had escaped from the confines of his English life, to walk among the columns of the Forum and Hadrian's villa, seeking some key to his future. He had found it in the forms of Roman architecture and sculpture and in the courage of the men who had left this immortal stamp upon the city, upon the Campagna and in the Tivoli hills.[61]

Stimulated by his Italian experience, Alfred became an antiquities collector, gracing his London and country residences with fine works of Greek and Roman art. A shared love for Rome and for the art of the classical past drew him to Eugénie, and she became a frequent visitor to their house.

By the 1920s the Mond collection had become sufficiently important that a published catalogue was needed. Eugénie seemed the ideal person to write it. However, she was ambivalent about the prospect. Most of the objects were Greek and by then her interests were focused on Roman and baroque art. She urged the rising young Greek archaeologist Bernard Ashmole to undertake the catalogue and provided him with the necessary introductions. Ashmole did some of the preliminary work but, in the end, abandoned the project.[62] Eugénie felt that, out of respect for the Monds and Henriette Hertz, she must finish the work. The task was made more difficult by the tensions that had developed between her and Ashmole in the wake of her 1925 dismissal from the British School. However, Strong saw it through to completion. In 1928, shortly before Alfred Mond's death, the Melchett catalogue appeared.

The passage of time and the trip to Greece served their purpose, and by the autumn of 1905 Eugénie Strong was again her old active self. Central to her new life was the librarianship at Chatsworth. The appointment of a woman to such a position in early twentieth-century Britain was unusual and a testimony both to the Duke's decency and Eugénie's talents. While librarians had a somewhat ambivalent place in the hierarchy of English country houses, theirs was a position of some status, and one that was generally reserved for men.

Mutual respect and affection clearly developed between Eugénie and the Duke and Duchess. However, her position was in many ways that of an educated servant, and some of her tasks required more tact than intellectual creativity. Neither the Duke nor the Duchess were distinguished for their learning and cultural awareness. However, they did not want to appear totally ignorant of their collection, especially when entertaining distinguished guests. Eugénie described the trouble she took in preparing the Duke and Duchess for their weekend gatherings by reviewing with them the artistic highlights of their holdings.[63]

Eugénie clearly enjoyed both the ambiance of Chatsworth and the challenge of mastering its magnificent collections. She spent extended periods at the house, working in the library. In later years she remembered with nostalgia her comfortable apartment and her walks on the manicured grounds. She continued Arthur's work of cataloguing and publication, and followed his policy of making the Chatsworth collections open to scholars and connoisseurs.

Her Chatsworth connections and the success of the Burlington show opened doors into most stately homes, and, never averse to controversy, Eugénie was soon involved in a curatorial debate related to English private collections, their study and preservation. She felt that the classical antiquities in private hands should become better known. In 1882 the German archaeologist Adolf Michaelis had published his pioneering *Ancient Marbles in Great Britain*. However, since then research on privately held antiquities had languished. Eugénie sought to change that. She encouraged younger scholars to prepare catalogues while she herself made important contributions. In 1908 her *Antiquities of the Collection of Sir Frederick Cook, Bart. at Doughty House, Richmond* appeared. The invitation to publish the Doughty House material came from Sir Frederick's son Herbert Cook, an antiquarian and art collector active in both the *Burlington Magazine* and the Burlington Fine Arts Club, who had become an enthusiastic Strong partisan after hearing one of her British Museum lectures.[64]

Eugénie also became active in the movement to preserve England's private art collections. That mission had an immediate urgency, since Continental and American museums and private collectors were on the prowl. Noble families beset by financial woes were increasingly willing to part with ancestral treasures. Eugénie was a traditionalist, sensitive to the importance of these old collections, not only for their artistic worth, but also as reflections of family traditions and changing tastes. She would have agreed with the art historian J. P. Richter: 'The art collection proper is not a mere assemblage of heterogeneous rarities, but an organism of which the parts mutually supplement and complement each other. It is the outcome of will, intelligence and taste and was brought into being at the expense of time and energy.'[65]

One major problem facing those who fought to save England's artistic heritage was that neither scholars nor government officials knew the exact contents of most country house collections. That ignorance, combined with what Strong saw as incompetence and shortsightedness on the part of British gallery and museum officials and a counter-productive set of death duties, led to a vast loss of patrimony. Eugénie lobbied for a national register and a flexible policy towards collection preservation. She argued: 'Rather than pass out of the country, works of art which come into the market should be secured without fail to an English public Gallery, but best of all would it be if by happy co-operation of private owners and a public body, our great houses should preserve their artistic contents.'[66] Her concerns about the dispersal of historic collections also extended to the Continent, and especially to Italy. She dreaded the day when the venerable Roman palaces would be emptied of their Greek and Roman art, and Rome itself would lose its place as one of the great repositories of ancient art.

Eugénie's interest in preservation naturally included England's architectural heritage. She led a special crusade to save the London home of the architect Christopher Wren. The building, located near St Paul's Cathedral, had for many years been used as a school. Even though it faced onto a squalid courtyard, both the exterior and interior preserved many features of its seventeenth-century elegance. Now the building faced demolition.

She threw herself into the preservation cause, rallying public opinion and writing forceful, persuasive letters to high London officials. To one she lamented:

Might not some of the energy now so lavishly directed towards the purchase of new works of art be employed preserving what we have here? The loss of a beautiful house like the one in Love Lane is as worthy of regret as the loss of a picture, and more so, for as the years pass examples of domestic architecture reaching back to the seventeenth century become fewer and fewer.[67]

One friend who aided the cause exclaimed in indignation: 'What vandalism! And how the English would screech if the poor Italians did such a thing. There is not much left in London now. They might spare us what there is.'[68] In spite of these protests their efforts were not successful.

The Chatsworth years also saw final breaks with her Munich past. In October of 1907 Adolf Furtwängler died of dysentery contracted during his excavations at Aegina.[69] Eugénie was deeply moved by the loss of the man who had done so much to make her a classical archaeologist. Friends wrote letters of sympathy as though she were a member of Furtwängler's family. She delivered a eulogy for him at Cambridge and dedicated lectures to his memory.

A few months earlier her other Munich mentor, Ludwig Traube, had also died. Unlike Furtwängler's sudden death, that of Traube had been long expected. Eugénie's post-Munich correspondence with Mary Lowndes and Adolf Furtwängler contained frequent references to Traube's health problems. Still, his passing was hard on her. While friends realized the impact of Furtwängler's death, few knew how close she had been to Traube.

Early in 1908 another death dramatically altered her life. On 24 March a telegram reached her in Rome to tell her that the Duke of Devonshire had passed away. It was first of all a great personal loss, for she had become a good friend of the old Duke. Violet Markham, whose own family connection with Chatsworth went back to the days of her grandfather Joseph Paxton, wrote in sympathy: 'I can well understand all that the Duke's death has meant to you. One is glad to have known those great figures in English social and political life before they are swept away by the rising tide of democracy.'[70] The Duke's death also created a professional crisis. The new Duke and his wife, Lady Evelyn Fitzmaurice, had different ideas about the use of Chatsworth. They had a large family and planned to live there more than had their predecessors. Lady Evelyn took a considerable interest in the house and its collections, and had definite ideas about the use and placement of objects. She was, in the words of her friend the architect Edwin Lutyens, 'a great restorer and preserver ... a perfectionist'.[71] Eugénie's robust personality soon clashed with that of the Duchess. She had been used to having her own way with the collections and did not easily accept what she deemed 'amateur interference'. Tensions mounted and to the surprise of some friends and the indignation of others, she resigned her position.

Among those most angered at her treatment was Violet Markham. She wrote to Eugénie after visiting Chatsworth: 'The whole stay makes me both sad and indignant – sad because one is sorry to see the traditions of a great household miserably upheld, indignant because it is more than I can bear that this couple, who ... are not fit to look at your shoes should have the impertinence to behave as they have done.'[72] Both the Duke and the Duchess were defensive about the course of events and claimed, probably correctly, that Eugénie had overreacted to legitimate efforts to assert their interests. The breach was not permanent, and the Duchess in particular kept up a cordial correspondence with Eugénie for many years. However, Eugénie's Chatsworth days were at an end, and she had once again to reassess her life and future.

8

Rome and the British School

With her resignation from Chatsworth, Eugénie once again faced very bleak prospects. Her financial condition was precarious, and there was still no future for her in the British archaeological establishment, where a forceful woman with a pronounced sympathy for German scholarship and a preference for Roman art found no welcome. Friends offered her financial assistance, but Eugénie was too proud to rely on even well-intentioned charity.

Suddenly a new, unexpected opportunity presented itself. The fledgling British School at Rome needed administrative support for its young director, Thomas Ashby. An older, seasoned academic with good scholarly credentials and administrative experience would be an ideal choice. Eugénie was offered the position and accepted. The official announcement of her appointment stressed her special qualities as teacher, scholar and organizer. The salary for the new position was £125 a year, hardly a princely sum, but a good supplement to her personal resources. In 1909, aged forty-nine, she moved to Rome, the city that would be her home until her death in 1943.

The British School of Archaeology in Rome had been established only in 1901, nearly a generation after its sister institution in Athens.[1] It was a small operation that was housed in the Palazzo Odescalchi, an elegant seventeenth-century palace in the centre of Rome. The first director had been G. McN. Rushforth, a respected Roman historian with an interest in archaeology and Italian art. He got the school off to a good start, but ill-health cut his tenure short.[2] Stuart-Jones succeeded him, but he also had to resign for reasons of health.[3] In 1906 Thomas Ashby, who had been the first student at the school and later the assistant director, became director.[4]

Ashby already had a long association with the city. In 1886 his father had sold his share of the family brewery and moved to Rome. There he had

111

developed a serious interest in archaeology and antiquarian studies and had begun building a formidable library on Roman subjects, a bibliophiliac tradition that his son continued.[5] The elder Ashby became a close friend of the Italian archaeologist and Roman topographer Rodolfo Lanciani, and frequently joined him in exploring the ruins outside the city.[6] This was the era when Rome, as the new capital of a united Italy, was developing rapidly, destroying much of the historic parks and other open spaces within the city walls. However, the countryside beyond the Aurelian walls that is today covered with apartments and factories was still largely uninhabited. It was the campagna of shepherds and aqueducts, ruins beloved of nineteenth-century British and American landscape painters. The Italian archaeologist and the retired British brewer explored the ruins of its villas, aqueducts and towns. Young Thomas accompanied them and began to acquire that knowledge of and love for the campagna that was to inspire him as an archaeologist and topographer.

Ashby had received a traditional classical education at Winchester and Christ Church, Oxford. He was a prized pupil of Francis Haverfield, an archaeologist with interests in both Roman Britain and Roman Italy.[7] Typically for a late Victorian British classicist, Ashby's immediate education had stopped with the BA, although he was awarded a D.Litt in 1904. He did not have any formal graduate training and lacked Eugénie's deep knowledge of German archaeological scholarship. He had some field experience, having worked at the Romano-British settlement at Caerwent in Wales, the Punic site at Motya in Sicily, and in Malta. However, his formal excavation training was limited.

Thomas was painfully shy and lacked anything approaching social graces. Rennell Rodd described his manner as that of an eternal schoolboy.[8] His personality made life difficult for subordinates at the school, and he often offended visitors. His lack of social skills did little to advance the cause of the fledgling establishment among the British elite, whose support was vital for the under-funded institution. In contrast, Eugénie brought social confidence and a developed network of connections to her new position. When she told Salomon Reinach of her appointment he observed that she would in reality be the director.[9]

112

Initially Eugénie and Ashby looked like an unbeatable team. The British School had in them two of the most respected scholars in Roman art and archaeology, and their interests complemented each other. Ashby focused on topographical research in the city and the campagna. He loved hiking that lonely countryside, recording the ruins of the Roman past. Former students recalled days spent with him 'trotting over the mountains and rushing for miles in an exhausted condition to catch the last train'.[10] He became a very skilled photographer and by combining image and text provided an invaluable record of an archaeological world that is now largely lost. He also established a tradition of survey archaeology at the British School that continues to the present day.

Eugénie turned immediately to the completion of the catalogues of the Roman municipal collections. Much preliminary work had been done by a young archaeologist named Alan Wace. While Wace is best known today for his later work as a Mycenaean archaeologist, his early research focused on Roman art.[11] However, he had left for Athens and Stuart-Jones was back in Oxford when Eugénie arrived in Rome. She became the on-site scholar, though returning periodically to Oxford to consult with Stuart-Jones. Years later she recalled 'hours spent at the Ashmolean, arranging photographs on a huge table, with Stuart-Jones bursting in at intervals, in his keen way, to offer criticism and encouragement'.[12] Progress was slow, and the publications took years to complete. The volume on the Museo Capitolino did not appear until 1912, while that on the Conservatori was only published in 1926.

Eugénie continued to lecture and to conduct guided tours. Her lectures in particular became popular events for the international community. Admission was generally by invitation only, and these were eagerly sought. Those attending represented the cream of Roman intellectual, ecclesiastical and diplomatic society. Oscar Browning of Eton and Cambridge fame was a frequent visitor to Rome during those years, and remembered her presentations fondly:

Her lectures were a joy and a delight and I never lost the opportunity of attending them. The first lectures of hers which I heard were given in connection with the Exhibition of 1911 … It contained copies of all the most distinguished works of Roman art throughout the world from the Palace of Diocletian at Spalato to the ancient cities of North Africa, a variety of subjects which gave ample scope to the genius and versatility of the lecturer.[13]

Ever since her days in Athens, Eugénie had been interested in excavation as well as museum archaeology. In Rome she assiduously followed the latest excavations. Her guide was often her close friend Giacomo Boni. Boni was a complex blend of early-modern scientific archaeologist and late-Romantic intellectual.[14] He had trained as a draftsman and architect in his native Venice and as a young man was influenced by the writings of John Ruskin and William Morris. He became active in the movement to preserve Venice's architectural heritage. He moved to Rome in 1888 and by 1898 had started to excavate in the forum. Boni pioneered the use of stratigraphic excavations and of other technical innovations such as balloon photography. His standards of archaeological analysis and documentation have only recently been equalled in Italian archaeology.

Eugénie possibly met Boni at the salon of her old friend Contessa Caetani Lovatelli. She became a regular visitor to his forum excavations, which were providing important new information on the early history of Rome. She also spent afternoons at his residence on the Palatine, where they delighted in watching the sun set over Rome while talking about topics as varied as the archaeology of early Rome and the human quest for immortality. She provided him with hospitality and introductions when he visited England.[15]

In spite of numerous activities and developing friendships, Eugénie's new life in Rome was not entirely easy, especially during the first months, when she lived in various hotels and pensioni. Violet Markham observed: 'I can read between the lines that the uprooting has not been an easy task and that you have had some sad hours and sad memories in Rome.'[16] However, Eugénie did not dwell long on past problems or present inconveniences; her position at the British School posed too many challenges. First and foremost the school needed to be placed on a firmer financial foundation. The French and German schools in Rome enjoyed generous state subsidies. The American Academy received both university and private support. The

British School had no government support and only limited private patronage. Ashby possessed neither the personality nor the connections to make him a success at raising money, so that task fell on Eugénie. She urged friends in London to press the Chancellor of the Exchequer for government subsidies. Such efforts, so contrary to the British government's general laissez faire approach towards cultural institutions, were not successful. However, she did better with private citizens. Attendees at her lectures often ended up as donors, and virtually any favour extended by her was accompanied by a request to contribute to the British School.

Important support came from the British Embassy in Rome. The ambassador, Sir Rennell Rodd, had known Eugénie since their London and Athens days (plate 14). He was a man of deep culture with a strong interest in the classics, and made the embassy a major social and cultural centre. Roma Lister, an Englishwoman living in Rome at the time, remembered his ambassadorship in all its brilliance:

> Since the time of the great Pro-Consul, the Marquis of Dufferin and his gifted wife, who had brought the embassy to the height of its popularity and brilliance, there have never been better ambassadorial hosts than Sir Rennell and Lady Rodd. Under their rule, the British Embassy was the social centre of Roman and cosmopolitan life. There was an atmosphere of poetry and art. Everything was original and beautiful. Lady Rodd initiated and other Roman hostesses followed.[17]

The brilliant, attractive, multi-lingual assistant director of the British School was an ideal addition to the embassy circle, and Eugénie soon became a regular at dinners and receptions. She even oversaw the design of costumes for their classically inspired fêtes. Her circle of embassy acquaintances extended beyond the ambassador and his family to a succession of younger diplomats who cultivated her friendship.

The pain of transition to Rome and the hurt of the Chatsworth resignation were soon eased by a special honour awarded by Girton College. In 1910 her old college elected Eugénie Strong research fellow for life. The fellowship was established for a woman 'who shall have distinguished herself in some branch of intellectual work', carried a stipend of £300, and had minimal residency requirements. The money was raised by a group of supporters, the chief donor being Mary Lowndes. Initially Eugénie felt a certain unease about accepting a position that had been created by her friends, but Katharine Jex-Blake persuaded her to suppress her qualms.[18] News of the fellowship produced a flurry of congratulatory letters. Mary Ponsonby saluted her 'on being recognized as the most distinguished English woman of the day'.[19] An old Girton friend wrote, 'You can't think how I enjoy the reflection that I prophesized great things of the young girl who Miss Welsh and Miss Bernard wanted to shove out of the classics tripos.'[20]

The fellowship fitted in well with Eugénie's new life. Late summer was a hot, dead time in Rome, and all who could fled the city. She regularly headed north and made Cambridge her base, from where she regularly visited her brother and sister-in-law as well as academic friends in Oxford. Ottoline Morrell described one evening spent with Eugénie: 'This little time in Oxford, when we all met fairly often – the Raleighs, Vernon Lee, Eugénie Strong, the Prices, Anne Sedgwick, Ethel Sands and Harry Norton, who was staying with us – gave me an idea of what a circle of friends could be. They all knew each other well, and struck sparks from each other.'[21]

The summers were not just devoted to socializing and relaxing in the cool corridors of Girton. She used the trips between Rome and London to tour archaeological sites and museums. In England she lectured and continued her research.

The Rome to which Eugénie moved in 1909 was very different from the city of the 1890s that she had known so well. The building boom had slowed. However, the social and economic problems caused by the rapid post-unification expansion had contributed to the radicalization of politics. One result was the election of the populist Ernesto Nathan as mayor in 1907.[22] Nathan belonged to a Jewish family who had befriended the Italian patriot Mazzini. His family also had strong English associations. He had been born in London, and English was the first language of his parental household. A key element in Nathan's success as a politician was his vigorous anti-clerical stance. His attempts to improve education and health services for the poor constantly brought him into conflict with Rome's conservative social elite, and with the Catholic Church and its political allies. Eugénie did not find him a sympathetic figure, but their futures were to be intertwined in complex and unexpected ways.

One of the most ambitious projects launched by Nathan was the 1911 exhibition celebrating the fiftieth anniversary of the proclamation of Rome as the capital of a united Italy.[23] Part of the exhibition was held in Turin and part in Rome. As was normal for such international exhibitions, foreign nations were asked to construct pavilions. The Roman exhibition grounds were divided between Prati on the right bank of the Tiber, north of the city, where the Italian pavilions were built, and the Valle Giulia on the left bank, where the international exhibits were located. A strong sense of triumphant Italian nationalism shaped the ideology of the exhibition, with modern Italy's links with ancient Rome highlighted. A major feature was an exhibit on Roman art and archaeology set up in the Baths of Diocletian. The displays dealt with ancient Rome and Roman Italy, but also with the Roman provinces. Casts, models and written texts were integrated to convey the diversity of the Roman imperial experience. The aim was as much inspirational as scholarly. In the words of the director and organizer Rodolfo Lanciani, the exhibition was to be a place 'where Italian youth may seek inspiration for all those virtues which rendered Rome, morally as well as materially, the mistress of the world'.[24] Such exaltations of Romanità had been important to the Risorgimento long before the Fascists came on the scene. It had shaped their archaeological policy and was one of the driving forces behind Italian colonial expansion in the Mediterranean. Significantly, in the year that the exhibition opened the Italians invaded Libya.[25]

Lanciani regarded the exhibition as the culmination of his long archaeological career that would link papal Rome with the Fascist era. Although trained as an engineer, he turned early to archaeology. After 1870 he diligently recorded the many archaeological finds made during Rome's rapid urban development. He also believed in the importance of informing the international community about the new discoveries. His archaeological 'Notes from Rome' were a popular feature in English magazines, as were his general books on the changing archaeological scene in the city.[26]

Lanciani drew on all his contacts in the Italian government and academic world to make the 1911 exhibition a success. His chief assistant was a rising young star of Italian archaeology Giulio Giglioli, who would become a major force in Fascist archaeology. Giglioli learned much from the 1911 experience and applied those lessons to the important archaeological exhibitions that he would organize during the Mussolini years.

Lanciani was especially anxious that Roman Britain be well represented in the exhibition. His enthusiasm was probably more to do with the important place that Britain held on the world stage than the significance of the British province within the Roman Empire. Eugénie's friend Robert Bosanquet observed ironically: 'Lanciani has written to me about the architectural exhibition two years hence. His ideas are gigantic. I gather that we must furnish the exhibit and Rome will return them. Still we'll do what we can to uphold the credit of the British province, but it was always an unproductive conquest.'[27]

Thomas Ashby was enlisted to organize the Romano-British section. That was to be expected, for Ashby was an old friend of Lanciani and a student of the premier Romano-British archaeologist Francis Haverfield. However, Ashby had very limited experience in organizing exhibitions. Eugénie, in contrast, had prepared a major show in London and had many contacts among curators and collectors. She played a major role in assembling the casts, models and photographs that were to be the key elements in the display.

Eugénie had long been interested in the then rather neglected and often despised art of the Roman provinces and had regularly visited the small museums of France and Germany. As early as 1895 she published a review of a catalogue of the Romano-Gallic material in the Museum St Germain-en-Laye and used the occasion to urge classical archaeologists not to neglect the Roman provinces.[28] She appreciated the important insight that these crude local products provided about the complex interaction between Celtic and Roman cultures. She also saw in those provincial works the innate vigour of native art forms asserting themselves against the increasingly academic classicism that became dominant in the Roman art of the High Empire.

Eugénie prepared a long review on Lanciani's exhibition for the first issue

1 Eugénie Sellers as a young woman.

2 Eugénie Sellers in peasant costume for a ball in Messenia, Italy. The photograph dates to *c*.1877 when she was visiting her mother's family in Sicily.

3 Girton College as it appeared in the era of Eugénie Sellers.

K. Dixon. A. Woods. L. Haynes E. Sellers.
Sub-Capt.ᵈ Head Capt.ⁿ Sub-Capt.ᵈ Secretary

S. Marks. M. Taylor. K. Jex-Blake. H. M. Sheldon.
Captain. Sub-Capt.ⁿ Captain Captain

Girton College Fire Brigade Officers.

4 Eugénie Sellers and the Girton College Fire Brigade.
Eugénie is the standing figure on the far right.

5 Katharine Jex-Blake as a young woman.

6 Mary Lowndes, Eugénie's closest friend
during her adult life.

7 Eugénie Sellers at Olympia during her 1888 tour of Greece with Wilhelm Dörpfeld.

8 The German archae-
ologist Wilhelm
Furtwängler and his
daughter.

9 The German philologist
Ludwig Traube. He and
Furtwängler were
Eugénie's mentors during
her years in Munich.

10 Eugénie Sellers Strong at the time of her marriage.

11 Eugénie Strong as sketched by Alphonse Legros shortly after
her marriage to Arthur Strong.

12 Eugénie Strong working at her desk in Chatsworth House,
while she was librarian (*c.* 1904-1909).

13 Thomas Ashby, the director of the British School at Rome during Eugénie Strong's years as assistant director.

14 Lord Rennell Rodd, British ambassador to Rome during Eugénie Strong's time at the British School. Rennell Rodd was one of her closest life-long friends.

15 The new quarters of the British School at Rome that Eugénie Strong occupied in 1919.

16 Eugénie Strong's apartment at the British School. This was the setting for her famous salons during her years as assistant director of the School.

17 Cardinal Merry del Val, secretary of state for Pope Pius X and important spiritual advisor for Eugénie Strong.

18 The English cardinal Francis Gasquet, Eugénie Strong's friend and principal spiritual advisor during her return to the Roman Catholic church.

19 Eugénie Strong in the apartment on the Via Balbo in
Rome that she occupied from 1925 to the outbreak of
World War II.

20 Eugénie Strong lecturing in Rome toward the end of her life.

of the *Journal of Roman Studies*. She used the occasion both to describe the exhibition and to praise the general cultural achievements of ancient Rome.[29] She personally identified with the underlying ideology of the exhibition and generally liked its organization and presentation. However, she did note mistakes in the reconstruction of certain monuments and expressed regret at the absence of certain important works. Her likes and dislikes within the body of Roman art were also made very clear. For her the Roman artists were most creative when they employed distinctive indigenous modes of expression. That could be seen in such works as the statues of the Dacian captives from the Forum of Trajan. In contrast, she regarded Roman art as least effective when it relied on 'abstractions, clothed in forms borrowed from decadent Hellenism'. Once again she was doing battle with classicism and the ghost of Winckelmann.

The 1911 exhibition had one major unexpected outcome for the British School. The British pavilion was an impressive neoclassical structure whose façade echoed the portal of Christopher Wren's St Paul's Cathedral. It was designed by that greatest architect of Britain's later imperial age, Edwin Lutyens.[30] Ernesto Nathan was so pleased with it that he offered the site to the British to be used for some cultural institution, and Colonel Charlton Humphreys, whose firm had built the pavilion, expressed a similar willingness to donate the structure itself. These offers coincided with discussions in London about expanding the British artistic and archaeological presence in Rome. Since 1907 the school had been hosting travelling architectural students sent out by the Royal Institute of British Architects.[31] Now leading figures in the arts wanted to make such studies part of the regular Rome programme. The British were ready to follow the Americans, who were merging their arts and classics schools into the American Academy in Rome.

The English already had a venerable arts institution in Rome known as the British Academy. However, that organization showed little enthusiasm for joining the archaeologists in the new Valle Giulia facility.[32] An alternative option presented itself. In London there existed an entity known as the Royal Commission of the Great Exhibition of 1851. Founded in the aftermath of the Crystal Palace exhibition, the commission controlled funds that were to be used for the advancement of education in the applied arts. In

119

1911 the Royal Commission recommended that some of that money be designated for scholarships for art students to study at the British School at Rome, and in 1912 the decision was made to create a combined school.[33] Thomas Ashby was appointed director and Eugénie Strong assistant director. In London, Evelyn Shaw, who had previously worked for the commissioners of the 1851 exhibition, became Honorary General Secretary of the British School at Rome, a post that he would hold until 1947.

This organizational restructuring of the British School forced a radical rethinking of the facilities' needs. A combined school would clearly require more space than was available in the pleasant but modest quarters of the Palazzo Odescalchi. However, the Valle Giulia site was not without its problems. The spaces behind the elegant neoclassical façade would have to be almost totally redesigned to meet the needs of the artists and scholars. While the façade conveyed a sense of grandeur appropriate to Britain at the height of its imperial age, it also suggested that the financially strapped institution was more prosperous than it really was. As one potential donor remarked to Eugénie, 'How is it that all the money was spent on a façade which you don't yet need, when you are short of money for so important an item as the Library?'[34]

Not all agreed with the decision to create a combined school or to move its operations to the outskirts of the city. Critics of the proposal felt that while the combination of artists and classical scholars in one organization was in theory a good one, in reality the differences between the two fields were too great to make sharing a facility easy. Others argued that the remote location in the Valle Giulia would cut the British scholars off from the monuments and museums and from the intellectual and cultural life of the historic centre of Rome.

The conversion of the exhibition building into a school facility proved to be no easy task. The pavilion was a temporary structure, and all of it, including the façade, had to be totally rebuilt. Limited funds forced Lutyens to scale down his designs; communications between London and Rome and between architect and builder became strained.[35] Unforeseen problems – such as the discovery that the channel of the Acqua Felice, a major source of drinking water for Rome, passed through the property – slowed construction. Since Eugénie was a much more practical person than Ashby she became involved in many redesign details, even though it proved to be an enormous drain on her time and energy. When the school officially moved up to the Valle Giulia in July of 1914, the interiors of the buildings were still not completed.

The year 1913 provided Eugénie with a welcome break from her arduous labours at the British School. She received an invitation from the Archaeological Institute of America to deliver the Charles Eliot Norton Lectures, which had been established in 1907 by the wealthy American connoisseur and classics patron James Loeb to honour the founder of the Archaeological Institute of America.[36] Before Eugénie, the lectureships had been held by such distinguished scholars as D. G. Hogarth and J. L. Myres of Britain, Christian Huelsen of Germany, and Franz Cumont of Belgium. She was the first woman so honoured.

Eugénie enthusiastically accepted this new offer. Since she was deep into research on Roman religion, she offered as one of her topics 'The Symbolism of the Afterlife'. However, her most popular talk on the circuit proved to be 'The Imperial Idea in Roman Art', what she described as 'a good subject ... showing the influence that a great modern state can have on art if, like the Roman Empire, it encouraged a central idea'.[37] Such a focus on the Roman sense of mission clearly appealed to a North American power entering its own imperial age.

Eugénie Strong sailed to Canada on 27 September 1913. The passage was uneventful, although the sighting of icebergs reminded British passengers of the *Titanic* tragedy of the previous year. Her tour got off to a disastrous start. She found her Canadian hosts so hapless and inefficient that she threatened to cancel the rest of her visit. Mitchell Carroll, the executive secretary of the Archaeological Institute of America, made an emergency trip to Rochester, New York, to pacify her. After that rough beginning, the circuit went reasonably well.

The strenuous tour took her to twenty-five local societies of the Institute, as well as to other universities and museums. Her itinerary included mid-western cities such as Buffalo, Cleveland, Chicago, Detroit, St Paul,

Minnesota and Madison, Wisconsin. St Louis was the farthest west that she journeyed. On the east coast she visited Richmond, Washington, Baltimore, Philadelphia, Princeton, Bryn Mawr, New York, Hartford, Providence and Boston. The audiences ranged from professional scholars to interested amateurs.

She was a great success. A Montreal paper praised her lecture, 'which exhibited as much grace of manner as it did power of thought and abundance of knowledge'.[38] Eugénie had always been a skilled, dynamic platform speaker, and the diverse North American audiences represented challenges similar to those of her early British Museum days. One of the most successful talks was at Mount Holyoke College in Massachusetts. There she not only lectured, but gave one of her famous 'demonstrations' in the college's well-appointed sculpture cast gallery. She also renewed an acquaintance with a member of the Mount Holyoke faculty, Louise Randolph, who had heard her lecture on the Acropolis in the spring of 1891.[39]

Eugénie showed interest in many aspects of America. She praised such neo-Roman structures as Pennsylvania and Grand Central Stations in New York, and found the autumn foliage of New England most beautiful. She visited some of the newly established private art collections in the United States, such as that of Henry Clay Frick in Pittsburgh. She even attended a Harvard–Yale football game. However, Eugénie would not have been herself if she did not have some critical comments on her American experience. She was not impressed with American museum methodology, and was especially critical of the new displays at the Boston Museum of Fine Arts.[40]

In advance of her Boston visit, Mary Berenson had written a letter of introduction to the formidable Boston collector Isabella Stuart Gardner:

A delightful friend of ours will be in Boston June the 11th to the 13th or 14th lecturing on Roman Art for the American Archaeological Soc., Mrs Eugénie Sellers Strong. Do go and hear her and be nice to her if the spirit moves you! I've given her no letter, because you may not feel like being bothered – but she is a distinguished scholar and a delightful woman.[41]

The two apparently met, but no details survive. It would be interesting to know more about the encounter between Mrs Jack Gardner, the premier art patron of Boston, and the equally formidable Eugénie Strong.

All in all, the tour provided the opportunity to meet with old friends and to forge new relationships. Most important was the time spent with Mary Lowndes and her students at Rosemary Hall School. At the end of the tour Eugénie returned to Ottawa to attend a special meeting for potential supporters of the British School. One aim of her Canadian lectures had been to rally support for the British School. Thomas Ashby had expressed dismay that the Canadians so vigorously supported the Archaeological Institute of America and neglected their British Empire connections.[42] She herself believed that the British School should serve the different countries of the Empire and promote the British imperial ideal. She had already been corresponding with Herbert Baker of Johannesburg about sending South Africans to the School. In Ottawa she waxed eloquent on the prospects of the new combined school. The mission appears to have been partly successful, for the Canadians continued to identify with the British School in Rome.

In spite of logistical problems, Eugénie regarded the tour as a success. She summed up her feelings to Mary Berenson: 'The tour has been shockingly mismanaged and I get torrents of letters after the lectures from people, who haven't been informed that they were going to take place. However, the tour has served its purpose. I have seen a great deal of America and got to know people more easily than would have been the case had I been on my own.'[43]

Although she never returned to North America, Eugénie retained a number of friendships from that visit and came away with a positive impression of the American scene. In later life she seldom manifested that condescension toward Americans that was so widespread in Europe among the educated elite.

In the late summer of 1914 the guns of August signalled the beginning of World War I. With its population of young and idealistic students, the British School quickly felt the impact of the war. No new students were sent out for the 1914–15 academic year, and many former fellows and prize-holders joined the military.[44] Eugénie desperately tried to maintain some sense of continuity at the school in spite of the cataclysmic events in Europe. Her efforts led one friend to observe: 'Personally I think that it would be good for the British public to know that just as Cudworth wrote his philosophy in the midst of our Civil War, so you are able to cultivate archaeology in a quiet corner of Armageddon.'[45] Ironically the last notice we have of Eugénie, just before her death in 1943, highlighted again her efforts to 'cultivate archaeology' in the midst of the next great Armageddon to engulf Europe.

Many alumni corresponded with Eugénie during the war years. Their letters convey a poignant sense of what she meant to the young students at the school. They had been raised in a male environment, where women were often marginalized and seldom given a chance to realize their full potential. They found in Eugénie Strong a female who was bright, well educated and caring, who was maternal yet at the same time attractive, a respected scholar and yet a sympathetic person who had time to serve them tea, listen to their tales, and help them through traumatic moments.

The early letters blended nostalgia and naivety. Robert Gardner wrote to tell her that he had resigned his Craven Fellowship to join the army. He was an archaeology student who had planned to study Italian polygonal walls. Not yet sensing what lay before him and his generation, he light-heartedly observed of his masonry: 'as it has already lasted for twenty-five centuries, it is not unreasonable to suppose that it will keep a year or two more for my special benefit'.[46] Often the boredom of military routine became overwhelming. Gilbert Ledward, a former student in sculpture, lamented that his one goal in life now was 'to bracket my target with high explosive shells'.[47]

As the years passed and the senseless slaughter mounted, this British School version of the 'Testament of Youth' underwent the expected change from idealism to resignation and cynicism. In their depressing and dangerous world the young soldiers idealized the warm days in Rome and sustained themselves with the hope of an eventual return. In early 1918, the painter Colin Gill wrote to Eugénie: 'After two years on the line, I find very little connected with war to interest me in the slightest, on the contrary, so that I, and I am sure the other men out here, would be excessively fed up and cheerless, if we had not the delightful prospect, the delightful contrast, of coming down to Rome and doing some real work after this inhospitable interlude.' He observed ironically that if he did return he would be 'a wretched pre-war survivor, of considerable interest to archaeologists'. Gill did survive and resumed his painting career after the war.[48] Another moving letter came from the first Roman scholar in architecture, H. Charlton Bradshaw. He described visiting his brother's grave at the Front, and then asked wistfully about the sketches and paints he had left at the school. He lived to design the final wing of the school building.[49]

Eugénie experienced the conflicts, tensions and divisions of the war on many levels. She had spent many pleasant years in Germany and had always counted Germans among her closest friends. Now hostilities strained long-standing relationships. An old friend, Marie Hays Hindenberg, British but married to a German, was deeply hurt that Eugénie would not visit her 'German house'.[50]

In Italy she saw with her own eyes the impact of the overcharged patriotic emotions produced by the war. She had long known and admired the archaeologist Emanuel Loewy, who had been brought to the University of Rome from Vienna to teach German archaeological scholarship. Eugénie appreciated his contribution to a new Italian classical archaeology: 'Loewy excelled as a professor, students flocked to his lectures, not in the least deterred by the austerity of his method; attested also by the genuine interest with which he watched their progress and the trouble he took in their advancement. A whole generation owed their scientific formation to him.'[51] Now, after nearly thirty years in Rome, he and other German and Austrian colleagues were removed from their academic posts. Loewy returned to Austria but had trouble finding a position, due in part to his Jewish origins. However, he was finally appointed professor at Vienna and remained there until his death.[52]

In spite of the war, Eugénie was able to travel between England and Italy with relative ease. Some of her activities were the expected 'women's war work', such as collecting funds for French soldiers whose families were trapped in German occupied territory. Early in the war she raised money for a small military hospital at Pont de l'Arche near Rouen. Later, her

Italian and her Church connections drew her into propaganda activities. Italy had become an important British ally, and both English and Italian publicists were busy stressing the cultural ties between the two countries. One Italian friend, Filippo di Filippi, a geographer married to an Englishwoman, was engaged in such work, and he recruited Eugénie to write articles on various cultural topics for his *Anglo-Italian Review*. The British were especially concerned with what they perceived as pro-German and pacifist sentiments in the Vatican, an anxiety heightened by Pope Benedict XV's 1917 plea for peace.[53] The British commissioned the prominent Catholic Hilaire Belloc to prepare the Allies' response, and Eugénie was recruited to use her Vatican contacts to get Belloc's manifesto circulated among influential clerics.

Most of Eugénie's time and energies were, however, still devoted to preparing the new school building for full occupancy and use. Thomas Ashby had joined a Red Cross ambulance unit on the north Italian front, and it was left to Eugénie to complete the preparations. The departure of Ashby was in many ways a benefit, for she could then manage day-to-day operations on her own. As she herself remarked, 'I am conceited enough to believe that if my Director is greatly my superior in all else, I can compete with him in accounts and the running of a household. After all he has never had one, and his parents always lived in hotels.'[54] Progress was slow; it was never easy to deal with Italian bureaucracy, and the war only made matters worse. Edwin Lutyens wrote to his wife about the frustrations that he, Rennell Rodd and Eugénie were experiencing, and though the building was officially handed over by the contractors in April 1916, many problems remained.[55]

The school library opened in November 1916 and Eugénie and her assistant, Kate Martin, moved into their quarters. Eugénie quickly evaluated the strengths and weaknesses of the new facility, and was direct in stating her concerns to the contractors and especially to Lutyens. As she put it to Evelyn Shaw, 'Lutyens and I are very good friends and I mean to point out defects to him quite frankly.' Lutyens found her formidable and not always appealing, but he listened.[56] The major problems were corrected, and by the time Ashby returned in 1919, the new school building was operative.

8. Rome and the British School

Eugénie could feel proud of her accomplishments. In managing this important transition she became one of the principal historical shapers of the British School at Rome.

9

Romance and Religion

During those early years in Rome, Eugénie underwent some of the most complex changes in her personal, spiritual and intellectual life. For the first time since Arthur's death she experienced romance. Her book *Apotheosis and the Afterlife*, published in 1915, was dedicated to Christian Mallet – 'Maréchal de Logis au XXIIème Régiment des Dragons IVème Escadron aux Armées, en campagne' – who was serving on the Western Front. In the dedication she evoked memories of the 'hours that we spent together in the Villa Giulia, trying to reconstruct some picture of the vanished civilization of the Latin race'; their time 'in the Vatican, where the masterpieces of Greek sculpture revealed to us the spell by which Greece held her grim conqueror captive'; and 'in the Baths of Diocletian, where we traced on the stelae of the provinces the religious beliefs that helped Rome to establish her imperial sway, and the soldiers of her legion to live and die faithful in her service'. She recalled 'that Easter eve on the Via Appia when a great red moon lay in the shallow of the Alban hills', 'the sombre garden on the Esquiline, under whose desolate paths lie the ruins of the Golden House built by the restless genius who was Nero', and 'the little flat on the Monte Tarpeo, and of the view, perhaps the noblest in the world'.[1] By the standards of the Victorian world in which Eugénie Strong had been raised it was a public document of extraordinary emotional openness and barely veiled eroticism.

Christian Mallet was the son of Etienne and Blanche Mallet of an old banking family with branches in both England and France.[2] Christian started his education in England and then returned to France to complete his baccalaureate. He spent two years informally attached to the British School and was introduced to Eugénie by Edwin Lutyens, who had done architectural work for the Mallet family and knew Christian's mother very well.[3]

Christian was a bright and charming young man who shared Eugénie's interest in art and archaeology. To most friends and family Eugénie referred to Mallet as her 'adopted son', and the age difference between the fifty-two-year-old British woman and the twenty-year-old Frenchman made the assertion a plausible one. In this guise, Mallet joined her on Rennell Rodd's yacht for a Mediterranean cruise during the summer of 1913. Her old friend Florence Wyndham wrote in early 1914: 'I am so glad that you are going to see your adopted son. The affection of a boy like that is a great trust, and as you say it is awfully difficult sometimes to know how to advise them when they turn to one for advice.'[4]

Other evidence suggests a passionate sexual relationship. In her diary for 1913, the year when the affair was at its height, Eugénie wrote an erotically charged meditation on the complexities of middle-age sexuality and the significance of a relationship between an older woman and a younger man. The intensity of their romantic involvement is confirmed by letters and postcards that passed between them. On one card from Christian in Paris to Eugénie in London the message reads: 'Can you come down for the weekend on Saturday the 17th. Please dearest do, I want you so much.' In another, Christian writes, 'Dearest, I am sure that you have not got the postcard in your collection. It will remind you of a department with a village and a house in the village, where you are eagerly expected.'[5]

Close friends were clearly aware that this was not just a filial attachment. When Eugénie returned hastily from her American tour, Mary Berenson expressed concern that it had been Mallet's health that had brought her back so suddenly. She sympathized: 'It would be dreadful to have him come into your life only to be an anxiety and cause of sadness. How dangerous it is to one's peace of mind to love anyone, and yet how empty life is without it.'[6] Marie Hindenberg sensed recklessness in Eugénie's behavior and warned her to be careful.

Mallet left Rome in 1913 for his military service. It looked like a prolonged but not dangerous situation, and Eugénie visited him at his garrison town. Then the outbreak of war changed everything. Mallet was involved in the early fighting and was seriously wounded in 1915.[7] He then transferred to the newly established flying corps. He corresponded regularly with Eugénie during the early months of the war, and she shared his moving letters with friends. Clearly the horrible events that he witnessed had a traumatic effect on his sensitive nature, and he suffered something approaching a nervous breakdown. However, he did write an account of his experiences. Eugénie worked hard to have Mallet's combat memoirs published and distributed copies to her friends.

Eugénie collaborated closely with his mother Blanche in helping French soldiers whose families were trapped behind German lines and could not provide the assistance necessary to supplement their meagre pay. She wrote letters to newspapers, distributed fliers and hounded friends for contributions. In the end she was able to send £170 to Blanche to purchase items like pipes and tobacco for the soldiers. Eugénie saved a stack of letters from French soldiers, who expressed touching appreciation for the simple gifts they had received.

Mallet survived the war, but the passion of their romance did not; there is little evidence of communication after 1915, and in 1917 Diane Watts promised to inform Eugénie if she heard from Christian. In 1919, Betty Montgomery, reading the dedication of Eugénie's *Apotheosis*, recalled 'their happy companionship in Italy and Greece', and then asked, 'I do not know if he came back safe and sound to you after the war and I hardly dare to ask you.'[8]

Christian Mallet died during the summer of 1920, a broken man addicted to the drugs he had used to relieve his pains during the war. One friend called him '[another] victim of the terrible war'. Ironically, it was the gruff Ashby who provided the most sympathetic picture of Mallet and what he meant to Eugénie. On hearing of his death he wrote:

I was very sorry to hear from my mother of Mallet's death. It seems such a terrible pity that one who promised so well should have not been able to fulfil what might have been hoped from him; I suppose that what he suffered in war had led him into taking drugs. They are indeed good servants, but terribly bad masters. I am very sorry indeed for you, for I know how devoted you were to him and with good cause; for he was very charming, attractive, and before the war came one felt he might have done great things and even after it. When he came through safely, he still had great possibilities though one was afraid his brilliance in other directions might have prevented him from realizing them and he was certainly a good and devoted friend to you and you to him.[9]

Eugénie maintained contact with Blanche Mallet long after Christian's death. In 1928 Blanche wrote on the face of a postcard to Eugénie, 'This is the chapel near Cannes that Christian loved.' On the reverse she wrote, 'Dearest friend, how precious the bibliography is to me. I am more than grateful for your kind thought and only wish I could go to Rome once more and kneel down in those "unique" churches a Roman Catholic.'[10]

Gradually the passions aroused by the hostilities cooled and Eugénie, who had been such a European cosmopolitan, re-established the international contacts that had been so central to her pre-1914 life. She articulated the ambiguities of her feelings in response to a request to contribute to a volume honouring Josef Strygowski: 'In old days I should have looked upon it as the greatest of honours to be asked to contribute to a *Festschrift* for Professor Strzygowski and I really don't see why, if yourself and Professor Bury think well of the scheme, one should not allow the painful and cruel memories of the war to efface one's debt of gratitude to so great a scholar.'[11] As librarian at the British School, she was able to provide more practical help. Answering the plea of a British diplomat in Vienna, she dispatched British School publications to that city's devastated libraries.[12]

Eugénie responded to the emotional upheavals of the war and her tragic friendship with Christian Mallet with a return to her spiritual roots. Although she had received a combined Catholic and Anglican religious upbringing, for much of her life she appears to have had no strong religious faith. Now she was increasingly drawn to the traditional rituals of the High Anglican and the Roman Catholic churches. Not surprisingly she became an early enthusiast for the young Catholic poet T. S. Eliot.[13] Close friends, such as the diplomat and writer Maurice Baring, were converting to Roman Catholicism, and her sister Charlie had become deeply religious.

Prolonged residence in Rome had made Eugénie familiar with the rich historical and cultural heritage of the Roman Catholic Church and had brought her into contact with many of the Church's most appealing clerical and lay intellectuals. Of her Vatican contacts the most important for her spiritual development was the sophisticated, cosmopolitan Cardinal Raffaele Merry del Val (plate 17).[14] His father had been a Spanish diplomat and his mother was English. He had been partly educated in Britain, and one of his personal spiritual missions was to bring the English nation back into the Roman Catholic fold. He belonged to the Franciscan order, but made his career as a Vatican official, rising to the position of Secretary of State under Pope Pius X. He was a conservative who consistently fought modernism within the Church.

Another cardinal, Gasquet, probably provided the main inspiration for Eugénie's return to the Church (plate 18). He was an English Benedictine known both as a spiritual leader and as a student of British monasticism. In 1907 he moved to Rome, where he became the leader of the English Roman Catholic community.[15] Gasquet fostered Eugénie's spiritual development and at the appropriate moment placed her under the guidance of Father Denis Sheil of Birmingham Oratory. Father Sheil led her through the final conversion process with common sense and good humour, and remained her friend for many years. His priestly example instilled in her a deep respect for the missions of the Oratorians of both England and Rome.[16]

A year after returning to the Church, Eugénie visited Cardinal Gasquet at his seaside retreat near Livorno. Upon her return to Rome she articulated her feelings about the impact he had had in her spiritual renewal:

I owe you already so much that perhaps it is only natural to add to the last the perfect holiday at Quercianella. It was a peculiar privilege to spend under your roof the first week during which, since the time of being received into the church, I found myself in harmonious surroundings away from the irritations, inevitable I fear, that come from living with people who however congenial in other ways think differently to oneself on the one point that matters. This morning I went to mass at 7:30 that it might be at your hour, not however

133

without a little tightening of the heart at the thought of receiving Holy Communion at other than your Eminence's hands. At your mass and in the little Franciscan Chapel to which you let me come with you I realized with intense gratitude how much interior peace had gradually come to me since my first visit to St Callisto when your eminence took me into the chapel. I was so frightened and bewildered that I could not bring myself even to kneel down.[17]

Theirs was more than just a spiritual friendship, for the cardinal was a frequent visitor to the British School. A soldier writing to Eugénie towards the end of World War I imagined her with 'the cardinal and all of the beaux-esprits of Rome sitting in the physical and intellectual cool of the School discussing the validity of Anglican Orders'.[18] However, not all activities at the school had equal appeal for Gasquet. With tact and good humour he turned down an invitation to the annual art show with the excuse that 'last time I came I was warned off certain rooms which contained pictures that a cardinal should not see'.[19]

Another close clerical friend was Monsignor Algernon Stanley, papal chamberlain and titular Bishop of Ammaeus, and brother of Eugénie's old mentor Maude Stanley. In his early years Algernon showed little promise as a student and suffered the appropriate English schoolboy punishments. When he visited his grandmother, Lady Stanley, the old lady observed him sitting gingerly on his lacerated posterior and remarked wearily, 'I have little faith in learning being flogged into a boy, but what else is to be done.'[20] He gradually improved in mind and spirit. His Anglo-Catholic enthusiasms drew him into the Roman Catholic Church and then into the priesthood.

As a friend of the Stanley family, Eugénie had known him for a long time, and their friendship continued until his death. She regarded him as a learned and pious cleric. Not everyone shared her view. His nephew Bertrand Russell described him as 'witty, fat and greedy'.[21] Nancy Mitford was equally unimpressed. 'He was a sad sceptic. A niece who was visiting him during Lent called attention to the fact that his board was groaning with beef and mutton. "Ah, my child," said the old bishop complacently, "Holy Mother Church sees to it that we don't starve."'[22] The Catholic writer

Hilaire Belloc accepted his foibles with amused tolerance, remembering him as 'delightful. Just like all his family as rude as a pig' but 'one of the nicest men I ever met … a priest to a ridiculous extent like the priests in books'.[23]

Forces more complex than spiritual enthusiasm shaped Eugénie's conversion. She had a scholar's respect for historical tradition, as she explained to an Italian friend: 'I will always be an archaeologist. I owe to archaeology, if I have understood, the historical authority of the Church and the conviction that only it can link for us the one and the other.'[24] Certainly her return to Roman Catholicism was related to her intense identity with Imperial Rome, for she saw the Church as continuing on the spiritual level the secular mission of the Roman emperors. Her close friend the German archaeologist Ludwig Curtius also emphasized the close connection between the scholar and the convert. Later, in his obituary of Eugénie, he wrote:

> From the Greek aestheticism of her youth she came to recognize the historical grandeur of Roman art and from that came to venerate the Catholic church. Wrongly many believed that she converted. She was baptized and raised as a Catholic but her devotion to the church was only a consequence of her Roman studies. She didn't have any mystical inclination … She loved the church as the living Roman Empire.[25]

However, Curtius underestimated the depth and complexity of her spirituality. She identified with Catholic intellectuals but also with the simple, saintly figures that are so much a part of Catholic religious history. She was drawn especially to the preaching order of the Dominicans. She lectured on the greatest of these, St Thomas Aquinas, and herself became a Dominican tertiary. However, Eugénie also had a special devotion to St Francis and lectured regularly on the religious and artistic legacy of that saint. She also felt close to that friend of Rome's poor and downtrodden, the sixteenth-century saint Filippo Neri.[26] She regularly worshipped at the Chiesa Nuova, dedicated to his memory.

Eugénie was very sensitive to the reactions of her non-Catholic friends to her reconversion. It was an era when the Roman Catholic Church was still regarded with suspicion in English elite circles. Some old friends like Betty

Montgomery responded very positively: 'I was so interested in hearing of your return to the Catholic church. I deeply sympathize though I don't think I shall ever do it myself as I become more and more of a free thinker.'[27] Others were not so positive. Mary Berenson was much concerned about the impact this spiritual turn would have on their long-standing friendship. Bernard calmed Mary by observing that whatever was happening in her religious life, Eugénie would still remain an archaeologist.[28]

Eugénie feared that her conversion had led to a cooling of her relationship with Gertrude Bell, although Gertrude's mother denied that.[29] She also felt that her Roman Catholicism played a role in her dismissal from the British School. In that she was probably correct.

Ludwig Curtius had certainly been right in seeing a connection between her spiritual life and her scholarly activities. Eugénie had long been interested in Roman religion; now it became one of the major foci of her scholarship. As she had with her earlier Furtwängler and Wickhoff books, she used a major translation to open a new direction in her scholarship. In 1913 she edited a translation of Alessandro della Seta's *Religion and Plastic Art*. Della Seta became one of the most important Italian archaeologists of the inter-war generation.[30] Eugénie first came to know him as a rising young archaeologist at the Villa Giulia Museum. By 1913 he had been made a professor at Genoa, and in 1919 he was appointed Director of the Italian School in Athens, a post he held until 1938. Della Seta was a strong Italian nationalist in the Risorgimento tradition. He also became an early Fascist supporter and under them his career prospered. However, della Seta was Jewish, and Mussolini's racial laws of 1938 led to his dismissal. He died in obscurity in late 1944.

Della Seta wanted to move the study of Greek art away from emphasis on magic and ritual and back to questions of form and narrative. For Eugénie the book represented a return to the conceptual world of Furtwängler. In her preface she sought to place della Seta's ideas in the wider world of scholarship on art and religion. She stressed her own respect for the usefulness of a comparative approach in understanding early Greek religion. She cited scholars like James Frazer, E. B. Tylor and William Robertson Smith, but significantly failed to mention Jane Harrison.[31]

The della Seta book was soon followed by her most important publication on Roman religion. In 1916 she published the lectures she had given during her Archaeological Institute of America tour as *Apotheosis and Afterlife*. Her completion of the book so soon after her return from the North American tour was an impressive achievement, since she faced the strains of war, the disruptions of the British School move, and the emotional turmoil of her intense friendship with Christian Mallet.

Eugénie opened the book with an 'Introductory Address to Students', an indication that she was seeking an audience beyond the world of specialized scholars. It was a plea for a balanced, positive appreciation of Roman art, one that avoided extreme positions. She was especially strident in her attack on Josef Strygowski and the Pan-orientalists. She was gentler but still critical of the die-hard Hellenist Gilbert Murray, who employed old stereotypes about Greek genius and the lack of Roman originality.[32] Eugénie praised the Romans' ability to incorporate outside influences while creating something new and distinctive. She highlighted the diversity of Roman art and the willingness of the Romans to allow 'nationalistic forces' inside the empire to 'shape their own destinies'. In short, she strove to counter the notion still prevalent that Roman art was uniformly bland.

Apotheosis and Afterlife was organized around two major themes. The first was the importance in Roman art of the ceremonies by which the Roman emperor was turned into a divinity. She related this emphasis on the apotheosis of the emperor to a popular desire for a more accessible immortality than was found in their traditional religion. An emperor made immortal through good works reinforced the hope of immortality among his subjects. This emphasis shaped artistic change. The importance of the divine emperor was conveyed to his subjects by the use of frontal representation. Traditional classical art had emphasized a self-contained narrative format separating viewer and viewed, deity and worshipper. In the new imperial Roman articulation, viewed and viewer confronted and interacted with one another.

Eugénie's second argument was that students of ancient art and religion underestimated the degree to which the ancient Greeks and Romans held well-articulated visions of the afterlife. For examples she turned to Hellenic and Hellenic-inspired art produced in Magna Graecia and Asia Minor. Most British classical archaeologists focused on Greek mainland art from the sixth to fourth centuries BC, and from that limited sample generalized about the entire Greek belief system. Eugénie had travelled often to southern Italian Greek sites and through her years at the British Museum had come to know the monuments of Lycia and Halicarnassus, which articulated a complex of Greek and local beliefs. This 'periphery' art expressed themes of immortality and the afterlife more diverse and complex than those found in Attica.

Eugénie's discussion of the afterlife in Roman art took her beyond the relatively small body of 'high art' representations. She was again innovative in her use of humbler artistic monuments to illustrate non-elite mortuary rituals and beliefs. Her detailed discussion of the tomb relief of a local Roman magistrate from the town of Amiternum and the great Romano-German funerary monument at Igel near Trier anticipated by decades the Italian art historian Rannuccio Bianchi-Bandinelli's advocacy of the importance of Roman popular art for understanding the social and intellectual complexity of the Empire.[33]

Eugénie's analyses were subtle and sophisticated, and she ranged widely over both classical and post-classical art. She considered beliefs concerning the dead prevalent in various 'primitive' societies, and drew on the latest discoveries on early Aegean religion made by Arthur Evans on Crete. Some of her interpretations can no longer be accepted: she certainly read too much religious symbolism into artistic representations. However, she provided imaginative approaches to the subject and demonstrated the spiritual seriousness of Roman art.[34]

The book was written when Eugénie had just reaffirmed her own faith, and it was therefore natural for her to stress the continuity between ancient and modern spiritual experiences. The last paragraph of *Apotheosis* emphasized such links both personal and professional:

We have travelled far from the primitive tombstones set up with magical intention to entrap the ghost. The dead man no longer lives in an obscure uncertain region, propitiated by acts of adoration born of fear. Magic had sought to imprison the soul; religion had effected her liberation and sent her soaring above the earth into the radiant spaces of heaven. A new era was to bring with it a still higher revelation of the soul's exalted destiny, but we have reached the goal of our present studies, and it is well to close them upon the vision of what Rome, by holding to spiritual ideals all but repudiated by classic Greece, contributed towards the emancipation of mankind from the haunting fear of death.[35]

The book was published in the darkest days of early World War I, and that crisis limited both the number of reviews and its scholarly impact. W. Warde Fowler of Oxford, the leading British authority on Roman religion, quibbled with some interpretations, but generally praised *Apotheosis* as a stimulating work of scholarship.[36] Stuart-Jones was especially impressed with her original discussion of the Roman funerary monuments.[37] An anonymous reviewer in the *Journal of Hellenic Studies* felt that she had been unfairly dismissive of the religious sensibilities of the Greeks, but praised her scholarship and her devotion to the Roman perspective in the often unsympathetic scholarly world of Britain.[38] Franz Cumont, the most respected Continental scholar of Roman religion, was very positive.[39] Less enthusiastic was Jane Harrison. Old personal antipathies blended with radically different approaches to ancient religion led to a lukewarm evaluation.[40]

In 1917 a major new Roman archaeological discovery provided Eugénie with an important new religious monument. Railway workers engaged in a construction project outside the Porta Maggiore in the eastern part of the city suddenly felt the ground sinking beneath them. Archaeological excavations revealed the remains of a well-preserved first-century underground basilica that had probably once belonged to the powerful Statilii Tauri family.[41] The walls were covered with complex stucco decorations, many of which clearly depicted mythological scenes. Some, like the suicide of the poetess Sappho, were very rare in classical art.

The discovery quickly attracted the attentions of experts in both Roman art and religion. Debates immediately started over the basilica's owner and purpose, and the significance of the scenes that decorated its walls and ceiling. Franz Cumont asserted that it had been a cult centre for neo-Pythagorean Romans, a sect that drew on the teachings of the fifth-century BC Greek philosopher Pythagoras and placed emphasis on the transmigration of souls in a complex afterlife.[42] Cumont's prestige and learning soon made his the dominant paradigm for understanding the basilica.

Eugénie visited the site soon after its discovery and became fascinated with the imagery. She added it to her programme of lectures and guided tours of Rome. Within eight years of the discovery she had already done forty presentations on the Porta Maggiore site. She also provided the first serious study of the basilica for English audiences. In a lengthy article which appeared in 1924 she and Norah Jolliffe, a Girton alumna and student at the British School, analyzed the basilica's artistic imagery.[43] It was a masterful example of Eugénie's precise but wide-ranging and imaginative scholarship. She analyzed the individual scenes carefully, providing parallels from other Roman monuments. She also tried to move beyond iconography to understand the basilica as an expression of Roman and specifically of Pythagorean and Orphic-based quests for the afterlife.

Work on the Porta Maggiore basilica strengthened her position as one of the leading scholars working on Roman religion in what many consider a golden age for that subject. The most distinguished of those was the Belgian scholar Franz Cumont.[44] In *Apotheosis and Afterlife*, Strong had praised Cumont as 'our leader here as in everything pertaining to the history of Oriental religions', and few scholars of her generation would dispute that judgment.[45] He had been educated in Belgium, Germany and Paris, taught at the University of Ghent and served as museum curator at the Musée Royaux de Bruxelles until academic politics exiled him from the Belgian academic scene. He used his private means to live as an independent scholar, building an immense personal library and living in rooms filled with beautiful objects. His research explored the rich variety of Roman religious experience, especially as it related to the afterlife. Cumont's emphasis on the symbolic interpretation of Roman religious iconography and his stress on the importance of the afterlife are now out of fashion among students of Roman religion. However, they were very influential when Eugénie worked in the field.[46]

Cumont inspired a whole generation of scholars and Eugénie was friends with most of them. Arthur Darby Nock was regarded as one of the most learned scholars of his generation. Students who heard him lecture, first at Cambridge and then at Harvard, remembered vividly the breadth of his interests and the depth of his knowledge.[47] He and Eugénie probably met through Cambridge connections, since Nock was a graduate and later a fellow at Clare College. He shared her interest in ancient religion and also her belief that the essence of religion lay 'not in philosophy or theology but in piety and cult'. It was how one practised religion on a daily basis that was important. That emphasis on religious action was a central thesis in his book *Conversion*, published in 1933.[48] Nock and Eugénie corresponded on a range of topics, from Roman archaeology to Edith Wharton. In Rome they toured archaeological sites together. In later years Nock fondly remembered the time spent with her in Rome: 'Geographical associations are very closely linked to personal associations and Rome implies for me also your friendship and your indomitable energy and goodness.'[49]

Similar interests and attitudes drew Eugénie and the French scholar Jerome Carcopino together. Carcopino, whose family came from Corsica, distinguished himself as a student first at the École Normale and then at the French School in Rome.[50] Like Eugénie, he was fascinated with the newly discovered Porta Maggiore basilica and in 1926 published the most important scholarly study of the monument.[51] Like so many outstanding *normeliens*, Carcopino went on to a brilliant academic career. He became a member of the French Academy and director of the French School in Rome. His conservative social attitudes, reflected in his best-known work *Daily Life in Ancient Rome*, fitted well with the ideology of Marshal Petain established after France fell to the Nazis, and he served as Minister of Education under the Vichy regime.[52]

Michael Rostovtzeff was the most interesting and ultimately the most important of this scholarly group. He came from a well-to-do, liberal Russian family, and received an excellent classical education during the last years of the Tsarist regime. Pompeii and the religions of Roman Italy became early research interests.[53] The Russian Revolution sent him into exile, first in Europe and then in the United States. However, he returned regularly to Europe and often met with Eugénie in Rome.

Eugénie's interests in art and religion had always extended well beyond the ancient period. With her conversion and her long residence in Rome she became fascinated with the Counter-Reformation and baroque art. The subject aroused little interest among English and American scholars of the time, for they were suspicious of the Counter-Reformation and of what they saw as the florid emotionalism of a Bernini or a Borromini.[54] Eugénie learned to appreciate the inherent beauty, great creativity and spiritual power of baroque art. Its oft-criticized lack of 'classical restraint' did not concern her, for she accepted those same 'emotional' qualities in both Hellenistic and Roman art. Years later Oscar Browning remembered how she articulated those continuities:

[The year 1917] was notable also for a series of lectures by Mrs Strong, in which she broke new ground in the preference of Asiatic Art to Athens. She showed how Pergamon was the progenitor of the Barocco, which is undoubtedly true. Our classical education has led us to attach too much importance to the Art of Athens both in sculpture and in literature and the neglect of that of Asia Minor.[55]

In 1920, Eugénie published her first article on Bernini. Two years later she presented the British Academy's Henrietta Hertz Foundation Lecture on 'Italian Sculpture of the 17th Century'. In 1929 she spoke on Bernini before the British Academy.[56] She displayed an impressive ability to convey to generally unsympathetic audiences the positive qualities of that often misunderstood and maligned art. Leo Ward, son of her old friend Mary Ward, wrote to her: 'You taught me for instance that I might admire (as well as like) the great Baroque churches such as the Gesu. I had always thought one must add "but this is heresy" – condemned solemnly by the 3rd volume of *Modern Painters*.'[57] Even those who could not share her enthusiasm for the baroque agreed that she had demonstrated the importance of Bernini as an artist. As a Dominican friend put it: 'My loves are earlier, less powder and paint, but if you will have paint and powder, Bernini is just a bit more honest.'[58]

Her most important publication on Counter-Reformation Rome was her

1923 guidebook to the church of Santa Maria in Vallicella, known popularly as the Chiesa Nuova. Her affection for Filippo Neri, one of the gentler and more appealing figures of the Counter-Reformation, went back a long time, and as it was the Oratorian fathers of London who had eased her way back into the Roman Catholic Church, she appropriately dedicated her little work to the fathers who served Cardinal Newman's Birmingham and London Oratories.[59]

The Chiesa Nuova and its attached oratorio and convent had been built in the later sixteenth century specifically to serve the needs of Neri's followers and their mission to the Roman urban poor. The church had been shaped by such artists as the architect Borromini and the painter Pietro da Cortona. Eugénie's account of the church's history drew on her deep knowledge of Rome in all periods. She described with insight and sensitivity the various people who had shaped Chiesa Nuova's spiritual and artistic development. Her written tour of the church was detailed and rigorous, yet also clear and easy to follow. She did not want the visitor to look at a few monuments and then depart, but rather to understand the church as a total environment whose central purpose was to promote pious and reverential worship. While her narrative was generally descriptive, she interspersed it with accounts of famous ceremonials associated with the church and biographical sketches of key people identified with it. Her work has stood the test of time and is much quoted in the most recent guide to the church.[60]

While Eugénie's *Chiesa Nuova* served the passing tourist well, no guidebook could recreate what it was like to visit the church under her tutelage. In 1945 her former young protégé Roger Hinks described a return visit, years after being guided through it by Eugénie Strong. On his own he found it 'a meagre and ugly thing, hardly better than Brompton Oratory (of Cardinal Newman)', while 'Mrs Strong used to have such a passion for this church that I had remembered it gilded with some of the radiance of her enthusiasm.'[61]

In 1920 Eugénie became the first woman invited to give the Rhind Lectures in Edinburgh. The Rhind Lectures had been established in 1876 to promote 'Archaeology, Ethnology, or Allied Topics' and had become one of the most prestigious lecture series in Great Britain. She used the opportunity to move her scholarship in yet another direction and chose Roman painting as her topic.

While most studies of Roman painting in English at that time were little more than reviews of styles and subjects based on the evidence from Pompeii, Eugénie approached the topic from a much broader perspective. Her expansive vision was made clear in her first lecture, when she ranged from Minoan frescoes to the landscape paintings of Nicholas Poussin and Claude Lorraine. She criticized others for concentrating too much on the abundant, well-preserved examples from the Pompeii region. While that material was obviously important, it represented a limited period and exemplified local elite taste, far from Rome. For her, the study of Roman painting had to incorporate all evidence, no matter how fragmentary, from the Republic to the early Middle Ages, with both Roman and provincial examples.

She then moved to the exploration of ancient Roman landscape painting. Not unexpectedly, she emphasized the religious themes expressed in the paintings, seeing them as manifestations of 'living Roman devotions to the divinities of earth and sea' and the art of a 'people painfully scrupulous in their religious observances and minutely attentive to every manifestation of divine power'. Only in the third lecture did Eugénie turn to Pompeii and the Bay of Naples. She acknowledged the importance of Greek influences on the development of Campanian painting; however, she emphasized that it was a regional Greek painting that had evolved dramatically during the centuries of contact with the native artists. For her, the true synthesis of Greek and Italo-Roman painting traditions came with the integration of figures and action in Pompeian works produced just before the city's destruction in AD 79. Her best examples were the recently discovered frescos from the Villa of the Mysteries at Pompeii. That cycle, depicting scenes associated with the cult of Dionysos, immediately became a subject of vigorous scholarly debate. Interpretations ranged from them depicting religious ceremonials, a wedding, or just random theatrical scenes. Eugénie, as was her tendency in interpreting Roman art, advocated a serious religious content in the frescos, seeing them as representations of the education of Dionysos.

In the fourth lecture she returned to the city of Rome itself and set out

144

an imaginative, if tentative, reconstruction of the development of painting at Rome from the Julio-Claudians to the Age of Constantine. That was a bold essay designed to demonstrate that the development of Roman painting did not stop with the eruption of Vesuvius in AD 79, but continued to evolve through late antiquity and into the Middle Ages. Her efforts were hindered by the fragmentary nature of the evidence and the poor publication of known materials. As with her Roman sculpture studies she did not limit herself to material evidence from the elite classes, but included examples of popular art like the paintings found in Ostia's apartment houses and private tombs. She finished her survey with catacomb painting, linking late antiquity with Christian and early medieval art.

Eugénie's last two lectures explored special topics, focusing first on portrait painting with special emphasis on the Fayuum mummy portraits, many of which had been discovered by her friend Flinders Petrie. One of the portraits that Petrie had donated to Girton featured an educated Greco-Roman woman named Hermione. It provided the opportunity for an aside that captured something of Eugénie's humour:

> Hermione Grammatica, a young lady professor with large eyes and scholarly pallor whose portrait stands appositing in the library of Girton College, where to quote Petrie she finds herself again surrounded by books and girl students whom she doubtless lived with before the Goth and the Arab had broken up her old culture.

She ended with a lecture on Roman mosaics, which she saw as a distinctly Roman contribution to Western art. Her lecture provided a wide-ranging overview that extended from the late Republic to the twelfth-century mosaics at the Church of St Clemente in Rome. Medieval mosaics provided her with a finale that highlighted this theme of continuity: 'I do not think there is a more splendid example of the marriage of what is best in Pagan art to what is going to be the best in Christian art and I would leave you with this image before you as a far more eloquent summary of what the art of Christianity owes to antiquity and to the Roman pictoral art and portraiture.'

The Rhind Lectures represented some of Eugénie's most creative scholarship. Regrettably, perfectionism and procrastination meant that she never published them. What is significant is that there was no work in English on Roman painting that combined her mastery of scholarship and breadth of vision. Indeed nothing of such a comprehensive nature appeared until the recent burst of publications on Roman painting.[62] If she had published these Rhind Lectures, the book would have been as pioneering as her *Roman Sculpture*.

During those years, Eugénie received honours rare for an English female academic. In 1920 she became the first of her gender elected to the Society of Antiquaries. Three years later she received her third honorary degree, this time from the University of Manchester. She was also granted honorary foreign membership by both the German Archaeological Institute and the Archaeological Institute of America. In Italy she received membership of the Pontifical Archaeological Academy and the Accademia dei Lincei. She was even inducted into the venerable Arcadian Academy, a literary society whose roots went back to the early eighteenth century. Her future seemed clear and promising.

10

Crisis at the British School

The British School continued to prosper. Thomas Ashby was in his most productive years as a scholar. His guided forays into the Roman campagna had become legendary; few knew its brooding ruins so well. He was equally at home with the topography and monuments of the city itself, and was completing the topographical dictionary of ancient Rome started with his late American friend Samuel Platner. He was also progressing on his research on Rome's aqueducts.

Eugénie was making her own important scholarly contributions, but also provided both intellectual outreach and a sense of community for the British School. She continued to lecture on subjects ranging from Etruscan art to the Sistine Chapel, and provided regular tours for British teachers who made instructional visits to Rome during their vacations. More important was the social role that she played at the school, whose director was a shy bachelor distinctly lacking in interpersonal skills. Her salons, with their mixture of clerics, academics, students and diplomats, continued to be the centrepiece of the school's social life (plate 16). Roger Hinks, a student during her last year as assistant director, provided an amusing account of her whirlwind, yet gracious, hospitality:

Surely I ought to have remembered from my Roman days of 1924–5 that on Saturday evening Eugénie Strong would change in a thrice from her old gum-beslobbered working dress and suffer the pencils to be taken out of all her pockets and even her hair and put on an all but identical though clean black dress with a silver cross on a ribbon deftly hanging round her neck and a comb stuck fiercely through her splendid leonine grey mane and there she was, welcoming cardinals

147

and ambassadors and lords and professors and clever little pioneering nobodies with a truly impartial hospitality.[1]

However, all was not idyllic in the Valle Giulia, and rumours began to circulate of increased tensions between Eugénie Strong and Thomas Ashby. These arose in part out of differences in style and personality. Axel Boëthius, the Swedish archaeologist who knew them both very well, contrasted Ashby, 'the restless, unpretentious expert on the Campagna and topography of Rome', with Strong, 'a brilliant personality of marked general culture with a leading position in Roman society'.[2] Edwin Lutyens was more biting in his description of the interaction between the two: 'I have likened Mrs Strong to a great big retriever and Ashby to a small wire-haired terrier that trots round after her.'[3]

Conflicts certainly existed. However, the extent of the hostilities has been considerably exaggerated in the lore of the British School. Their correspondence from those years documents a civil, and at times rather friendly, relationship. Ashby even invited her to his beloved summer home at St Margaret's Bay in Sussex, a significant gesture for that shy, reclusive man. Eugénie had nothing but high praise for Ashby as a scholar.

The social situation at the British School became more complicated during the summer of 1921, when to the surprise of almost everyone the forty-seven-year-old Ashby married Miss Caroline May Price-Williams. For much of his adult life, Ashby had lived with his mother, who even shared his apartment at the school. Old Mrs Ashby was a formidable personality; Eugénie remarked tartly that before his marriage, Ashby 'lived entirely in the shadow of his mother's petticoats'.[4]

Thomas Ashby met his future bride through her cousin Walter Ashburner, a school friend of Ashby and director of the British Institute in Florence. They were both middle-aged.[5] However, May Ashby was a very different person from her husband and even more different from Eugénie. As a clergyman's daughter, May had limited cultural and intellectual horizons. She spoke only English and seemed apart from the sophisticated Euro-British society living in Rome. None of this prevented her from asserting her place as wife of the Director of the British School at Rome: old Mrs Ashby was moved out, and the new Mrs Ashby moved in. Tensions developed immediately. Eugénie's salons, with their diplomats, German scholars and cardinals, overshadowed Mrs Ashby's 'At Homes' with their 'drawing room plays and acts'. Eugénie sensed impending trouble almost immediately and tried to have the parameters of her position as assistant director more precisely clarified. Still, unseemly conflicts developed over social roles and the allocation of living and entertainment space at the British School.[6]

The conflicts between Mrs Strong and Mrs Ashby were not contained within the walls of the British School. Mrs Ashby shared that English interest in fighting cruelty to animals. When, in 1921, the Italian government decided to invigorate the manly spirit of its youth by bringing back the macho sport of bullfighting, she rallied friends of animals to oppose the spectacle. At the height of the controversy a rumour was spread that Eugénie had actually encouraged students at the School to attend the bullfights. She vehemently denied the charge and produced several testimonials from students and employees at the School, all stating that she had in fact discouraged attendance. However, the story persisted. It reappeared at the time of her dismissal and is still part of the anti-Strong lore. She herself responded petulantly to the calumnies by asserting that, even though opposed to the sport, she would use an upcoming trip to Spain to attend any bullfight she could.

Ashby was the last person to be able to mediate between two such strong-willed individuals. Eugénie lamented that Thomas Ashby, 'whether through love or fear of her always gives in', and described their relationship as 'not amorous but uxorious'. In the midst of one battle Strong realized 'how tired and nervous Ashby had become', took pity, and yielded the field to her rival.[7]

Then, in 1922, a major scandal struck the British School. While it demonstrated Eugénie's skills as an administrator, ironically it fuelled the desire of certain School bureaucrats in London to change the staff in Rome. It had been decided that the School needed a new Roman administrative secretary to assist with the expanding operational responsibilities. The successful candidate was a young Oxford graduate R. Gordon George, a man of considerable culture and charm who had spent periods of time in Rome. Because he had recently lost much of his fortune through bad business decisions, the British School offer was most welcome, and as a recent convert to Catholicism, he appealed to Eugénie. His English references were good, and little effort was made to contact his former Italian employers. George was a young English gentleman and that was enough to recommend him for the post.

Both Strong and Ashby were away when he assumed the position, but by the time Eugénie returned in June, the School was in turmoil. She soon discovered that George was not only arrogant towards her and the staff, but also incompetent as a businessman and lazy to boot. He spent work time writing articles in the School garden rather than paying bills and, in the Italian custom, getting to know the tradesmen who did business with the School. As Eugénie put it, he thought, with her around, he 'would have a good time and that I would let him do as he liked. He had a rude awakening'.[8] Belated local investigations disclosed that his previous Roman employer thought poorly of him, that he had been blackballed by an English club in Rome, and that his record at the passport office showed compromising information.[9] By early autumn, Eugénie, on the advice of the School's Roman lawyer, had suspended him.

George made his way to London, where complaints of ill-treatment at the hands of Eugénie Strong found a receptive hearing from A. H. Smith, the chair of the School's archaeology faculty and someone who had never had great enthusiasm for his dynamic assistant director. However, a careful review of the facts convinced the faculty and Evelyn Shaw, that possessive bureaucrat who ran the day-to-day operations for the School in Britain, that she had acted correctly in suspending George. Still, the fiasco reinforced the view held by key members of the School that Eugénie was someone constantly surrounded by turmoil, and that she was becoming 'too big for her job'.[10] Ironically, two years later when the School was preparing to release her, a notice appeared in an Italian newspaper that a certain Englishman named 'Giorgio Gordon' had been arrested near Florence for attempted sexual abuse of a minor. Someone placed the article carefully in the School's Gordon George file.[11]

Tensions at the School continued to mount. When Ashby left in 1924 for a lecture tour in Canada, the officers in London were forced to make it clear to Mrs Ashby that, as wife of the director, she did not have any special powers. Friends and colleagues sensed impending trouble and urged Eugénie to exercise maximum discretion and restraint. She received an admonitory letter from that wily old Vatican diplomat Cardinal Merry del Val, who urged that she act with caution and extreme tact. Those qualities were never present in abundance in Eugénie Strong.

She had by now a firm notion of how the School should develop and vigorously pushed her schemes with powerful friends outside the School. Those activities aroused resentment in London, especially with Shaw. As early as 1919 he sent Eugénie a sharply worded message reminding her of the limits of her position: 'If Lord Esher [chairman of the British School] and others hear that there is talk of anyone doing what they have set out to do, you will find yourself high and dry and I will be forced to promptly resign.'[12] The storm clouds continued to gather, however, and the management of the School grew increasingly alarmed. The personnel concerns combined with general financial problems created an atmosphere of crisis. Powerful patrons felt that the programmes in Rome had become too ambitious, and that retrenchment was needed.

The sequence of actions that led to disaster for Strong, Ashby and the School began in the Faculty of Archaeology, History and Letters. That group directly controlled Eugénie's fate, for her salary was paid from their budget. The faculty was chaired by A. H. Smith, with whom Eugénie went back a long way, although their relationship had never been warm. Smith presided over the British Museum's Classical Department in one of its more somnolent phases, and was a painful reminder of how it had declined since the more dynamic days of Sir Charles Newton. Eugénie was the more creative and productive scholar and a better museum professional. Of this she was proud, and at times a bit boastful.[13]

Smith and the faculty now set about getting their revenge. They recommended to the Executive Committee of the School that the position held by Mrs Strong be abolished, and that her employment be terminated at the end of the 1924–25 academic year.[14] The criticisms used to justify their actions were insubstantial and petty, centring on what they saw as Eugénie's failures as a library cataloguer. This rebuke was a sad but telling indication of what Smith and his colleagues saw as a suitable role for an internationally respected female scholar at the British School. Their rather petulant and narrow-minded charges drew from Rennell Rodd the caustic observation that 'Between ourselves I always thought that those old gentlemen on Bloomsbury Square looked at things rather from the clerk of the catalogues point of view, who as Whistler said "file the fifteenth century and pigeonhole the antique" and did not quite realize that the telescope has a big as well as a small end and they were looking through the wrong one.'[15]

Even the archaeology faculty knew that they could not justify the dismissal of a distinguished figure like Eugénie Strong on the grounds of minor failures in librarianship. Their public statements focused on the dire financial situation at the school that made necessary the termination of the position.

The faculty's decision was referred to the school's Executive Committee. They formed a subcommittee consisting of Lord Balcarres, Rennell Rodd and the chairs of the relevant arts faculties to review the report. The group was to consider the financial problems, the personality conflicts and the long-term needs of both archaeologists and artists at the school. Rennell Rodd and Lord Balcarres were old friends of Eugénie, and she should have been safe in their hands. A verbatim transcript of one meeting preserved in the archives of the British School at Rome provides a frank picture of the views of the participants.[16]

In the privacy of their meeting, Smith stated bluntly that the decision of the archaeology faculty was based first and foremost on the continuing friction between the director and assistant director. Sir David Cameron of the Faculty of Printing and Engraving quickly rose to Eugénie's defence. He praised her efforts on the part of the students and placed special emphasis on the role her famous Saturday teas played in introducing the students to important people in Rome. He stated bluntly that 'Mrs Strong is the only one as far as I know to take any pains with them. Dr Ashby does not seem to.'[17] At that point Lord Balcarres weighed in and added that Mrs Strong 'represents in the eye of Rome that sentiment that Great Britain is performing a function in the School – that impression is not conveyed by Dr Ashby'. In spite of all these spirited defences and the reservations expressed about the decisions of the Archaeology Faculty, the subcommittee did not override that group's decision. After all it was that faculty's funds that paid Eugénie Strong.

At a special meeting on 24 June 1924, the full Executive Committee agreed that the position of assistant director should be abolished. The Archaeology Faculty had made no judgment on Ashby, but the committee now went after him. The representatives of the arts took the occasion to criticize the manner in which the director had handled the artists, and sought his head. No serious defence of Ashby was mounted, so he too was sacrificed. It was decided that a new director would be appointed with primary responsibility for classical studies. Rennell Rodd was instructed to draft the appropriate letters to Strong and Ashby.

Eugénie did not appreciate the gravity of developing events in London. Even while decisions to terminate her job were being made, she made requests for improvements in her apartment. A letter of 12 June from Shaw should have warned her. He stated ominously:

As all correspondence passing between Rome and the office is now seen by the Executive Committee, it is necessary for me to adopt an official style of address. So please do not be alarmed at my apparent hardness of heart. Will you also treat me as part of this office furniture and whenever you have a comment to make which requires consideration for a reply please make it as frigid and 'departmental' as you can.[18]

On 25 June, a letter signed by Shaw was dispatched to her from London. It opened with the formal, chilling words:

Madam,
I am directed to inform you that the question of the reorganization of the administration of the British School at Rome is engaging the anxious consideration of the Authorities and that as a result of the decision already come to by the Faculty of Archaeology with regard to the suppression of the office which you at present hold as the Assistant

Director and Librarian, the Executive Committee are unable to extend the term of your appointment as Assistant Director beyond the 30th June, 1925.[19]

There followed the usual expressions of thanks and good wishes. It was a highly insensitive ending to the career of a person who more than any other had made the British School at Rome a major research presence on the international scene. Thomas Ashby received exactly the same letter.

The joint actions split the supporters of the school badly and set back its reputation for a generation. The powers at the school retreated behind arguments of cost containment and the need for new administrative direction in an attempt to present a common front to a very vocal opposition. The chairman, Viscount Esher, was a distinguished courtier and government official.[20] He had long been associated with the school, and it owed a great deal to his efforts. Like many of his generation and social class, he had a strong interest in the classics: his country home was named 'The Roman Camp' and his memoirs of a close friendship were entitled *Ionicus*. Now he avoided the public and designated Shaw to speak for him.

Doubts and recriminations about the decisions surfaced immediately within the elite of the school. Sir Reginald Blomfield, who represented the architectural faculty, went to Rome. He found Ashby and Strong on good working terms, 'united by the bonds of affliction'. He observed sadly:

I fear the late heads have been harshly treated. It is a serious matter for both of them and particularly for Ashby to lose their jobs and I did not realize till I came here how much they have both done for the School. I learn that they have both made considerable donations to the School from their own libraries and their own resources and I gather that little or no acknowledgment of this has been made by the authorities responsible.[21]

Blomfield further articulated his concerns in a memo to the committee. However, Smith stuck rigidly to the decision of the archaeology faculty. To

Blomfield's relatively benign suggestion that the two directors, who had served so long and well, be encouraged to maintain contact with the school, Smith replied coldly that he 'would prefer that touch were not kept'.[22]

Rennell Rodd, who also expressed reservations, found himself in an especially uncomfortable position. He wrote to Shaw: 'Almost anyone I meet deplores the decision because other things apart our school was the only one which could compete in any way with the German Institute with its great library ... In spite of Ashby's eccentricities he had the regard of the Italian archaeologists.'[23] When Shaw sent Esher a copy of one of Rennell Rodd's exculpatory letters, Esher scribbled testily in the margin, 'He was one of the persons responsible for the changes. He cannot escape it.'[24] However, Esher himself passed the word to Eugénie that the real culprits were the archaeology faculty, although a member of that faculty returned the blame to the Executive Committee. Shaw naturally denied that the decision was the result of any intrigue or 'hole and corner agitation'. He asserted emphatically that 'it was not based on prejudice or any exaggeration of trifles'. He tried to placate Strong by claiming that 'they could not replace Dr Ashby or yourself in any way adequately, but that the committee wished to inaugurate a new policy which under existing circumstances could not be carried out'.[25]

Evelyn Shaw was placed in a very difficult position. He was a consummate administrator with a great appreciation of bureaucratic fine points. He and Eugénie Strong had very different personalities, and he could be petty and spiteful. In 1920 he had visited Rome while she was away, soliciting grievances from the residents and issuing such orders as prohibiting Strong's assistant Eunice Howard from eating with the students.[26] However, there is no clear evidence that Shaw played a major role in shaping the decision to sack Strong. He was certainly happy to be rid of her dominating presence, but he must have realized that she was a better administrator than most of the men associated with the school.[27]

These firings continued to haunt the school for years. The old wounds were reopened by Ashby's tragic death in 1931. School officials could not avoid reference to the events of 1924–5, but they did not want to resurrect all the grim details. The director Ian Richmond was delegated to prepare the memorial minute on Ashby, but his first version was judged too honest. The school was negotiating with Mrs Ashby to obtain her husband's impressive library and Shaw and Smith feared that even a hint that 'the real reason for dismissal was the quarrel of two women' would 'raise a hornet's nest and probably lose us Ashby's library'.[28] Richmond revised the minute and wrote back to Shaw: 'I think that I have arrived at a version which comes very near the truth, without stating it and which one side would read as though we were rather sorry, while the other would judge that we are sticking to our guns and silence, anyway, is enjoined by Ashby's example.'[29]

A. H. Smith was preparing his own obituary of Ashby. Again, Shaw tried to shape the outcome:

> I think it unwise to attempt to tell the truth which we did our best officially to disguise. Your words strike me as being rather harsh and might appear to others as being aggressive and as the whole trouble has now been forgotten it would in my view be a mistake and fundamentally wrong to blame Ashby's capacity or personal qualities as a Director when his damnable silly wife's bickering with Mrs Strong was the sole cause of his retirement.[30]

It was ironic, sad and unfair to Strong and Ashby that a sordid tale of academic narrow-mindedness, bureaucratic rigidity and the betrayal of friendship and trust had been recast as the 'quarrelling of two women'. Yet this is the view of the events still held by many today.

Eugénie felt she deserved better support from friends of the school, and especially from Rennell Rodd. She became especially annoyed when he emerged as an enthusiastic partisan of the new director, Bernard Ashmole. She was not alone in that complaint. Her friend George Wyndham wrote that Rodd's explanation of events in *The Times* 'was a most shameful display and disgraceful action after all the devotion you and Ashby had shown in carrying out his grandiose and almost impossible schemes'.[31]

Needless to say, Eugénie did not accept the decisions meekly, but turned to powerful friends for support. She also worked to ensure that the 'catastrophe' would alienate powerful people connected with the school. Her old friend Alfred Mond had just joined the managing committee when the dismissals took place. Mond was the type of wealthy, cultured industrialist whose financial support the school very much needed. In addition to his own wealth he had important connections in the establishment press. Strong felt that he was in a position to

> rope in the Press Lords to take an interest in a concern as important to the Dominions as to Great Britain. The conventional when not pompous reports that the well meaning Mr Shaw sent year after year to the 'Times' were productive of nothing – probably never read by rich or influential people, mere food for old ladies like so much BSR stuff produced during its arid existence.[32]

After the shabby treatment of his old friend, Mond asserted 'he would do nothing for what he called "that rotten concern"'.[33]

Eugénie felt that her Catholicism had played a role in her dismissal. She lamented to Salomon Reinach that 'a little coterie of not more than three or four free thinkers should have imposed their narrow minded tyranny worse than any exerted by the Inquisition upon a naive body like our Committee, who fell into the trap. At the bottom of it all there is a lady who has never loved me'.[34] She returned to the 'Catholic problem' in a letter to Eric Maclagen, then director of the Victoria and Albert Museum:

> I wished to have my say and give the old croakers who it seems have complained of my using lectures on art for purposes of religious propaganda something to talk about. You perhaps knew, for everyone else except myself until quite lately seems to have known it, that this was a common accusation brought against me. What idiots people are, and how narrow-minded and inquisitorial are all so-called free thinkers.[35]

Eugénie had the grace to feel great sympathy for Thomas Ashby and to understand what the dismissal had meant for him. She acknowledged his limitations as an administrator, but praised his record of distinguished scholarship, which had brought great prestige to the school. As she remarked to her brother-in-law: 'I think that Ashby has been treated very badly. They have got rid of a great scholar and one who was very much respected in Italy.'[36] She saw that the little world of the British School was even more central to his life than to her own, and had premonitions that greater tragedy lay ahead. A year before his fatal accident she warned about possible suicide, noting that his father had ended his life in that way.

In his obituary of the former director, A. H. Smith observed that 'the notification came as a surprise and disappointment to Ashby'. That was certainly a serious understatement; Ashby was shattered by the decision. While Strong had reached normal retirement age and had already done many things in her life, Ashby was only a little over fifty, and had devoted almost his entire career to the British School. Now he was left without his central reference point in his scholarly universe. He chose to remain in Rome and to continue his topographical and historical researches. He managed to complete his classic work, *The Roman Campagna in Classical Times*, in 1927, and a year later *The Topographical Dictionary of Rome* was finished.[37] However, his friends, including Eugénie, became increasingly concerned about his physical and mental health.[38] They felt that he needed a fixed academic position and worked to obtain one appropriate to his scholarly distinction.[39] Finally, in 1930, Ashby was appointed a research student at his alma mater, Christ Church College, Oxford. The position, very similar to the one held by Eugénie at Girton, required that he spend only thirty days a year in residence. On 15 May 1931 he boarded the train at Southampton for London to start his first residency. He never completed the journey. His body was found by the tracks. Some said that he had fallen from the train; others judged it a suicide. A letter was found on his body, but its contents were never revealed. The coroner was clearly divided on what judgment to render, and in the end stated rather ambivalently that the evidence did not justify a verdict of suicide.[40] Thomas Ashby was buried at St Margaret's Bay.

Eugénie was to render one last service to her old colleague. In 1935 his monumental *The Aqueducts of Rome* appeared, and she was asked to use her Roman contacts to ensure that complimentary copies reached both Mussolini and the Pope. Monsignor, later Cardinal, Tisserant asked her to make the formal presentation to the Pope on Mrs Ashby's behalf, claiming somewhat naively that Eugénie's 'friendship with the late Dr Ashby and his wife qualify you for presenting the volumes'.[41]

Ashby was more fortunate in his posthumous fame than in his later years. After World War II the British School's new director, John Ward Perkins, focused the institution's research programme on survey archaeology in the rural areas around Rome. Those surveys, which stressed settlement reconstruction based on the collection and analysis of surface artefacts, were very different from Ashby's practice of recording standing ruins.[42] Nevertheless, the pre-war topographer was turned into a patron saint for the new British survey archaeology.

The Ashby–Strong replacement as Director of the British School was the extremely ambitious, well connected, but young and as yet undistinguished classical archaeologist Bernard Ashmole.[43] Ashmole had studied classical archaeology with Percy Gardner at Oxford and had been a student at the British School in Athens. He was not yet thirty, knew little about Roman art and archaeology, and lacked the scholarly prestige of his predecessor. However, he was personable and 'married to a lady who is from all accounts thoroughly fitted to occupy the position of Director's wife'.[44] He went on to a distinguished career in Greek archaeology, holding professorships at London and Oxford and the keepership of Greek and Roman antiquities at the British Museum.

Eugénie felt a real sense of betrayal at his appointment after the churlish dismissals of Ashby and herself. She had seen Ashmole as a protégé and helped advance his early career, recommending him to Stuart-Jones to help in the completion of the Conservatori catalogue, and to that end providing him with access to important private collections. Eugénie was not one to bear a grudge, and she tried to establish a working relationship with him.[45] Yet Ashmole was not interested in mending fences, and she remained *persona non grata* at the institution she had done so much to build.

Eugénie was not the only person to regard the dismissal of the directors as a major blow to the prestige of the school. The American ancient historian Tenney Frank remarked, 'We have all called the British School blessed in its fortunate management.'[46] Ludwig Pollak commented sadly that 'at that point the brilliance of the English School ended'.[47] Alice Lion, a French philosophy student who became a friend and supporter of Strong, remembered:

> It was then with profound emotion that the Roman intellectual world received the news of the departure of these two famous savants from the institute which owed to them all of its Scientific prestige. It is still difficult for me to enter into the beautiful library of the School where Mrs Strong claimed to have herself put each volume in its place, and in the austere places where Dr Ashby offered with generosity not only the riches of his personal library and his marvellous collection of prints, but furthermore all the special insights which made him the most eminent topographer of the campagna and Rome.[48]

Ashmole and his successors were unable to stop the school's decline. Ashmole himself resigned as director in 1927 to take up the Chair of Archaeology at London. A. H. Smith, now retired from the British Museum, succeeded him. His regime was mainly characterized by a fussy formality that did not endear him to the younger residents of the school.[49] Eugénie, hardly an impartial observer, commented in 1929 to Salomon Reinach: 'The British School has gone down terribly and poor Arthur Smith, kind though he is, has neither the vitality nor the reputation that should enable him to rival men like Curtius or like Male.'[50]

Ongoing administrative and financial problems continued to haunt the school until the outbreak of World War II. Smith was succeeded by the young and promising Ian Richmond. However, health problems cut his directorship short.[51] Smith returned briefly as interim director, but was soon replaced by the classicist Colin Hardie. Growing hostility between England and Italy, especially over Ethiopia, forced the school to curtail its activities and even briefly close its doors.[52] The medieval archaeologist C. A. Ralegh Radford succeeded Hardie in 1938 and ran the school until the outbreak of the war, but the BSR was not to regain its sense of mission and stature until the mature years of John Ward Perkins after World War II.[53]

11

The Golden Years of a Scholar

Forced retirement from the British School came as a shock to Eugénie and initially produced considerable bitterness. Friends who saw her in the months after her dismissal commented on her depression. Portrait sketches and busts made at the time show that she had aged considerably during this emotionally charged period of her life. There were even hints that she was drinking excessively.[1] However, she soon righted herself and began to plan the next phase of her life. For her, retirement was much more in the order of things than for Ashby. She was sixty-five, had weathered many changes in her life, and had a vast network of friends and enough projects to consume more than one lifetime.

Eugénie's retirement was marked with appropriate honours. She was made a Commander of the British Empire in the New Year's Honours List of January 1927. It added to the list of honours that made her one of the most recognized women of her generation. As Raymond Asquith put it, she 'was probably a doctor of more universities and a fellow of more learned societies than any woman in the world'.[2] Letters poured in from friends and admirers.

On 14 July 1925, Eugénie was fêted at a ceremonial dinner held at the Cecil Hotel in London. The attendees included old friends like Mary Lowndes, important academics, a cross-section of the nobility, as well as of the cultural and political elites. Former Prime Minister Herbert Asquith, now the Earl of Oxford, presided.[3] Lord Balcarres gave the principal speech, and her old friend Salomon Reinach sent a Latin couplet to be read on the occasion:

> I, dea Roma, rector, lonqinquo laeta volatu
> Votaque Romulidum perfer ad Eugeniam

Eugénie saw a certain irony in the presence of some who had been involved in the recent unpleasantness at the British School. As she observed to her brother-in-law, Thomas Strong, 'The dinner is something of a puzzle, as so many of the Executive Committee of the School are organizing it and many others are coming to it. There seems to me to be a consensus of opinion that I was not to blame for the happenings.'[4] Strong experienced considerable anxiety over the upcoming event, but in the end carried it off with her usual style and flair, her speech of thanks including gracious praise of Thomas Ashby.

As part of the retirement celebrations, the sculptor David Evans prepared a bust of Eugénie.[5] She despised it, exclaiming: 'I quite own its cleverness as a work of sculpture, but I was taken at a disadvantage, when I was very ill and very nervous, for reasons that you know and the portrait is so disagreeable to me.'[6] Clearly the vanity of a woman who had been one of the Victorian beauties was offended.

With the celebrations behind her, Eugénie once again had to think about her future. She made clear in her speech at the London banquet that she did not consider herself retired, and indeed needed to remain active in order to supplement her slender income. There was no doubt that she would remain in Rome, but she had to establish a life there tailored to her restricted financial resources. The British School provided no retirement assistance even after long years of service, so her income comprised her Girton fellowship and some personal savings. Fortunately the cost of living in pre-war Rome was low, and in spite of occasional protests she felt no real privation until the outbreak of the war.

One reason for Eugénie's financial security was the continued assistance she received from Mary Lowndes. Mary had long subsidized their apartment in London; now she offered to do the same in Rome. By early September 1925, Eugénie had established herself in an apartment at Via Cesare Balbo 35 on the Viminal hill near the basilica of Santa Maggiore. This was to be her home until the outbreak of World War II. The building was located on what is still today a pleasant side street near the early medieval church of Santa Pudenziana. It was not far from the Fascist Ministry of the Interior, and Strong could observe Mussolini's frequent visits to it. The apartment building's architecture was turn-of-the-century Umbertine eclectic, with rustication and balconies. Photos of the interior show comfortable rooms crowded with bookshelves. In one, a now white-haired Mrs Strong, dressed in black, is shown sitting at a desk decorated with a crucifix and photographs of clerics (plate 19).

At Via Balbo, Eugénie continued the cosmopolitan salons that had been such an important part of her life at the British School. Her apartment became the venue for what Ludwig Curtius described as the last international salon in Rome.[7] At her Saturday afternoon 'at homes' assembled diplomats, distinguished archaeologists and learned cardinals, but also young students and artists just beginning their careers. Newcomers were quickly charmed. The author Norman Douglas, admitting he had always been afraid to meet her, changed his mind when a mutual friend assured him that any such fears would be 'dispelled two seconds in your presence'.[8]

Young and old retained warm memories of those Saturday gatherings. Joan Yeo Marsh, Eugénie's personal secretary from 1929–31, recalled:

> I was invited to her Saturday evening reception – 'at Home 6–8, a tres petit comité' – as I later found the invitations ran. I remember the room, closely packed with people ... Above all – Mrs Strong, turning with apparent equal ease from English, to French, to German, to Italian – and I can see her now, as the guests began to depart – bidding farewell to one of them in English – 'How wonderful if we could excavate Sybaris.'[9]

Marsh also provided insight into the social dynamics and the openness of the occasions: 'One party I remember vividly began with a cardinal and a principessa; one ended in Mrs Strong asking me to take an Irish artist out to supper. He had come, doubtless with some good introduction, complete with several paintings. Until one of these was sold there was apparently no money.'[10] She recalled some of the more interesting guests:

> The main body of the parties was of course scholars – professors, and some students from various schools. Prof. Ludwig Curtius of the

German Academy, Ernst Robert Curtius, of different fame, were around with the Herziana set … Maurice Baring I remember well, having been absorbed in 'Cats Cradle', and now cherishing the Anthology he called 'Something to Declare'. There were the Gladwyn Jebbs on their honeymoon.

The warmth and excitement of those evenings remained vivid to Eugénie and her friends long after the outbreak of World War II ended them and the world that they embodied. As she lay dying in war-torn Rome, Eugénie reminisced with the Swedish archaeologist Axel Boëthius about the delight of those afternoons at Via Balbo 35.[11]

While the cultural and scholarly elite of Rome made their way to her apartment, Eugénie herself was very much involved in the social and intellectual life of the city. She attended and gave lectures at most of the major Italian and foreign institutes. Visitors to Rome were constantly calling on her, and she was most generous in providing tours of the archaeological sites and museums. She continued to travel, returning every summer to England. In Cambridge, Girton was her home. In London the Albemarle Club, with its elegant rooms decorated in the style of Robert Adam, provided her with comfort and ambiance.

Eugénie had always had a marvellous ability to begin and maintain friendships. People were attracted by her wide-ranging intellect and vivacious and determined personality. Her group of friends, like the stratigraphy of a complicated archaeological site, represented associations preserved from each phase of her life. Rare was a Jane Harrison, where a deep friendship ended definitively. Distance, over time or place, proved to be no barrier to continuing relationships, because Eugénie corresponded regularly with most of her friends. She provided a classic example of female friendships maintained during long periods of physical separation, a subject that has interested feminist historians.[12]

By the Via Balbo years, most friends of her early life, as well as youthful mentors like Maude Stanley and Mary Ponsonby, had died. The deaths of Furtwängler and Traube in 1907 had broken the major links with her Munich days. The most important friendship surviving from her pre-marriage days was that with Rennell Rodd. She had felt betrayed by his lack of support during the British School crisis, but they had had too many years of friendship to remain estranged for long. Their correspondence, with its salutations of 'My dear Hypatia', soon resumed, and he visited the Via Balbo whenever he came to Rome.[13] Their friendship even weathered their differences over the British–Italian crisis of 1935–6 and the resulting closure of the British School at Rome.

It was fitting that Joan Marsh should highlight the presence of Maurice Baring at Eugénie's evenings, for he was one of her oldest and dearest friends. He belonged to a distinguished banking family and had received an appropriately elite education.[14] He entered the diplomatic corps, serving at embassies in Paris, Copenhagen, Rome and St Petersburg. However, his heart was in literary studies, and he resigned from the Foreign Service to devote his life to writing. He was a man of impressive culture, well versed in the literatures of Europe, and especially interested in the classic Russian writers, doing much to make them better known in England. He wrote essays, plays, novels and memoirs. Like Eugénie he became a devout Roman Catholic, and his Catholicism was central to his writing.

Some people, like Mary Lowndes, found Baring rather too precious. One friend described him as a 'troll living between reality and fairyland',[15] and Hilaire Belloc joked that no one in Baring's novels had less than £5,000 a year.[16] However, most saw him as an appealing ambassador of culture. One admirer observed: 'I cannot but believe that at the General Resurrection Maurice Baring, of all men now living, will be the most warmly greeted by the greatest number and variety of his fellow creatures from every country and continent and from every walk of life.'[17]

The Strong–Baring correspondence preserved at Yale's Beinecke Library and in the Girton College Archives conveys the richness of their friendship. It also mirrors the changing politics and cultural concerns of their era. In a letter from 1900, Baring admitted his ambiguity about the Dreyfus affair: 'as long as Dreyfus was in prison, I should have sacrificed my antipathy against the Dreyfusards. Now that he is free, I am also free to hate the Dreyfusards.'[18] Generally, their letters centred on literature, music and art. They discussed Goethe, Dante, Milton and George Eliot; Schubert, Mozart and Wagner. Baring was one of her great supporters during Arthur's final illness and death, and his newly published novel *The Cat's Cradle* provided a welcome distraction for her during the dreary months after her departure from the British School. The letters from the late 1930s, when Baring was living in the countryside near Brighton and Strong in Fascist Rome, became increasingly sad. Once more Europe was descending into chaos, and that community of culture they both valued so much was falling apart. Baring suffered from a painful, debilitating illness. However, a shared devotion to the faith and rituals of the Roman Catholic Church provided a strong bond. In a letter written in the Easter season of 1939, Baring remarked, 'I always think of you today, Holy Saturday, which I think is the cause of the most beautiful ritual in the whole liturgy.'[19] The outbreak of war separated them for ever. Baring survived Eugénie by two years, dying on 14 December 1945.

Eugénie's friendship with Bernard Berenson had pre-dated her marriage. They continued to see each sporadically while Arthur was alive, but the intense rivalry between the two men made the relationship difficult. The Berensons saw Arthur as a major enemy in the vicious world of the international art market and Arthur resented Eugénie's past relations with Berenson. As Mary put it in a letter to the American collector Isabella Stuart Gardner,

> Most of these tales go back to a Mr S. Arthur Strong, librarian of the House of Lords, who was at one time bitterly jealous of B.B. because the lady he was in love with (and has since married) had broken her engagement with him and come to travel in Italy with us. This, we think, started Mr Strong's hatred, but, as he is of a bitter envious nature, it continues still although he has got the lady in question.[20]

Ironically, this letter was written three days after Arthur's death. When Mary was informed, she merely observed that she hoped his demise would improve Bernard's art business.[21] With Arthur's death and Eugénie's move to Rome, her friendship with the Berensons was renewed. Bernard had become a central figure in the international art market, and had used his income as an art consultant to purchase I Tatti, a splendid villa outside Florence where he held court for leading figures in the world of art and culture. Eugénie was one of the regular visitors during the 1920s and the 1930s. Such encounters were stimulating but often stormy, as Eugénie was not about to grant Berenson the intellectual deference that he increasingly came to expect.[22] He observed on one occasion: 'You have a way of exciting and stimulating and rousing that is unique. You have always been and remain a fascinating woman, no little of a Siren and a good bit of a Circe and at times a Medusa.'[23]

Many of their disagreements arose from differing views on art and aesthetics. Berenson was imbued with an aesthetic classicism, which placed the high points of Western art in fifth-century Athens and the Italian Renaissance. He had no great enthusiasm for Hellenistic art or for that of the baroque. He did not understand Eugénie's passion for Roman art, especially its more 'primitive' manifestations in the monuments of the provinces and of the Late Empire. He had little liking for the art of late antiquity and less sympathy with the scholarship of revisionists like Wickhoff.[24] His last book savagely attacked the late-antique aesthetic values represented by the sculptured reliefs of the arch of Constantine.[25] His emphasis on stylistic analysis and the use of very general aesthetic terms like 'tactile values' differed significantly from Eugénie's more historical approach.

Eugénie's friendship with Mary also revived after Arthur's death. By the 1930s they were again mellow old friends, touring the towns of Tuscany and Umbria together, arguing over art and talking about friends from the past. Eugénie's increasing infirmities prevented her from keeping pace with the aging but more vigorous Bernard on regular visits to Rome, but she arranged soirées where he could meet young Italian intellectuals like the novelist Alberto Moravia and the architect Marcello Piacentini.

The last surviving letter Eugénie Strong sent to the Berensons is dated 28 December 1941, shortly after the Americans entered the war. All were now threatened by the hostilities. Eugénie, as an English subject, had suffered first. However, after Pearl Harbor the situation became worse for Bernard, for he was both American and Jewish. He elected to stay in Italy and, through luck and the devoted support of friends, survived. He returned after the war to I Tatti, where he spent his sunset years acting the role of a great cultural sage.[26] The visits of old acquaintances revived memories of times past and friends deceased. Roger Hinks remembered one evening when they evoked the spirits of Logan Pearsall Smith, Salomon Reinach and Eugénie Strong.[27]

Another old friend was the artist and art critic D. S. MacColl. Their association dated back to her early days when they socialized with Jane Harrison, Mary Lowndes and Eugénie's sister Charlie. MacColl had decorated Eugénie's study in her London apartment and helped her through various intellectual and personal crises. Years later she recalled the anxieties and uncertainties of that time: 'When I first knew you, I was very unhappy and uncertain about my own studies and about criticism in general. I hated the narrow pedantic and self-righteous atmosphere all around me, but was too young and crude and ignorant myself to be able to react.'[28] Their long friendship was often punctuated by disagreements over art and art history. In the early years, MacColl, who approached art from an aesthetic perspective, opposed her commitment to German scientific archaeology. He pictured her in Athens 'sliding upon the Ilissos or that other classic drain that Dörpfeld is attached to'.[29] Their disagreements became more heated and stimulating as Eugénie matured from hesitant student to self-confident scholar.

MacColl was increasingly upset by what he saw as the too-close integration of her personal Catholic identity and her advocacy of baroque art. After one lecture he admonished: 'the absence of any critical element suggests to me that the missionary spirit of propaganda, mingled with the real religious motive, have carried you beyond the point where the evidence of the eye is attended to.'[30] Eugénie responded vigorously, hitting what she saw as his aesthetic weak points: 'You simply violently assert what you feel and express your own likes and dislikes. I try to show that each of these men was making manifest the ideas of his time. If we dislike the ideas, that is another matter … The art critic's business is to show the relation of *form* to *idea* and from the measure of the artist's success in equating the two must spring our criticism of his work.'[31]

Eugénie's most important archaeological friend during those years was

Ludwig Curtius, who, like Eugénie, had been a student of Adolf Furtwängler.[32] They first met on a train in Greece shortly after Arthur's death, and became fast friends. They shared a devotion to classical art and a broad humanistic culture, although Eugénie was sceptical about Curtius's enthusiasm for Winckelmann.[33] She admired his dynamic leadership of the German Institute from 1928 to 1933 and liked to contrast his directorship with what she considered the hapless and ineffective leaders of the British School.

As Germany changed, Curtius faced major ethical dilemmas. He sympathized with the efforts of scholars like Werner Jaeger to advance the cause of a new classically based humanism. However, he increasingly felt the tensions between his own Goethian values and the monstrous regime that was coming to power in Germany. His inability to support the Nazis led to an early retirement from the institute.

Another regular at the Via Balbo was the medievalist Ernst Robert Curtius.[34] The grandson of the great nineteenth-century archaeologist Ernest Curtius, he was born and raised in Alsace and derived from that a lifelong appreciation for French as well as German culture. Curtius must have reminded Eugénie of her Munich mentor Ludwig Traube. All three shared a European cosmopolitanism and a common appreciation for the Roman heritage. The latter found expression in Curtius's great work, *European Literature and the Latin Middle Ages*.[35] They frequented each other's salons in Rome and corresponded for years about books and friends.

Rome of the 1920s and 1930s was still a major centre for antiquarian research, collecting and the trade in antiquities. As a museum archaeologist, Eugénie had many friends in these circles, although she was ambivalent about the growing trade in classical art. She knew John Marshall, long the chief purchaser for the Metropolitan Museum of Art in New York, from the days of her Burlington exhibition. His elegant apartment off the Spanish Steps had become a gathering place for aesthetes, dealers and scholars.[36]

At Marshall's apartment and other venues, Eugénie crossed paths with Gisela Richter of the Metropolitan Museum, who was often in Rome purchasing classical art for that institution.[37] Eugénie had known her art-historian father, and watched young Gisela mature into one of the most respected classical art historians of her generation. Richter saw in Eugénie

Strong not only a distinguished Roman archaeologist, but also an exemplar of a woman who had carved out a successful career in her selected profession.[38]

Eugénie had long been a close friend of the Czech-Jewish art dealer and connoisseur Ludwig Pollak.[39] Pollak had studied classical archaeology and art history at Prague, and by the early 1890s had made his way to Rome. There he lived a cultivated lifestyle as a private scholar, art dealer and advisor to collectors. His residence was one of the most elegant and cultured spaces in Rome. He knew the museums, private collections and antiquities market intimately and was friendly with most of the players in the international art trade that prospered between the wars.

Eugénie's frequent visits to the Vatican collections fostered a close friendship with Bartolomeo Nogara. He had come to Rome from Lombardy and spent much of his archaeological career in the Vatican museums, where he was appointed director in 1924.[40] They shared an interest in classical archaeology, a deep religious faith, and a strong Christian humanism. Nogara remained loyal to the end, visiting Eugénie during her last months in war-torn Rome and even arranging for her funeral and burial.

Unlike many aging people, Eugénie always remained open to the young. The English archaeologist Stanley Casson praised her for being the 'only archaeologist who sees that after all there is a new generation of archaeologists that needs help and encouragement'.[41] Closest among her young protégés was Jocelyn Toynbee.[42] Jocelyn came from a family that combined scholarly interests with social concerns. Her brother was a famous historian, and the family had helped found the settlement house at Toynbee Hall where Eugénie had lectured in her youth. Jocelyn read classics and archaeology at Cambridge with Percy Gardner and became interested in second-century Roman art. Gardner sent her to study with Eugénie, who was still the leading scholar in the field. Although Eugénie had little interest in the neo-Hellenic revival of the Hadrianic period that fascinated Toynbee, she saw in the young woman a very promising student and did everything possible to help her career.[43]

Toynbee responded with deep affection for the aged scholar of the Via Balbo, with whom she shared not only an appreciation for Roman culture but also a deep Catholic faith. Toynbee found her academic home in Newnham College, Cambridge, ironically the place where Jane Harrison had held court for many years. She became a highly productive scholar, almost alone in keeping interest in Roman art alive in Britain during the immediate post-war years. Her final act of piety to her mentor was to help preserve Eugénie's papers after World War II.

Another young female academic drawn to Strong was the medieval historian Eileen Power.[44] They shared a Girton connection, since Power was both a student and tutor at Eugénie's old college. Power soon established a reputation in both Cambridge and London as one of the most creative medievalists of her generation. The older woman saw in the bright, pretty, lively Power a younger version of herself, while Power found a role model in the respected senior scholar. Power wrote chatty letters to Eugénie, and regularly sent friends and colleagues to visit her in Rome.

Young men as well as young women received Eugénie's friendship and support. The closest that Eugénie Strong had to a collaborator after Katherine Jex-Blake was Gilbert Bagnani, who had been educated in Italy, but knew England well, for his father had served as military attaché in London. [45] He was the type of young cultured cosmopolitan whom Eugénie adored. Their shared love for Rome, its history and its monuments led them to plan a historical guide to the city and its surrounding countryside, although sadly the project was never completed.

Among the younger Italian intellectuals she was especially drawn to Mario Praz. Their mutual friend Maurice Baring probably drew them together. Praz was a learned scholar of English literature and an aesthete, with a special interest in the decorative arts of the eighteenth and nineteenth centuries, collectables little appreciated among connoisseurs at the time.[46] His collection of objects from that era filled his Roman apartment, which became the 'memory palace' vividly described in his book *La Casa di Vita*. Praz and Strong were kindred souls, and his essay about her written after her death was one of her most moving memorials.[47]

In 1922, Eugénie wrote enthusiastically to Israel Gollancz of the British Academy about a young friend: 'I have just seen a very brilliant and interesting young relative of yours M. Leon Kochnitzky, who seems to be a man of great promise. I am reading his *D'Annunzio*, though it is not the work of his that I like best. Leon is a great dear as well as a real intellectual and when he is settled in Rome, as he was last week, I see him constantly.'[48] Kochnitzky indeed knew d'Annunzio, the Italian novelist and poet, well, for he had served as an official propagandist for his Fiume Republic.[49] That increased his appeal for Eugénie, for she too had long admired d'Annunzio.

Kochnitzky was Belgian-Jewish in origin, but in later life converted to Roman Catholicism.[50] To his early reputation as a poet he added that of a knowledgeable art and music critic, and shared with Eugénie a devotion to the international baroque art form. His deep humanistic culture and appealing personality attracted all who knew him. He was, throughout his life, a restless wanderer, who sent Eugénie a succession of letters and post-cards from diverse locations. As a strong anti-Fascist, he spent the war years in the United States. Among his unpublished papers was found a perceptive essay on Eugénie Strong.[51]

It would be wrong to regard the Eugénie Strong of the inter-war years as merely a cultured socialite. She remained an active scholar, perhaps not as productive as she wished, but by the standards of her English and American contemporaries highly visible. She published three books, presented important lecture series, wrote articles, gave many talks, and was engaged in ambitious research projects up to the time of her death. However, she was never totally satisfied with her scholarly legacy, and feelings of inadequacy haunted her as she grew older. In 1929 she returned to Berlin, but the experience saddened her. She reflected on 'the meaning of all that here in this very Berlin I planned to be and do … and I have accomplished nothing'.[52] She expressed similar disappointments in a printed edition of her bibliography that she sent to the Mistress of Girton.[53] Expressions of thanks for the years of support were followed by apologies, for the 'results are not such as College and donors were entitled to expect'.

In spite of such doubts and regrets, Eugénie remained a hard-driven scholar, who placed high demands on herself and on collaborators. Joan Marsh provided a vivid insight into Eugénie's working methods:

I had letters to type, and address correctly to distinguished persons in several nationalities (some knowledge of German was a requirement for the post, and French was assumed). I must admit to occasions when I returned to find an envelope slashed with corrections when both knowledge and imagination had failed me over some title. Mrs Strong, although sometimes explosive, was basically very patient with me. I had been told, on setting out for the post, that no secretary for Mrs Strong lasted very long, so the sense of adventure sustained me through ups and downs.[54]

Eugénie's research continued to focus on Roman art and archaeology. Central to her efforts was a revision of her classic *Roman Sculpture*. New discoveries and new scholarship had made her 1909 work outdated, and she had long contemplated a revised edition. Finally, in 1923–5 there appeared a new two-volume Italian version entitled *La scultura romana da Augusto a Constantino*. An English translation was promised but never appeared. While the overall organization followed the old work, the new text was substantially revised and improved. Moreover, it had nearly three times the number of illustrations, many in a larger, more user-friendly format. The work was on the whole well received.

More innovative was her *Art in Ancient Rome from the Earliest Times to Justinian*, published in 1928. It was a small-format, two-volume work which also had French and Italian editions and was part of an art-history series directed by her old friend Salomon Reinach. Eugénie now presented a more inclusive view of Roman art than had been possible in her Roman sculpture books. She extended her time-frame backwards to Italian prehistory and forwards to the early fifth century, and discussed architecture as well as the visual arts.

The book had been long in the making. In the preface she thanked her friend and fellow art historian Katharine Esdaile, recalling how 'we worked together during tragic and unforgettable weeks at the beginning of the War, and I often think of how we strove to cheat the anxious hours by steeping ourselves in the problems offered by the art of Eternal Rome'.[55] She acknowledged her debt to many Roman archaeologists, but her warmest tribute was reserved for Thomas Ashby: 'My more personal thanks are due to Dr Thomas Ashby for the encouragement accorded me in this and other works during an official association of sixteen years; for the privilege of free access to his rich library, and for generously loaning to me so many of his own valuable photographs of Rome and the Campagna, before he had published them himself.'[56]

In the preface she declared: 'My aim throughout has been to show, as clearly as in me lay, that the diverse phases of Roman art correspond to as many phases in the spiritual and political life of the Roman people.' It was intended to be, as Jocelyn Toynbee observed in a review, 'the study of Rome's political and spiritual development as expressed in her art'.[57] It was also a study of the persistence of the Roman spirit. Eugénie stressed that:

> The indestructibility of the Roman type is patent throughout the story. As it had resisted Hellenistic influences under the Republic, so under the Empire it was proof against the strong oriental currents which, it is often asserted, threatened its very existence. But these currents simply brought with them new seeds of life and thus averted the sterility which inevitably overtakes any art impervious to extraneous influence.[58]

For the first time Strong systematically explored the art of the Republic. Beginning with the prehistoric roots, she traced the complex development of Rome's artistic culture in relation to internal political and social forces and to outside influences. Architecture, sculpture, painting and even such neglected arts as terracotta work received full attention. It was in many ways her most 'archaeological' book in the way that the material culture was presented. While recent discoveries have made many sections outdated, it remains a model of how ancient art history should be written.

The book was an ambitious undertaking and one that she felt was not totally successful. She thought that because of its small format, it did not receive the attention it deserved. She lamented to the Danish archaeologist Frederick Poulsen, 'That is the worst of writing little books. They give a lot of trouble and nobody learned notices them.'[59]

In her review of the work, Jocelyn Toynbee rightly chastised Eugénie for her disclaimers about the work's usefulness for archaeologists. Eugénie was more sensitive than most art historians to the potential of 'dirt' archaeology, and it was true that she had never participated in an excavation, something almost impossible for a woman of her generation. However, from the moment that her translation of Schuchhardt brought the discoveries of Schliemann to the English public, she was very attuned to what archaeological discoveries could contribute to an understanding of antiquity. Throughout her life she counted among her friends some of the best field archaeologist of the day. She enjoyed warm relations with Giacomo Boni and knew Arthur Evans, the excavator of Knossos, well. Among younger archaeologists she cultivated Mortimer Wheeler, one of the best field archaeologists of his generation, and made a special point of visiting his model excavation at the Iron Age hillfort of Maiden Castle.[60] Most interesting, and in some ways surprising, was her long friendship with the austere Egyptologist Flinders Petrie. They came to know each other during their early London days, for he and Arthur were colleagues at the University of London.[61] Their friendship continued beyond Arthur's death. Shared archaeological interests and enthusiasms are captured in a letter she wrote to him in early 1928, suggesting a visit together to the newly opened Museum of the Roman Provinces in Rome:

I want very much to hear you talk again on the subject of archaeology versus art. You express so well what I have been trying in my insufficient manner to preach for many years that some of the Schools here and also the universities at home make the mistake of considering that archaeology is the study of art and that the study of art means the extolling of one period at the expense of another. It has been as disastrous to the study of aesthetics which is quite a subject by itself as to that of archaeology proper.[62]

In the preface to *Art in Ancient Rome*, Eugénie stressed the work's valedictory quality, evoking the words of the Latin mass: 'But I shall at least sing my *nunc dimittis* in peace.' However, another scholarly challenge lay ahead.

She was commissioned to write for the *Cambridge Ancient History*, the most important work of British classical scholarship in the inter-war period.

She was the only woman asked to contribute, and her chapter on 'The Art of the Roman Republic', part of Volume Nine, appeared in 1932. It opened with a detailed and sensitive discussion of the Italic, and especially the Etruscan, roots of Roman art. Her discussion of the creativity of later Etruscan art was very original. The analysis of Romano-Italic art benefited from her willingness to consider the creations of artisans working in the smaller centres of Roman Italy. She anticipated in many respects the post-war scholarship of such Roman art historians as Rannucio Bianchi Bandinelli and Diana Kleiner. The importance of Greek art for Roman art was not ignored, but she refused to see Rome as some late provincial manifestation of Hellenic creativity. Most dated has become her discussion of Roman architecture. She did try to include the most recent archaeological discoveries such as the Republican temples recently excavated in the Largo Argentina in central Rome. However, Roman architecture was never one of her major interests, and it is a field where new discoveries and interpretations have forced the most substantial revisions of her positions.

The chapter on Augustan art, published in 1934 in Volume Ten, focused on the Roman-Italic world of Augustus. It was a topic not only dear to Eugénie, but also central to the historical ideology of the Fascists who then governed Italy. Key to her interpretations was the Ara Pacis that Mussolini's archaeologists had recently reconstructed. Her arguments on the central themes of Augustan art were well supported by examples drawn from both Italy and the provinces, and by new discoveries. She explored topics that have only recently received much scholarly attention, such as the representation of women and children in Roman art.[63] Discussion of Roman high art was again complemented by consideration of provincial works and products of popular art such as columbarian tomb paintings and stuccoes. The section devoted to architecture drew heavily on recent discoveries by Fascist archaeologists in Rome.

The *Cambridge Ancient History* chapters were accompanied by a host of major projects started but not completed: reviews, short articles, letters to newspapers and lectures. If anything, Strong divided her formidable energies too much, and important undertakings were never completed. A good example was the book, *Rome and Her Treasures*, which she proposed to write with her young friend Gilbert Bagnani. She described her aim:

> I think that the point of having a keen and young archaeologist like Bagnani to write one part and an old and somewhat experienced hand like myself to write the other is to bring out what is new and also what has been shamefully neglected. We do not want to repeat the old rubbish about the Renaissance and the Baroque, though I am going to give its full share to the Renaissance. People always complain of its non-existence in Rome. I endeavour to show them what an amount of beautiful examples there are of both medieval and renaissance work, enough to content even Ruskin.[64]

Both authors moved forward; indeed the book appeared so close to completion that the publisher announced its imminent appearance. That rash action drew a sharp rebuke from Eugénie, who protested that new archaeological discoveries in Fascist Rome forced constant revisions and delayed its completion. She never did finish her section, while Bagnani published his in a 1929 book, *The Roman Campagna and Its Treasures*. The loss was great, for the book would have provided Eugénie with an opportunity to share her deep knowledge and love of the city.

The decade after Eugénie's departure from the British School was in many ways one of the happiest in her life. Rome still retained many aspects of its old-fashioned charm and she demonstrated a diverse productivity that would have been impressive in someone much younger. The loneliness that she must have felt after the years of community life at the British School was mitigated by the presence of faithful servants and loyal friends. However, political forces in both Italy and Europe were to produce changes that dramatically affected both the later life and reputation of Eugénie Strong.

12

A Life and Death in Fascist Rome

In 1936, Bernard Berenson hurriedly ended a letter to his friend Clotilde Marghieri saying that he had to dash off to Mrs Strong's to meet the Sarfattis.[1] Marguerita Sarfatti was a major figure on the Fascists' cultural and journalistic scene. In 1926 she had published *Dux*, an influential biography of Mussolini.[2] She was for many years his mistress, but by the early 1930s had fallen out of favour. Marguerita Sarfatti was Jewish, and the Italian racial laws instituted in 1938 ultimately forced her to flee to Latin America.

Marguerita Sarfatti provides an appropriate introduction to the complex relationship between Eugénie Strong and the Fascist regime, an association that has become the most controversial part of her legacy. She had been assistant director of the British School for thirteen years when, in 1922, the Fascists marched on Rome, and Benito Mussolini became the *de facto* ruler of Italy. By 1925, when she settled into Via Balbo 35, the crises of early Fascism had passed, and Mussolini was established as the head of what proved to be a long-lived, stable and, for many contemporaries, a very successful regime. In that year Eugénie praised the decision of a young friend to join the Fascist movement, calling it 'the best and healthiest thing for Italy'.[3] She encouraged her young protégé Aline Lion to write a biography of Mussolini, although does not appear to have been vociferous in her support of the dictator.[4] One friend wrote, 'I don't believe I have ever heard your opinion of that great enigma and you must know so much of him.' In fact, she did not meet Mussolini until four years after his march on Rome, and during all her years in the city appears to have met Il Duce twice, both times at archaeological ceremonies.[5]

Later events, from the Ethiopian invasion to the debacle of World War II, have led modern students of Fascist Italy to forget the high level of support that Mussolini and his policies received from the British and American governments and the elite of those countries.[6] Rennell Rodd, that experienced student of Italian affairs, provided this judgment on Mussolini in his memoirs:

> But I may add here that the personality of the actual Prime Minister in Italy has always suggested to me to the type which impressed itself on the early history of the Renaissance by the possession of those characteristic qualities of primeval vitality, of courage, intellectual ability and forceful will to achieve a purpose which Machiavelli indicated in the word *virtu*.[7]

Il Duce restored order to Italy. As his apologists proclaimed, he had after all made the trains run on time. Public-works projects such as the draining of the Pontine marshes gave Italy the appearance of an increasingly modern country. Building went on everywhere.

In 1929 the Fascist government and the Vatican signed the Lateran Concordat. For the first time since 1870 official relations existed between the Roman Catholic Church and the national government. The extra-territorial status of the Vatican was recognized, and the Church assumed an important role in areas such as education. Clerics and individual Catholics could now participate more fully in the civic life of Italy.

Throughout her life Eugénie had shown relatively little interest in politics. In her voluminous correspondence, spanning the years from the Franco-Prussian War to World War II, she rarely discussed contemporary events. Only the Dreyfus Affair received significant attention, and that was due more to her close personal connection with significant players than to any strongly held views of her own. Even the rise and triumph of the Fascists passed with relatively little notice. Politically and socially her reaction to Mussolini was similar to that of most of the British and American ex-pats. In the words of Mario Praz: 'Eugénie Strong with her eye turned on Cola di Rienzo and Augustus, believed in Mussolini. And it is necessary to say that among the English she was not alone.'[8] The Mussolini of the later 1920s represented order and a progressive social policy. Restoration of good relations between Church and state was appealing to her religious sensibilities.

None of Eugénie's close acquaintances in England or Italy identified closely with Fascism. She was not friendly with conservative intellectuals like Hilaire Belloc who favoured them.[9] In fact her friends were more likely to be opponents of Fascism like Leon Kochnitzky and the archaeologist Umberto Zanotti Bianco. Where her attitude most differed from that of her English contemporaries was in response to Mussolini's invasion of Ethiopia in 1935. Eugénie was vehement in her defence of the Italian action, while her friends in England were equally outspoken in their condemnation. Even the deep friendship with Mary Lowndes was strained. Both sides shared an equally colonialist view of the Ethiopians, but disagreed on the positions taken by the League of Nations and the British government. The decision to close the British School in the aftermath of Ethiopia led to heated exchanges between Eugénie and Rennell Rodd.[10] She was clearly influenced by Italian propaganda and by conservative Englishmen like Evelyn Waugh who visited Ethiopia and provided her with their rather biased perspectives.

Eugénie was especially drawn to the new regime because of its close identification with ancient Rome; she had long stressed the civilizing mission of the Roman Empire. Her views were similar to those of mainstream pre-Fascist Italian archaeologists Rodolfo Lanciani and Giacomo Boni, who welcomed the Fascists. She was also an old friend of the art historian Corrado Ricci, who inspired and guided Mussolini's excavations of the fora of the Caesars in the centre of Rome.[11]

The most important link for her between the old and new worlds of Italian archaeology was Giulio Giglioli, the most powerful archaeologist in the country under Mussolini.[12] Their acquaintance went back to the days of the 1911 exhibition, when Giglioli had served as Lanciani's chief assistant. In 1913 Giglioli joined the staff of the Villa Giulia Etruscan Museum, and in 1919 became its director. The museum was located close to the British School, and Eugénie and her students often worked there. His high standing with Mussolini's government was indicated by his appointment as the director of the Museo del Impero in 1926, a new museum established to glorify both the Roman past and Fascist imperial policies.[13] He and Eugénie remained on cordial terms, and he was to call on her services when planning the 1937 Mostra Augustea. However, he was never one of her close circle of intimate friends.

Eugénie was much closer to the anti-Fascist archaeologist Umberto Zanotti Bianco. He was a dashing, handsome man, who one female contemporary described as 'an incarnation of a Greek hero', an archaeological romantic who 'acts and occasionally succeeds like Schliemann'. He was also an old-fashioned political liberal, whose views on a whole range of issues got him in trouble with the regime. His archaeological research focused on Magna Graecia, but that was part of his larger agenda promoting the interests of southern Italy's neglected regions.[14]

Eugénie's interest in Magna Graecia went back to her travels with her father and her youthful encounter with François Lenormont. She showed great interest in Zanotti Bianco's research and supported organizations such as the Societa Magna Grecia that advanced his archaeological agenda. Among the greatest pleasures of her later years were the trips taken with him through southern Italy. The bond between two such people is a clear refutation of the common view that Eugénie Strong was a doctrinaire supporter of the regime.

However, as an archaeologist she certainly found the Fascist years an exciting time to be in Rome, since archaeological excavation soon became an important part of Fascist cultural politics.[15] In the capital that meant massive programmes of excavation and restoration, and the systematic isolation of major Roman monuments from their surrounding urban fabric. These archaeological excavations were closely co-ordinated with building programmes in central Rome. The most dramatic example of this was the parade route built between the Colosseum and the Piazza Venezia, where large areas of Caesar's, Augustus's and Trajan's fora were cleared of medieval and post-medieval overlays to provide a Roman imperial backdrop for parades and processions.[16] By the time of his death, Mussolini ranked with the Emperor Augustus and the great Counter-Reformation popes such as Sixtus V as one of the major physical transformers of the city.

Eugénie looked on these developments with interest but also with considerable ambivalence. While she was enthusiastic about the archaeological discoveries and appreciated the glorification of the ancient Roman achievements, she was saddened by the destruction of familiar landmarks and concerned about the excessive damage done to the historical fabric of the city. Many years before, she had campaigned to save Christopher Wren's London home, and now she felt the need to resist what she saw as the Fascist urban excesses. In 1926 she wrote: 'We are founding here a small society called the Friends of Rome, which I trust may be of use in controlling public opinion as regards building Vandals.'[17] Most members of the society were Italian, and both they and resident foreigners like Eugénie had to be careful lest they offend the authorities. Some modest successes were achieved, with a few buildings saved, but they could do no more than slow the officially sponsored urban destruction.

Complementing the excavations and the opening of new museums were special expositions celebrating Fascist achievements, commemorating important political anniversaries and linking the regime with past Roman glories.[18] Most important of these for the archaeologists was the Mostra Augustea, launched in 1937 to commemorate the bi-millennium of Augustus's birth. Mussolini's identification with Augustus, which also found expression in the excavation of the Forum of Augustus and the restoration of the Altar of Peace, now culminated in this major exhibition.

Eugénie became very much involved in the Augustus exhibition. She shared with many classicists of her generation a deep admiration of Augustus, regarding him as the statesman who had saved Rome from the chaos of the late Republic and laid the foundations of an enduring imperial system. He had also been the great patron of the arts who presided over Rome's cultural golden age. This 'establishment' view of Augustus was captured by her friend John Buchan's 1937 biography of the emperor, a book that became an enormous commercial success. Buchan was a classically educated diplomat and statesman.[19] In his view Augustus more than Julius Caesar was the 'great man' of Roman history, the leader who embodied 'all the virtues of a dictator, when a dictator was needed'.[20] However, he stressed Augustus's stance as a man of peace, at his best when he realized the limits of empire. Eugénie agreed with him on the historical greatness of Augustus, and was a great admirer of the biography.[21]

Two years after the Buchan work a very different portrait of Augustus caught the imagination of the classical world. In 1939 the young Roman historian Ronald Syme published *The Roman Revolution*. His was a cynical, opportunistic Augustus, who anticipated many of the negative qualities of Benito Mussolini. Chapter headings such as 'Dux' and 'The March on Rome' drove home the similarities between Augustan past and Fascist present. Eugénie, ever attentive to bright young scholars, had come to know Syme, and had heard about his iconoclastic work. He confirmed the rumours: 'Your information is correct. I have written a rather shocking book about the history of Rome in the period 60BC–AD14. Nobody will like it.'[22] *The Roman Revolution* proved to be one of the most important works of its generation, and Syme's view of Augustus remained dominant during and after World War II.[23]

As the planning for the Mostra Augustea moved forward, Giglioli contacted Eugénie for assistance in obtaining Romano-British material for the exhibition. She responded enthusiastically, remarking to Mary Berenson that 'the Mostra Augustea ties me to Rome by invisible but strong chains. I am glad to have lived to see it.'[24] She used her yearly trips to Britain to gather the material. In spite of Anglo-Italian political tensions, British archaeologists like Robin Collingwood supported her efforts. Unlike most British classical archaeologists she had long been interested in the archaeology of Roman Britain. Collingwood, the leading Romano-British archaeologist of his generation, described her as 'the chief authority on important aspects of Roman Britain'.[25] Through her efforts a good selection of Romano-British material was displayed in the Mostra Augustea, providing a representative picture of that distant province and highlighting 'the results obtained by English archaeologists by the use of scientific archaeological methods'.[26]

The Augustan exhibition was installed in the Palazzo di Esposizioni on the Via Nazionale. The neo-baroque front of the late nineteenth-century exhibition hall was covered with a temporary façade in Fascist classical-modern style.[27] Over the entrance were inscribed the words 'Bimillenio di Augusti, Mostra Augustea della Romanità', while the word *dux* was repeated in large letters on each side.

The exhibition relied heavily on casts and models (some 21,000 in all).

The displays made striking use of sophisticated juxtapositions of images and texts. The various exhibitions presented a wide-ranging review of Rome's history and accomplishments with obvious stress on the links between Imperial Rome and Fascist Italy. As one Italian archaeologist wrote: 'The great undertaking, conceived by il Duce and entrusted to the scientific and organizational ability of Giulio Quirino Giglioli, has been brought to completion. It appears to us as worthy of fascist Italy, result of a driving force realized in a climate of spiritual unity in which the glorious memories of the past appear in direct connection with the possibilities of the present.'[28]

The first part of the exhibition traced the historical development of the Roman Republic. The reign of Augustus was then highlighted as the moment when both the imperial system and the Christian religion came into being. Succeeding sections depicted the historical evolution of the Roman Empire and explored particular topics such as architecture, engineering, religion and social life.

Eugénie provided the *Journal of Roman Studies* with a full and very positive evaluation of the exhibition.[29] It was an interesting complement to the review of the 1911 exhibition that she had done more than a quarter of a century before. For the British Catholic magazine *The Tablet* she took a different tack, stressing how the 1929 Concordat with the Vatican had made possible the important contribution of the Roman Catholic Church.[30]

During the 1930s the Italian government increasingly treated Eugénie Strong as a spokesperson for the British and American archaeological communities in Rome, of which she was the most distinguished. The directors of the British School during those years were generally young, relatively unknown scholars, and the leading American archaeologist, Albert Van Buren of the American Academy, had nothing like her record of distinguished scholarship. Her publications received very positive reviews in the Fascist press, and presentation copies were conveyed to Il Duce.[31] In 1938 she was awarded the City of Rome's gold medal. In the same year she also received the Serena Medal for Italian Studies from the British Academy. Earlier recipients had included such distinguished British Italophiles as Rennell Rodd and G. M. Trevelyan.[32]

The high point of Eugénie's involvement with Fascist archaeological propaganda came on 23 September 1938 when she delivered an address of greeting to Mussolini at the dedication of the reconstructed Ara Pacis in the Campus Martius. The original altar, which was erected between 13 and 9 BC, had been one of the most important monuments in Augustan Rome. After the fall of the Roman Empire many of the sculptural fragments had been scattered in museums in Italy and abroad and the architectural remains buried under later buildings. Mussolini's archaeologists had excavated fragments from the original altar site and recovered most of the pieces in museums. The altar was rebuilt near the newly cleared tomb of Augustus. Altar and tomb represented one of the most striking examples of Mussolini's identification with the Roman past.[33]

The dedication occurred at a time when relations between Italy and England had reached their lowest point. The Italian invasion of Ethiopia precipitated a break with England, and Mussolini was moving ever closer to Hitler. Many felt that Eugénie, as a British subject, should have excused herself from the occasion. However, she saw herself merely as a representative of the foreign scholarly community in Rome. At a time when both Hitler and Mussolini were rattling their sabres, she laid great stress on Augustus as a man of peace. She praised the restored Ara Pacis as

> The outstanding monument that the emperor Augustus – that great pacifier who always preferred to celebrate a restored peace than the related victory – built as the perpetual reminder of a wise policy reawakened in our day under your auspices. The marvellous restoration of the Ara Pacis will be to us all a new challenge of that which can be accomplished by an elected official like yourself who works under the inspiration of that divine force that your Pliny defined as the 'Immense Majesty of the Roman Peace'.[34]

In justifying her presence at such a politically charged event Eugénie argued that in spite of the Anglo–Italian crisis, two centuries of close friendship should not be forgotten. Moreover she felt great gratitude to the regime that had restored the greatest monument of Roman art to something like its former glory.[35]

However, the changes taking place in Europe were deeper and more troubling than she was willing to acknowledge. By 1938 the Nazi regime was firmly established in power in Germany. Archaeologist friends like Ludwig Curtius and Karl Lehmann resigned their positions or fled to America. The Germany that she had known in her youth was fast disappearing. Sadly representative of that change were the steps the Nazis took to obliterate the record of the great debt they owed Henrietta Hertz for providing the library that formed the foundation of the great art-history library in the German Institute in Rome. Her name was erased from the title of the institute and her bust removed from its honoured place in the building.[36]

During the summer of 1938 Eugénie received a letter from Ludwig Pollak informing her of the death of their old friend Emanuel Loewy. Loewy, who had lost his Rome professorship during World War I because he was Austrian, had faced an even worse fate because he was Jewish. Pollak reflected: 'It was a great gift of God that he died just before the terrible events of March in Vienna happened. The dying of the old Austria had killed him surely. He was a convinced Austrian and as that he died. Honour to his memory. He was a great savant.'[37]

Pollak was not to be so lucky. He was killed at Auschwitz a few years later.

Germany and Italy were becoming closely linked through their 'pact of steel'. In 1938, on a visit to Rome, Hitler was shown around the archaeological sites by the rising young Italian archaeologist Ranuccio Bianchi-Bandinelli.[38] In the autumn of 1938, Mussolini applied Nazi-style racial laws to Italy and scholars like Alessandro della Seta lost their positions. Even foreign members of Italian honorary institutes had to prove their Aryanism. Many hoped that Neville Chamberlain's concessions at Munich had brought peace. This was especially true of the English community in Italy. In his memoirs, Harold Acton recalled how so many deluded themselves that Il Duce would not drag his country into conflict.[39] But the Germans invaded Poland in 1939 and Italy joined them in the hostilities against Britain and France in June 1940.

Eugénie was placed in a difficult situation. Friends and family urged her to leave Italy. Her sister, whose son was in the British diplomatic service, considered using his contacts to bring her through Portugal to England. In the summer of 1939, Eugénie was in Lausanne, Switzerland, and contemplated staying there. However, she was assured that conditions were safe in Rome that had not yet joined the war, so she returned.

Along with such expatriates as the Americans Albert Van Buren and Bernard Berenson, Eugénie elected to pass the war years in Italy.[40] She was now eighty years old, and for over thirty years Rome had been her home. She had always been ambivalent about living in England, and she had few remaining connections there. She trusted, rightly, in the friendship and gentle humanity of the Italians. Old friends like Ludwig Curtius could provide her with support within the German community, and she could count on the assistance of representatives of neutral countries like the Swedish scholars Axel Boëthius and Eric Sjöqvist.

Her major problems became financial as the hostilities cut off her funds from England. Since America did not enter the war until the end of 1941, Mary Lowndes continued to send money, although with each passing month the transactions became more difficult. Mary's letters also provided her with news of friends in England and America and a view of the world from outside censored, embattled Italy. Descriptions evoked memories of the past. News of the death of Rennell Rodd in 1941 led Mary to recall 'the attaché in Athens, so good looking, suave and dilettante'.[41] Accounts of the London Blitz recalled memories of destroyed monuments that had inspired them in their youth. A poem by D. S. MacColl in *The Times* evoked their days together in Kensington, when MacColl 'decorated your study in flame red and purple'.[42]

Touchingly, one of the mutual friends whom Mary mentioned was a young archaeologist from the American Academy, Erling Olsen, who had been a fellow at the Academy just before the war. His special interest was Roman sculpture, and he had begun a research project on the Arch of Septimius Severus.[43] Eugénie befriended him in the last months before the American students were forced to leave. Now he was back in the United States waiting to join the army. He came to know Mary Lowndes and visited her in Connecticut. In one of her last letters, she wrote to Eugénie about the appealing young American, who 'spoke with warmth of your kindness to him in Rome'. Sadly Olsen never returned to Roman archaeology. He was killed in action in France in July 1944.[44]

The last letter from Mary Lowndes to Eugénie Strong is dated 16 October 1941. Soon Italy and the United States were at war, and Eugénie was now totally cut off from outside news and financial support. Remaining at the apartment on the Via Balbo was becoming increasingly difficult. She managed to stay on there until the summer of 1941, but then was forced to move into the Hotel Regina on the Via Veneto, where kindly Italian officials provided her with free accommodation. Although over eighty years old and in increasingly poor health, Eugénie remained an active scholar. Ludwig Curtius described her hotel room piled high with books and research notes.[45]

The atmosphere of her last days in Rome were captured by an article in the London *Sunday Express* of 3 October 1943 entitled 'A Woman in Rome':

> While Rome was in tumult on the days just before the surrender to the Germans, an elderly Englishwoman sat writing in her room in an hotel in the city. Italians fought with Germans in the streets. She heard the thunder of guns in the distance. But because the woman knew that she had not long to live, she wrote on, praying for strength to complete the task begun five years ago.

This last project was an art-historical study of the development of the papal palaces in the Vatican. In spite of many difficulties she maintained the pace of her research. Contacts within the Italian government and the Holy See ensured that she could visit the Vatican regularly, and the Swedish School even placed a carriage at her disposal. The manuscript was nearly completed when she died and miraculously her writing survived the chaos of the war. She certainly would have wanted it published. However, her executors, the classicists Hugh Last and F. E. Adcock, felt that too much work was required and decided against it. Her sister deposited typescript copies in several British libraries.

Though incomplete, the manuscript represents an impressive accomplishment for an aged, infirm woman working in a war-torn city. She set out to trace the history of the papal residences at St Peter's from the first simple lodgings built next to the Constantinian basilica down to the elegant palaces of the Renaissance. The surviving manuscript took the history into the papacy of Gregory XIII, who died in 1585. It was a work of great ambition in the tradition of such scholars of Rome and the papacy as Ferdinand Gregorovius and Ludwig Pastor, who she admired so much. She blended history and art history in a lively manner. Impressively, she had not lost her ability to speak to general audiences. While she was clearly sympathetic to the Church, she was not a blind apologist.

The traumatic events she was experiencing in her final months occasionally intruded into her narrative. When she described the cutting of the aqueducts during the sixth-century BC Roman-Gothic Wars, she digressed to current water shortages in Rome: 'Those of us who during this greater war have known the threat of a similar calamity and have even experienced the total absence of water for a day or more owing to the rupture of the conduits that fed the Acqua Marcia will understand what the cutting of the aqueducts meant of horror and misery.'[46] The Norman sack of Rome in 1083 led her to reflect: 'They had come to save and stayed to destroy. Their actions may be compared to what would happen today were the allies of Italy summoned to rid Rome of an occupying enemy force, and they carried out their threat to bombard Rome until not one stone was left upon another.'[47]

War and infirmity increasingly limited Eugénie's activities. She walked in the neighbourhood, visited the convent where her books were stored, and attended mass at the church of San Camillo de Lellis a few blocks from her hotel. However, in spite of physical infirmities her mind remained sharp and her opinions forceful. In her last letter to her close friend Mother General Mary Amadeus, she asked that a copy of the *Life of Mother Connelly* be given to the Vatican Library, but added: 'I wonder how much he, or indeed others of his colleagues of the Curia seems to know about either Mother Connelly or Mary Ward. Since Cardinal Gasquet no one seems to have worried much about either – and since the days of dear Urban VIII no Pontiff seems to have given a thought to women, even as intellectual and educational forces.'[48]

It was appropriate that the Girton pioneer in male-dominated Cambridge should at the end of her long life be concerned about the role of women in another very patriarchal institution.

Friends who remained in Rome came to visit and talk about past times.[49] Both Albert Van Buren and Ludwig Curtius put in appearances. Members of the Pasolini family called. Among her younger Italians visitors were Mario Praz and Ranuccio Bianchi Bandinelli. She maintained contact with Ludwig Pollak and with Umberto Zanotti Bianco. The Swedes, as neutrals, were given relative freedom to move around the city. The Swedish scholar Axel Boëthius described his last visit to Eugénie and his final walk from her hotel across the Villa Borghese to the Swedish School:

> For me Rome will never be our Rome, the Rome of our most immemorial years without Mrs Strong and Via Balbo. I felt in November that she understood that – not as a sentimental phase but as a real thing and a sorrow and debt, that at the same time are a treasure to have. On the photograph she gave me ... she wrote 'Addio Via Balbo' and so we parted. It was late. The Villa Borghese was dark. All Rome was dark.[50]

In spite of these visitors Eugénie's life was lonely. As a British citizen she was suspect, and those academic institutions that still operated were reluctant to invite her to their meetings. For someone who had been such a prominent force in the Roman conference scene this was especially distressing. Pathetically, she wrote to the Accademia di San Lucca, complaining she had not received invitations to their events. She suggested that it all might have been a clerical mistake, but surely in her heart she knew that the omission was intentional.[51]

To visit her was a sad experience. Mario Praz remembered taking his young daughter to call. The aged, bent figure frightened the little girl, who saw in her not the Diana or Helen of Eugénie's youth, but the wicked witch from some fairy story. Praz, the subtle student of memory, reflected on the irony of the situation and the fleeting impressions that even bright and beautiful people leave:

> More than the pages, one records her words, her appearance that no Reynolds had fixed for ever on canvas. Who remembered her at sunset among Attic forms. Who remembered her as another Helen whose

face had launched a thousand ships. Images from Leighton, far from us as that *fin de siècle* world to which she belonged.[52]

By the summer of 1943, it was clear that Eugénie Strong was dying. Cancers ravaged her weakened body. On 10 September, the day the Germans occupied Rome, she was moved from her hotel to a local clinic. The timing was providential, not only because she probably never knew of the German occupation, but also because the Nazi seizure of the Hotel Regina would have forced her to move again. It was tragic that, as her friend Axel Boethius observed, Eugénie Strong, who 'had hoped and wished to promote in Rome's name her ideals of an universal culture ... should end her days in a bombed and occupied Rome'.[53]

The end came on 16 September 1943. Ludwig Pollak noted in one of the last entries in his diary that Eugénie 'had died in Rome aged eighty-six years as a third order Domitian'.[54] Mario Praz provided a more dramatic setting for her death: 'The German cannons thundered on Rome in those first days of September 1943, when Rome had fallen to the lowest point in its history, this setting of confusion and abasement formed a setting of indescribable tragic pathos for the death of the great exalter of Romanità.'[55]

Eugénie was laid out in her Dominican robes. A photograph taken at her death shows a handsome, aged woman. In a Rome under siege the funeral had to be simple. She had wanted it that way. Although she had been at the centre of social scenes for her entire life, she stipulated that no notice of her death was to be disseminated until after her burial, as 'she disliked "fuss and a lot of people"'.[56] The good sisters who had cared for her in her last days disobeyed her wishes, for they felt that her closest friends would want to attend her funeral. The service was held at the church of San Martino ai Monti, not far from the Via Balbo, its structure embodying that sense of continuity and tradition that Eugénie loved in Rome. One of the earliest Christian gathering places in the city, it had been rebuilt many times, and incorporated the remains of the Baths of Trajan in its foundations.[57]

The directors of the Swedish, Dutch and German Institutes were present, along with friends from the Roman nobility, Italian academic colleagues like Filippo Magi and Bartolomeo Nogara, her servants and many of the nuns who had cared for her in her last illness. She was laid to rest in the section reserved for foreigners in the Campo Verano cemetery near San Lorenzo fuori i Muri. On her tomb were inscribed, in now fading letters, the words from Paul to the Galatians: 'qui autem seminat in spiritu de spiritu metet vitam aeternam'.

Mussolini, whose career Eugénie had followed with such interest, had fallen from power in late July. Germans, British and Americans were locked in mortal combat in southern Italy. On 19 July, Allied bombs fell on the area near San Lorenzo, where Strong would soon be laid to rest. One month after her death the Germans rounded up the Jews of Rome for shipment to the extermination camps. Among those who perished was her friend of fifty years Ludwig Pollak.[58] The cultured, open, cosmopolitan world that Eugénie had loved seemed doomed.

Obituary writers noted her long and distinguished career, her many honours, and her importance as an advocate for the place of Roman art in the Western cultural tradition. As *The Times* put it, 'Of all her achievements the most memorable was her discovery or rather rediscovery of Roman art as no mere pallid reflection of Greece, but with a history and character of its own.'[59] Considering that the war in Italy was still bitter and bloody, the newspapers handled her sympathies for Mussolini and her decision to stay in Italy during the war with tact. The evocative article in the *Sunday Express* has already been quoted. The *Star* merely noted that 'because of her work, even the Fascist government respected her and when they plunged into war, they allowed her to continue to live in Rome without the slightest disturbance'.[60]

She was not forgotten in England. A mass was celebrated in her honour at Westminster Cathedral with the bishop officiating. Those who attended were a palimpsest of her life. The British School at Rome, Girton, the Hellenic Society, the Roman Society and the Society of Antiquaries were all officially represented. Probably the oldest friend was D. S. MacColl, who recalled not only Eugénie Strong the eminent scholar, but Eugénie Sellers the great Victorian beauty.[61]

After the war, two of her Italian archaeological friends, Bartolomeo

Nogara and Alberto Colini, arranged for a private memorial mass in the San Filippo Neri chapel at the Chiesa Nuova. This was a rare privilege, but the Oratorians felt it was an appropriate honour for Strong, who had been so devoted to the 'apostolo di Roma'.[62] The memorial mass was followed by a ceremony at the Verano cemetery. Old Roman friends ranging from Carlo Cecchelli to Albert Van Buren were present, but except for the diplomatic delegate to the Vatican, the British were absent.

Ironically, Eugénie made the British School the executor of her will and the chief beneficiary of her estate. Ultimately over £4,000 went to the school, one of its most substantial benefactions at that time.[63] Many of her books were donated to the library of the Pontifical Academy of Archaeology and to the Pontifical Institute of Christian Archaeology at Rome. In her safe deposit box were found her gold medals from both the City of Rome and British Academy, a decoration of the British Empire, a sixteenth-century book decorated with the arms of the kings of England, nine family miniatures and an early Renaissance crucifix.

Given the wartime conditions of 1943, it is not surprising that the publication of Eugénie's obituaries in scholarly journals was slow and sporadic. The complex politics of the period and the obvious desire of some to disassociate themselves from the events and attitudes held before and even during the war, produced a certain moralizing at the expense of the deceased. She may not have identified any more with Mussolini than most of her contemporaries, but she was dead and could not rewrite her own history. Representative of that attitude was the obituary of Charles Picard. He closed his memorial in *Revue archeologique* by remarking smugly: 'Mme E. Strong a été longtemps une des reines de la vie intellectualle de l'Urbs. Les erreurs de la politique mussolinienne lui causerent les premieres deceptions, qui transformerent a vie.' ('Mrs E. Strong had for a long time been one of the queens of the intellectual life of the city. The errors of Mussolini's politics produced the first deceptions that transformed her life.')[64] Others, such as Gisela Richter in the *American Journal of Archaeology*, stressed her important contributions to archaeology, especially to Roman studies.[65]

Afterword

Eugénie was a woman in many ways ahead of her times. In 1929 Virginia Woolf published her own call for a woman's literary identity in a slim volume entitled *A Room of One's Own*. Strong read the book and was moved by it, even though she commented negatively on some details. The work was based on lectures that Woolf had delivered at Cambridge, where Eugénie Sellers had pioneered as a female student. Woolf emphasized the importance of Emily Davies, the founder of Girton, in raising women's consciousness of themselves in opposition to society's consciousness of women. The three women writers whose accomplishments Woolf had highlighted, Jane Harrison, Vernon Lee and Gertrude Bell, had all at one time been friends of Eugénie.

Eugénie had been blessed with an independent income, although not as much as the £500 a year Woolf thought necessary. She had created, literally and figuratively, a series of rooms of her own, the last being the famed apartment on the Via Balbo. She had lived almost all of her adult life independently, without husband or family. She had pushed the new possibilities open to women to the limit, as a first-generation student at Girton, as a student at the British School at Athens, as librarian at Chatsworth, and as assistant director of the British School at Rome. Her scholarship in Roman art and that of the baroque represented an independence of spirit not to be found among many of her male contemporaries.

Eugénie would have wanted to be remembered as a pioneer in classical archaeology. The importance of her contributions to Greek archaeology is demonstrated by the fact that both her translation of Schuchhardt's account of Schliemann's excavations and her study of Pliny have been reprinted in recent years. However, her role in stressing the importance of Roman art to the Anglophone scholarly world represents her most important legacy. When Eugénie Strong published her *Roman Sculpture* in 1907, scholars in the English-speaking world knew or cared very little about Roman art. That book and her other works on Roman art began the slow process of changing attitudes and outlooks. The worship of Greek art in the tradition of Winckelmann remained strong, and only a few disciples like Jocelyn Toynbee immediately continued her legacy.

A greater appreciation for the creative aspects of Roman art only came after World War II. Much of the stimulus for this rethinking of old paradigms came from German refugee scholars in America such as Otto Brendel, Karl Lehmann and George Hanfmann.[1] This interest in Roman art has increased dramatically in the last fifteen years. New scholarly approaches to the subject vary, and many would not have won Eugénie's total approval. However, she always encouraged the young, appreciated innovation, and tolerated dissent.

In this moment of new interest in both women's history and Roman artistic studies, it is important that Eugénie's story be told. Eugénie Sellers Strong manifested many of the limitations of her time and place in history. However, she used her life well and accomplished much. With all of her defects she remains an inspiration not only for women, but for all who respect the life of the mind and the life of the spirit.

Bibliography

Note: Eugénie Sellers Strong published under varied surnames and initials. In both the endnotes and bibliography items have been listed under the name used in the publication.

Archival and Manuscript Sources

Beinecke Archives   The Maurice Baring Papers, Beinecke Library, Yale University, New Haven, Ct, USA

BSR Archives   The Eugénie Strong Papers, in the archives of the British School at Rome

Chatsworth Archives   The Devonshire Collections, in the archives at Chatsworth House, Bakewell, Derbyshire, United Kingdom

Colby College Archives   Vernon Lee Papers, in the archives of Colby College, Waterville, Maine, USA

Girton College Archives   Eugénie Sellers Strong Papers, in the archives of Girton College, Cambridge, United Kingdom

Houghton Library Archives William Rothenstein Papers, at Houghton Library, Harvard University, Cambridge, Mass., USA

I Tatti Archives   The Bernard Berenson and Mary Costelloe Papers, in the I Tatti Berenson archives, Villa I Tatti; The Harvard University Center for Italian Renaissance Studies, Florence, Italy

Published Sources

Ackerman, R. (1972), 'Jane Ellen Harrison: The Early Work', *Greek, Roman and Byzantine Studies* 13 pp. 209–30.

——— (1987), *J. G. Frazer, His Life and Work* (Cambridge).

——— (1991), *The Myth and Ritual School: J. G. Frazer and the Cambridge Ritualists* (New York).

'A.C.T.' (1903), '*Reproductions of Drawings by Old Masters in the Collection of the Duke of Devonshire at Chatsworth* with an Introduction by S. Arthur Strong', *Burlington Magazine* 1 pp. 391–5.

Acton, H. (1970), *Memoirs of an Aesthete* (New York).

Adams, P. (1996), *Somerville for Women* (Oxford).

Alföldy, G. (1993), 'The Two Principes: Augustus and Sir Ronald Syme', *Athenaeum* pp. 101–22.

Allingham, H. & D. Radford (eds) (1907), *William Allingham: A Diary* (London).

Amelung, W. and H. Holzinger (notes by the English editor E. Strong) (1906), *The Museums and Ruins of Rome* (London).

Andren, A. (1969–70), 'Commemorazione di Axel Boëthius', *Rendiconti della Pontificia Accademia Romana d'Archeologia* 42 pp. 3–11.

Anon. (1893), 'Lost Masterpieces of Greek Sculpture: *Meisterwerke der griechischen Plastik* von Adolf Furtwängler' (Leipzig/Berlin), *Quarterly Review* 180 pp. 61–87.

Anson, H. (1949), *Thomas Strong* (London).

Anstruther, I. (1983), *Oscar Browning: A Biography* (London).

Anstruther-Thomson, C. (1969), *Art and Man: Essays and Fragments* (Freeport, New York).

Arias, P. (1976), *Quattro archeologi del nostro secolo* (Pisa).

Arlen, S. (1990), *The Cambridge Ritualists* (London).

Arnal, O. L. (1985), *Ambivalent Alliance: The Catholic Church and the Action Française* (Pittsburgh).

Arnold, D. (ed.) (1994), *Belov'd by Ev'ry Mus* (London).

Ash, R. (1997), *Lord Leighton* (London).

Ashby, T. (1927), *The Roman Campagna in Classical Times* (London).

—— (1935), *The Aqueducts of Ancient Rome* (Oxford).

Ashmole, B., 'Sir John Beazley (1885–1970)', in D. Kurtz (ed) (1985), *Beazley and Oxford* (Oxford), pp. 57–71.

—— (1994), *Bernard Ashmole: An Autobiography* (edited by D. Kurtz) (Malibu, CA).

Auchmuty, J. J. (1945), *Lecky* (Dublin).

Bagnani, G. (1919), 'The Subterranean Basilica at Porta Maggiore', *Journal of Roman Studies* 9 pp. 78–85.

—— (1929), *The Roman Campagna and its Treasures* (London).

—— (1929), *Rome and the Papacy* (London).

Bagot, R. (1912), *My Italian Year* (Leipzig).

Bailey, C. (1945), 'John William Mackail, O.M. 1859–1945', in *Proceedings of the British Academy* 31 pp. 244–55.

Balcarres, MP, Lord (1905), 'A Memoir', in S. A. Strong, *Critical Studies and Fragments* (London).

Barbanera, M. (1993), *Museo dell'arte classica, Gipsoteca I* (Rome).

—— (1998), *L'archeologia degli italiani* (Rome).

—— (2003), *Ranuccio Bianchi Bandinelli* (Milan).

Barbieri, C. et al. (1995), *Santa Maria in Vallicella* (Rome).

Baring, M. (1922), *The Puppet Show of Memory* (Boston).

—— (1951), *Have You Anything to Declare?* (London).

Barker, G. et al. (1986), *Thomas Ashby: un archeologo fotografa la campagna romana tra '800 e '900* (Rome).

Barry, W. (1905), *Ernest Renan* (New York).

Bather, A. G. (1897), 'Pliny's Chapters on Art', *The Classical Review* 11 pp. 458–60.

Beagon, M. (1992), *Roman Nature: The Thought of Pliny the Elder* (Oxford).

Bibliography

Beard, M. (1993), 'Casts and Cast-Offs: The Origins of the Museum of Classical Archaeology', *Proceedings of the Cambridge Philological Society* 39 pp. 1–29.
—— (2000), *The Invention of Jane Harrison* (Cambridge, Mass., 2000).
Beck, R. (1984), 'Mithraism since Franz Cumont', *Aufstieg und Niedergang der römische Welt* II.17.4 pp. 2002–115.
Beckwith, J. (1970), *Early Christian and Byzantine Art* (Harmondsworth).
Bell, Lady (1927), *The Letters of Gertrude Bell* (New York).
Bell, Q. (1995), *Elders and Betters* (London).
Bell, V. (1998), *Sketches in Pen and Ink* (London).
Belli, C. (1974), 'Francois Lenormont, Archeologo Adventuroso' *Atti del tredicesimo convegno di studi sulla Magna Graecia* (Naples) pp. 7–41
Benson, A. C. (1907), *Walter Pater* (London).
Benson, E. F. (1930), *As We Were: A Victorian Peep Show* (London).
Berenson, B. (1954), *The Arch of Constantine or the Decline of Form* (London).
—— (1963), *Sunset and Twilight* (New York).
Berenson, B., and C. Marghieri (1989), *A Matter of Passion: Letters of B.B. and Clotilde Marghieri* (edited by Dario Biocca) (Berkeley).
Berg, M. (1996), *A Woman in History: Eileen Power 1889–1940* (Cambridge).
Bessborough, Earl of (1955), *Georgiana, Duchess of Devonshire* (London).
Bianchi-Bandinelli, R. (1981), *Archeologia e cultura* (Rome).
—— (1998), *Roma: la fine dell'arte antica* (Milan).
—— (1996), *Diario di un borghese* (Rome).
Bieber, M. (1955), 'Necrology: Ludwig Curtius', *American Journal of Archaeology* 59 pp. 64–5.
Binkley, R. (1935), *Realism and Nationalism, 1852–1871* (New York).
Birley, E. (1966), 'Sir Ian Archibald Richmond 1902–1965', *Proceedings of the British Academy* 52 pp. 293–302.
Blanshard, B. (1984), *Four Reasonable Men* (Middletown, Ct).
Blegen, C. (1958), 'Alan John Bayard Wace (1879–1957)', in *Yearbook of the American Philosophical Society* pp. 162–71.
Blennerhassett, R. (1905), 'Arthur Strong' *Quarterly Review* pp. 632–40.
Boardman, J. (1985), '100 Years of Classical Archaeology in Oxford', in D. Kurtz (ed.), *Beazley and Oxford* (Oxford), pp. 43–55.
Boethius, A. (1943), 'Eugénie Strong: A Great English Archaeologist', translated from *Svenske Dagbladet* (in Girton College Archives).
Bolitho, H. (1933), *Alfred Mond, First Lord Melchett* (New York).
Bolton, G. (1970), *Roman Century* (New York).
Bonnet, C. (1997), *La correspondence scientifique de Franz Cumont* (Brussels-Rome).
Borland, M. (1995), *D. S. MacColl: Painter, Poet, and Critic* (Harpendon).
Borowitz, H. and A. Borowitz (1991), *Pawnshop and Palaces* (Washington, DC).
Bowersock, G. W. (1994), 'Ronald Syme: 1903–1989', *Proceedings of the British Academy* 84 pp. 539–63.
Bowen, J. (1989), 'Education, ideology and the ruling class: Hellenism and the public schools in the nineteenth century', in G. W. Clarke (ed.), *Rediscovering Hellenism* (Cambridge), pp. 161–86.

Bradbrook, M.C. (1984), *'That Infidel Place': A Short History of Girton College, 1869–1969* (Cambridge).
Breay, C. (1999), 'Women and the Classical Tripos 1869–1914', in C. Stray (ed.), *Classics in 19th and 20th Century Cambridge* (Cambridge), pp. 49–70.
Brendel, O. (1979), *Prolegomena to the Study of Roman Art* (New Haven).
Briggs, W. W. & W. M. Calder (ed.) (1990), *Classical Scholarship: A Biographical Encyclopedia* (New York).
Brilliant, R. (2000), 'Winkelman and Warburg', in A. Payne, A. Kuttner and R. Smick, *Antiquity and its Interpreters* (Cambridge).
Brittain, V. (1960), *The Women at Oxford* (London).
Browning, O. (1910), *Memories of Sixty Years at Eton and Cambridge and Elsewhere* (New York).
—— (1923), *Memories of Later Years* (London).
Lord Bryce (1921–3), 'Lord Reay, 1839–1921', in *Proceedings of the British Academy* 10 pp. 533–9.
Buchan, J. (1937), *Augustus* (London).
Burton, A. (1999), *Vision and Accident: The Story of the Victoria and Albert Museum* (London).
Calder, W. (1998), 'Jane Harrison's Failed Candidacies for the Yates Professorship (1888–1896)', in *Men in their Books* (Zürich), pp. 145–66.
Calloway, S. (1998), *Aubrey Beardsley* (London).
Campbell, A. (1988), 'The British School at Rome, A Valuable Asset in Cultural Diplomacy', in *Apollo* pp. 189–91.
Campbell. F. P. (1914), *Memorials in Verse and Prose of Lewis Campbell* (London).
Cannadine, D. (1990), *The Decline and Fall of the British Aristocracy* (New Haven).
—— (1994), *Aspects of Aristocracy* (New Haven).
Cannistraro, P. and B. Sullivan (1993), *Il Duce's Other Woman* (New York).
Caracciolo, A. (1993), *Roma capitale* (Rome).
Carcopino, J. (1926), *Etudes romaines: la basilique pythagoricienne de la Porte Majeure* (Paris).
—— (1944), *Souvenirs de Sept Ans, 1937–1944* (Paris).
—— (1968), *Souvenirs romains* (Paris).
Cederna, A. (1981), *Mussolini urbanista, lo sventramento di Roma negli anni del consenso* (Bari).
Chadbourne, R. (1957), *Ernest Renan as an Essayist* (Ithaca, NY).
Chanler, W. (1934), *Roman Spring* (Boston).
Chapman, G. (1972), *The Dreyfus Trials* (New York).
Church, J. E. Jr. (1908), 'Adolf Fürtwangler, Artist, Archaeologist, Professor', in *University of Nevada Studies* 1, 2 pp. 61–6.
Ciucci, G. (1989), *Gli architetti e il fascismo* (Turin).
Clark, K. (1974), *Another Part of the Wood* (London).
Clarke, G.W. (1989), *Rediscovering Hellenism* (Cambridge)
Clarke, J. (1991), *The Houses of Roman Italy 100 BC–AD 250* (Berkeley).
Coarelli, F. (1995), *Roma* (Rome-Bari).
Colvin, S. (1921), *Memories and Notes of Persons & Places 1852–1912* (New York).
Connor, P. (1989), 'Cast-collecting in the nineteenth century: scholarship, aesthetics,

connoiseurship', in G. W. Clarke (ed.), *Rediscovering Hellenism* (Cambridge), pp. 187–235.

Conway, Lord (1932), 'Salomon Reinach', *Burlington Magazine* 61 p. 288.

Conway, R. S. (1926), 'Sir William Ridgeway 1853–1926', *Proceedings of the British Academy* 12 pp. 327–36.

Cook, A. B. (1931), *The Rise and Progress of Classical Archaeology* (Cambridge).

Courtney, J. (1931), *An Oxford Portrait Gallery* (London).

Cox-McCormack, N. (1929), 'Giacomo Boni, Humanist-Archaeologist of the Roman Forum and the Palatine', *Art & Archaeology* 28 pp. 35–44.

Craster, H. H. E. (1920), 'Francis Haverfield', *English Historical Review* pp. 63–70.

Crawford, A. (2001), "The Artist Scholars (1913–1939) in A. Wallace Hadrill, *The British School at Rome* (Rome), pp. 145–158.

Crowe. J. A. (1895), *Reminiscences of Thirty-Five Years of My Life* (London).

Cumont, F. (1918), 'La basilica souterraine de la Porta Maggiore' *Revue archeologique* pp. 52–75.

———— (1922), *After Life in Roman Paganism* (New Haven).

Cunningham, G. (1927), *London* (London).

Curtius, E. R. (1963), *European Literature and the Latin Middle Ages* (New York).

Curtius, L. (1929), 'Geist der römischen Kunst', *Die Antike* 5 pp. 187ff.

———— (1930), 'Winckelmann under unser Jahrhundert', *Die Antike* 6 pp. 94–126.

———— (1943–6), 'Eugenia Strong, Commemorazione', *Rendiconti della Pontificia Accademia Romana d'Archeologia* 21 pp. 29–32.

———— (1950), *Deutsche und antike Welt* (Stuttgart).

———— (1957), 'Adolf Furtwängler', *Torso* (Stuttgart) pp. 213–24.

Dakers, C. (1999), *The Holland Park Circle* (New Haven).

Daniel, A. M. (1908), '*Roman Sculpture from Augustus to Constantine* by Mrs Arthur Strong', *The Classical Review* 22 pp. 85–7.

Daniel, G. (1992), *Writing for Antiquity* (London).

Darroch, S. J. (1976), *Ottoline* (New York).

Davids, T. W. Rhys (1903–04), 'Oriental Studies in England and Abroad', *Proceedings of the British Academy* 1 pp. 183–97.

DeBruyne, L. (1960–1), 'Commemorazione del socio Carlo Cecchelli (1893–1960)', *Rendiconti della pontificia academia romana di archeologia* 33 pp. 39–51.

deGrummond, N. (1996), *Encyclopedia of the History of Classical Archaeology* (Westport, CT).

Delamont, S. and L. Duffin, eds. (1978), *The Nineteenth Century Woman: Her Cultural and Physical World* (London).

DeLaura, D. (1969), *Hebrew and Hellene in Victorian England* (Austin, Texas).

della Seta, A. (1914), *Religion and Plastic Art*, translated by Marion Harrison with preface by E. Strong (London).

DeLuca, G. (1949), 'Amica di Roma', *Osservatore Romana* 13 June 1949.

De Ruyt, F. (1947), 'Franz Cumont (1868–1947)', *L'Antiquité Classique* 16 pp. 5–11.

Devonshire, Duchess of (1987), *Chatsworth, The Home of the Duke and Duchess of Devonshire* (Derby).

Diggins, J. P. (1975), *Mussolini and Fascism: The View from America* (Princeton).

Dimier, L. (1905), 'Un exemple d'esprit classique en Angleterre, Arthur Strong', *L'Action Française* 15 October 1905 pp. 103–9.

Dodds, E. R. and H. Chadwick (1963), 'Obituary: Arthur Darby Nock', *Journal of Roman Studies* 53 pp. 168–9.

Dörpfeld, W. (1896), *Das griechische Theater* (Berlin).

Dowling, L. (1994), *Hellenism and Homosexuality in Victorian Oxford* (Ithaca, NY).

Drake, R. (1980), *Byzantium for Rome* (Chapel Hill, NC).

Drinkwater, J. (1931), 'Edmund Gosse', *Quarterly Review* 257 pp. 116–32.

Drower, M. (1985), *Flinders Petrie* (London).

Dyson, S. L. (1998), *Ancient Marbles to American Shores* (Philadelphia).

Easterling, P. (1999), 'The Early Years of the Cambridge Greek Play: 1882–1912' in C. Stray (ed.), *Classics in 19th and 20th Century Cambridge* (Cambridge), pp. 27–47.

Editorial (unsigned) (1971), 'Munich: City of the Arts', *Apollo* Nov. 1971 pp. 332–345.

Edwards, A (1883), *A Girton Girl* (London).

Einstein, L. (1968), *A Diplomat Looks Back* (New Haven).

Eisner, R. (1991), *Travellers to an Antique Land* (Ann Arbor).

Ellmann, R. (1988), *Oscar Wilde* (Harmondsworth).

Elsner, J. (2000), 'The Birth of Late Antiquity: Riegl and Strzygowski in 1901'. *Art History* 25 pp. 358–379.

Emanuel, A. (ed.) (1989), *A Bright Remembrance: The Diaries of Julia Cartwright 1851–1924* (London).

Esher, Reginald, Viscount (1923), *Ionicus* (London).

—— (1938), *The Captains and the Kings Depart* (London).

Evans, A. R. (1970), *On Four Modern Humanists: Hofmanstahl, Gundolf, Curtius, Kantorowicz* (Princeton).

Evans, J. (1954), *John Ruskin* (New York).

Faber, G. (1957), *Jowett: A Portrait with Background* (Cambridge, Mass.).

Faber, R. (1995), 'Humanistische und fascistische Welt: Über Ludwig Curtius', *Hephaistos* 13 pp. 137–167.

Farnell, L. R. (1934), *An Oxonian Looks Back* (London).

Ferro, M. (1973), *The Great War 1914–1918* (London).

Festugiére, A. J. (1948), 'Franz Cumont 1868–1947', *Gnomon* 21 pp. 272–4.

Fifoot, C. (1971), *Pollock and Maitland* (Glasgow).

Fitton, L. (1991), *Heinrich Schliemann and the British Museum Paper 83: Department of Greek and Roman Antiquities* (London).

Fitzgerald, P. (1997), *Edward Burne-Jones* (Stroud, Gloucestershire).

Fitzroy, Sir Almeric (1923), *Memoirs* (New York).

Flanders, J. (2002), *A Circle of Sisters* (Harmondsworth).

Flasch, A. (1902), *Heinrich von Brunn: Gedächtnissrede* (Munich).

Fletcher, S. (1980), *Feminists and Bureaucrats: A Study of the Development of Girl's Education in the Nineteenth Century* (Cambridge).

Foreman, A. (1998), *Georgiana: Duchess of Devonshire* (London).

Fowler, R. (1982–3), 'On Not Knowing Greek: The Classics and the Woman of Letters', *Classical Journal* 78 pp. 337–49.

Fraser, A. (1974), 'Maurice Baring', *The Times Saturday Review*, 27 April 1974 p. 7.

Bibliography

Frend, W. (1996), *The Archaeology of Early Christianity: A History* (London).

Fry, R. (1913), 'The Case of the Late Sir Lawrence Alma Tadema, OM', *The Nation* 18 January 1913 pp. 666–7.

Furtwängler, A. (1895), *Masterpieces of Greek Sculpture*, translated by Eugénie Sellers (London).

—— (1896), *Intermezzi* (Leipzig/Berlin).

—— (1901), 'Ancient Sculptures at Chatsworth House', *Journal of Hellenic Studies* 21 pp. 209–28.

—— (1904), 'On the Ancient Sculptures Exhibited at the Burlington Fine Arts Club – A Reply', *Classical Review* 18 pp. 419–20.

—— (1912), *Kleine Schriften* (herausg. von J. Sieveking & L. Curtius) (Munich).

—— (1965), *Briefe* (herausg von W. Riezler) (Stuttgart).

Furtwängler, A. & H. L. Urlichs (1914), *Greek and Roman Sculpture* (London).

Gabrieli, V. (ed.) (1966), *Friendship's Garland: Essays Presented to Mario Praz on his Seventieth Birthday* (Rome).

Gardner, B. (1987), *The Lesbian Imagination, Victorian Style: A Psychological and Critical Study of Vernon Lee*

Gardner, E. A. (1894–5), 'Sir Charles Newton, KCB', *Annual of the British School at Athens* 1 pp. 67–77.

Gardner, E. A. et al. (1892), *Excavations at Megalopolis 1890–1891* (London).

Gardner, P. (1889), *Classical Archaeology at Oxford* (Oxford).

—— (1896), 'Sir Charles Newton', *Biographische. Jahrbuch* 19 pp. 132–42.

—— (1901), 'Review of F. Wickhoff *Roman Art*' *Classical Review* 15.

—— (1907), 'Adolf Furtwängler', *The Classical Review* 21 pp. 251–3.

—— (1933), *Autobiographica* (Oxford).

Gathorne-Hardy, R. (ed.) (1963), *Memoirs of Lady Ottoline Morrrell* (New York).

Gaunt, (1952), *Victorian Olympus* (London).

Gellner, E. (1994), 'James Frazer and Cambridge Anthropology', in R. Mason, *Cambridge Minds* (Cambridge), pp. 204–17.

Gentile, E. (1994), *Il culto del littorio* (Bari).

Giglioli, G. Q. (1928), 'Origine e sviluppo del museo dell'impero di Roma', *Capitolium* 4 pp. 303–12.

—— (1928–9), 'Rodolfo Lanciani', *Bullettino della Commissione Archeologica Comunale di Roma* 56–7 pp. 367–84.

—— (1935), 'Corrado Ricci e l'archeologia romana', *In Memoriam di Corrado Ricci* (Rome) pp. 247–50.

—— (1938), 'La mostra augustea della romanitá', *Bullettino Comunale* 66 pp. 55–9.

Girouard, M. (1978), *Life in the English Country House* (New Haven).

Girton College Register 1869–1946 (1948) (Cambridge).

Goldsmith, J. (ed.) (1984), *The Gymnasium of the Mind, The Journals of Roger Hinks 1933–1963* (Salisbury, Wiltshire).

Goodman, S. (1985), *Gertrude Bell* (Leamington Spa).

Griffin, N. ed. (1992), *The Selected Letters of Bertrand Russell*, Vol. 1 (Boston).

Guarducci, M. (1980), 'La cosiddetta fibula prenestina: antiquari, eruditi e falsari nella Roma dell'ottocento', *Memorie della Accademia Nazionale dei Lincei.* VIII.24.4 pp. 415–574.

Guedalla, P. (1926), *Palmerston, 1784–1865* (London).

Gunn, P. (1964), *Vernon Lee* (London).

Hadley, R. O. (1987), *The Letters of Bernard Berenson and Isabella Stewart Gardner 1887–1924* (Boston).

Hake, T. and A. Compton-Rickett (1916), *The Life and Letters of Theodore Watts-Dunton* (London).

Hamilton, A. (1971), *The Appeal of Fascism: A Study of Intellectuals and Fascism 1919–1945* (New York).

Hapgood, H. (1939), *A Victorian in the Modern World* (New York).

Hapgood, N. (1930), *The Changing Years: Reminiscences of Norman Hapgood* (New York).

Harrison, J. (1882), *Myths of the Odyssey in Art and Literature* (London).

—— (1892), *Introductory Studies in Greek Art* (2nd ed.) (London).

—— (1895), 'Some Points in Dr Furtwaengler's Theories on the Parthenon and its Marbles', *CR* 9 pp. 85–92.

—— (1915), *Alpha and Omega* (London).

—— (1918), 'Greek Religion and Mythology', *The Year's Work in Classical Studies* 12 pp. 88–92.

—— (1925), *Reminiscences of a Student's Life* (London).

Harrison, J. and M. Verrall (1890), *Mythology and Monuments of Ancient Athens* (London).

Haskell, F. (2000), *The Ephemeral Museum* (New Haven).

Haverfield, F. (1907), 'Henry Francis Pelham', *Proceedings of the British Academy* 8 pp. 365–70.

—— (1911), 'An Inaugural Address Delivered before the First Annual General Meeting of the Society, 11th May, 1911', *Journal of Roman Studies* 1 pp. xi–xx.

Hawkes, J. (1982), *Adventurer in Archaeology* (New York).

Haynes, R. (1949), 'Review of G. S. Thompson's *Mrs Arthur Strong*', *Time and Tide* 23 April 1949.

Hazeltine, H. D. (1949), 'Sir Frederick Pollock, Bart.', *Proceedings of the British Academy* 35 pp. 233–56.

Hill, G. (1937), 'Percy Gardner 1846–1937', *Proceedings of the British Academy* 23 pp. 459–69.

Hilton, T. (1985), *John Ruskin: The Early Years 1819–1859* (New Haven).

Hingley, R. (2000), *Roman Officers and English Gentlemen* (London).

Hirsch, P. (1998), *Barbara Leigh Smith Bodichon* (London).

Hodges, R. (2000), *Visions of Rome: Thomas Ashby, Archaeologist* (London).

Hodgkin, R. H. (1936), 'Robert Carr Bosanquet', *Archeologia Aeliana* pp. 1–8.

Holland, S. (1911), *The Life of Spencer Compton, Eighth Duke of Devonshire* (London).

Horgan, P. (1970), *Maurice Baring Restored* (London).

Howe, M. (1942), *Holmes-Pollock Letters: The Correspondence of Mr Justicce Holmes and Sir Frederick Pollock 1874–1932* (Cambridge, Mass.)

Hutchinson, H. G. (1920), *Portraits of the Eighties* (New York).

Hutton, C. A. (1893), 'Inscriptions on Pottery from Naukratis', *Classical Review* 7 pp. 82–3.

—— (1896–7), 'On Three Bronze Statuettes', *Annual of the British School at Athens* 3 pp. 149ff.

—— (1897), 'Votive Reliefs in the Acropolis Museum', *Journal of Hellenic Studies* 17 pp. 306–18.

Isager, J. (1991), *Pliny on Art and Society* (New York).

Isnenghi, M. (1979), *Intellectuali militati e intellectuali funzionari. Appunti sulla cultura fascistica* (Turin).

Iversen, M. (1993), *Alois Riegl: Art History and Theory* (Cambridge, Mass.).

Jackson, H. (1950), *The Eighteen Nineties* (Harmondsworth).

Jackson, P. (1994), *The Last of the Whigs* (Rutherford, NJ).

Jackson-Stops, G. (ed.) (1985), *The Treasure Houses of Britain* (Washington, DC/New Haven).

Jann, R. (1983), 'From amateur to professional: the case of the Oxbridge historians', *Journal of British Studies* 22 pp. 122–47.

Jebb, R. C. (1878), 'An English School of Archaeology at Athens and Rome', *Cambridge Review* 33 pp. 776–791

—— (1883), 'A Plea for a British Institute at Athens', *Fortnightly Review* 33 pp. 705–14.

—— (1895), 'Sir C. T. Newton', *CR* 9 pp. 81–5.

Jenkins, I. (1983), 'Frederic, Lord Leighton, and Greek Vases', *Burlington Magazine* 125 Oct. 1983 pp. 597–605.

—— (1992), *Archaeologists and Aesthetes: In the Sculpture Gallery of the British Museum 1800–1939* (London).

Jenkyns, R. (1980), *The Victorians and Ancient Greece* (Oxford).

—— (1991), *Dignity and Decadence: Victorian Art and the Classical Inheritance* (London).

Jex Blake, K. & E. Sellers (1967), *Pliny the Elder's Chapters on the History of Art* (with preface by R.V. Schoder) (Chicago).

Jolliffe, N. C. (1943), 'Obituary: Eugénie Strong', *The Cambridge Review*, 20 November 1943 pp. 92–3.

Jones, S. (1996), 'Leighton the Academic', in S. Jones et al. (eds), *Frederic, Lord Leighton* (New York), pp. 55–68.

Journal of the Royal Asiatic Society (1904), 'Obituary of S.A. Strong' pp. 387–93

Kalavrezou-Maxeiner, I. (1984), 'Franz Wickhoff: Kunstgeschichte als Wissenschaft', in S. Krenn, M. Pippel (eds.), *Wien und die Entwcxklung der kunsthistorische Methode* (Wien), pp.17–22

Kaschnitz-Weinberg, G. von (1956–7), 'Commemorazione del socio Ludwig Curtius', *Rendiconti della Pontificia Accademia Romana di Archeologia* 29 pp. 155–64.

Kenyon, F. G. (1930), 'Sir Israel Gollancz', *Proceedings of the British Academy* 16 pp. 424–38.

—— (1941), 'Arthur Hamilton Smith 1860–1941', *Proceedings of the British Academy* 27 pp. 393–404.

Kestner, J. (1989), *Mythology and Misogyny: The Social Discourse of Nineteenth Century British Classical Subject Painting* (Madison, Wisc.).

Kleiner, D. (1992), *Roman Sculpture* (New Haven).

Kochnitzky, L. (1983), *Carmées d'autrefois* (Brussels).

Kostof, S. (1973), *The Third Rome, 1870–1950: Traffic & Glory* (Berkeley).

Krenn, S & M. Pippel (eds.), *Wien und die Entwicklung der kunsthistorische Methode* (Wien).

'K.T.B.' (1947), 'In Memoriam: Mary Elizabeth Lowndes', *Girton Review*, Michaelmas Term 1947 pp. 24–6.

Kuhn, W. M. (2002), *Henry & Mary Ponsonby* (London).

'L. D.' (1904), 'S. A. Strong', *Athenaeum* 3978, 23 January 1904.

Lago, M. (1996), *Christina Herringham and the Edwardian Art Scene* (New Haven).

Lago, M. and K. Beckson (1975), *Max and Will* (Cambridge, Mass.).

Lameere, W. (1947–8), 'Sur le Tombe de Franz Cumont', *Alumni* 18.3 pp. 99–158.

Lanciani, R. (1894), *Ancient Rome in the Light of Recent Discoveries* (Boston).

——— (1897), *The Ruins and Excavations of Ancient Rome* (Boston).

——— (1988), *Notes from Rome* (Rome).

Lang, A. (1887), 'M. Renan's Later Works', *Athenaeum* 41 pp. 50–60.

Las Vergnas, R. (1938), *Chesteron, Belloc, Baring* (trans. C. C. Martindale) (London).

Leach, E. W. (1988), *The Rhetoric of Space* (Princeton).

Leaf, W. (1892), 'Review of *Schliemann's Ausgrabungen im Lichte der heutigen Wissenschaft dargestellt* and *Schliemann's Excavations: An Archaeological and Historical Study*', *Classical Review* 6 p. 132.

Lee, V. (1906), *Leaves from a Diary* (London).

Leedham-Green, E. (1996), *A Concise History of the University of Cambridge* (Cambridge).

Lehman, H. (1989), 'Wolfgang Helbig (1839–1915)', *Mitteilungen des Deutschen Archaologischen Instituts, Römische Abteilung* 96 pp. 7–86.

Lehmann, K. (1945), 'Erling C. Olsen', *College Art Journal* 4 p. 107.

Lemerle, P. (1942–3), 'Joseph Strzygowski (1862–1941)', *Revue Archéologique* pp. 73–8.

Lenormont, F. (1881–4), *La Grand-Grece: paysages et histoire* (Paris).

Letley, E. (1991), *Maurice Baring: A Citizen of Europe* (London).

Lewis, D. (1973), *Prisoners of Honor* (New York).

Lindsay, W. M. (1907), 'Obituary: Professor Traube died June, 1907', *The Classical Review* 21 pp. 188–9.

Ling, R. (1999), *Stuccowork and Painting in Roman Italy* (Brookfield, VT).

Lion, A. (1927), 'Les études d'art romain et Madame Eugénie Strong', *Le Correspondant* 10 August 1927 pp. 413–24.

Lister, R. (1926), *Reminiscences, Social and Political* (London).

Liversidge, M. and C. Edwards (1996), *Imagining Rome: British Artists and Rome in the Nineteenth Century* (London).

Lovat, L. (1948), *Maurice Baring: A Postscript* (New York).

Lowndes, M. E. (1898), *Michel de Montaigne: A Biographical Study* (Cambridge).

——— (1905), 'A Distinguished Librarian', *Longman's Magazine* 46 (June 1905) pp. 117–30.

——— (1909), *The Nuns of Port Royal* (Oxford).

Lucas, E. (1928), *The Colvins and their Friends* (London).

——— (1938), *Two Englishwomen in Rome 1871–1901* (London).

Lugli, G. (1931), 'Thomas Ashby', *Bulletino Comunale* 59 pp. 287–95.

—— (1943–6), 'Rodolfo Lanciani', *Rendiconti della Pontificia Accademia Romana di Archeologia* 21 pp. 33–7.

Lullies, R. (1988), 'Adolf Furtwängler 1853–1907' in Lullies and Schirmer *Archäologenbildnisse,* pp. 110–11.

—— (1988a), 'Heinrich Brunn 1822–1894' in Lullies and Schirmer *Archäologenbildnisse,* pp. 47–8.

—— (1988b), 'Ludwig Curtius 1874–1954' in Lullies and Schirmer *Archäologenbildnisse,* pp. 186–7.

Lullies, R. and W. Schiering (eds) (1988), *Archaologenbildnisse* (Mainz).

Lumsden, L. (1933), *Yellow Leaves: Memories of a Long Life* (Edinburgh).

Lutyens, M. (1991), *Edwin Lutyens* (London).

MacColl, D. S. (1931), *Confessions of a Keeper and Other Papers* (London).

MacDonald, G. (1919–20), 'F. J. Haverfield 1860–1919', *Proceedings of the British Academy* 9, pp. 475–91.

MacDonald, W. (1982), 'Excavation, Restoration and Italian Architecture of the 1930s' in H. Searing (ed.), *In Search of Modern Architecture, A Tribute to Henry-Russell Hitchcock* (New York), pp. 298–320.

Macioti, M. I. (1995), *Ernesto Nathan* (Rome).

MacKendrick, P. (1976), *The Mute Stones Speak* (New York).

Mack Smith, D. (1982), *Mussolini* (New York).

MacLachlan, B. (1994), 'Bagnani, Gilbert Forrest' in W. W. Briggs (ed.), *Biographical Dictionary of North American Classicists* (Westport, Ct) pp. 30–1.

Macleod, D. (1996), *Art and the Victorian Middle Class* (Cambridge).

MacMullen, R. (1981), *Paganism in the Roman Empire* (New Haven).

Magi, F. (1955–6), 'Commemorazione di Bartolomeo Nogara', *Rendiconti della Pontificia Accademia Romana di Archeologia* 28 pp. 109–19.

Magnus, P. (1964), *King Edward the Seventh* (New York).

Maiuri, A. (1931), *La villa dei Misteri* (Rome).

Mallet, C. (1916), *Impressions and Experiences of a French Trooper* (New York).

Manacorda, D. and R. Tamassia (1985), *Il piccone del regime* (Rome).

Manvell, R. (1968), *Ellen Terry* (New York).

Marcaccio, M. (1977), *The Hapgoods, Three Earnest Brothers* (Charlottesville, VA).

Marchand, S. (1996), *Down from Olympus* (Princeton).

Marchetti Longhi, G. (1934), 'La Via dell'Impero', *Capitolium* 10 pp. 53–84.

Mariano, N. (1966), *Forty Years with Berenson* (New York).

Marsh, E. (1939), *A Number of People: A Book of Reminiscences* (London).

Marsh, J. Y. (1929), 'With Mrs Strong at 35 Via Balbo', unpublished memoir in the Chatsworth Archives.

Marsh, J. and P. G. Nunn (1997), *Pre-Raphaelite Women Artists* (Manchester).

Marshall, G. (1998), *Actresses on the Victorian Stage* (Cambridge).

Mason, R. (ed.) (1994), *Cambridge Minds* Cambridge

Martinelli, V. (1960), 'Antonio Munoz', *Studi Romani* pp. 195–6.

Masson, G. (1965), *The Companion Guide to Rome* (New York).

Masterman, J. C. (1975), *On the Chariot Wheel* (Oxford).

Mazgaj, P. (1979), *The Action Francaise and Revolutionary Syndicalism* (Chapel Hill, NC).

Mazzotti, M. (1964), 'Corrado Ricci', *Studi Romani* 15 pp. 306–10.
McCartney, D. (1994), *W. E. H. Lecky, Historian and Politician 1838–1903* (Dublin).
McDonald, W. and C. G. Thomas (1990), *Progress into the Past* (Bloomington, Indiana).
McMillan, J. (1991), *Napoleon III* (London).
Meacham, S. (1987), *Toynbee Hall and Social Reform 1880–1914* (New Haven).
Mengarini, M.T. (1907), 'Seine Schülern' in L. Traube, *Nomina Sacra* (Munich) pp. 1–xii
Michaelis, A. (1882), *Ancient Marbles in Great Britain* (Cambridge).
Miller, E. (1974), *That Noble Cabinet* (Athens, Ohio).
Misciatelli, P. (1928), 'Die Bibliotheca Hertziana in Rome', *Italien Monatsschaft für Kultur und Literatur* Jahr 1, Heft 3.
Mitford, N. (1968), *The Stanleys of Alderly* (London).
Mitten, D. (1987), 'George Maxim Anossov Hanfmann, 1911–1986', *American Journal of Archaeology* 91 pp. 259–66.
Moltesen, M. (1987), *Wolfgang Helbig* (Copenhagen).
Momigliano, A. (1994), 'From Bachofen to Cumont', *Studies in Modern Scholarship* G. W. Bowersock & T. J. Cornell (eds.), (Berkeley) pp. 315–328.
—— (1966), 'M. I. Rostovtzeff', *Studies in Historiography* (New York), pp. 91–104.
Morey, C. R., E. Herzfeld and W. Koehler (1942), 'Josef Strzygowski', *Speculum* 17 pp. 460–1.
Mosley, C. (ed.) (1996), *The Letters of Nancy Mitford and Evelyn Waugh* (Boston).
Muirhead, G. (1933), *Shorter Guide to London* (London).
Munoz, A. (1934), 'Ricordo di Corrado Ricci', *Capitolium* 10 pp. 326–31.
Munro, J. & P. Sirton (1998), *The Society of Three: Alphonse Legros, Henri Fantin-Latour, James McNeill Whistler* (Cambridge).
Myres, J. L. ('JLM') (1940), 'Sir Henry Stuart Jones 1867–1939', *Proceedings of the British Academy* 26 pp. 467–78.
—— (1943), 'Mrs Arthur Strong CBE', *Nature* 1 October 1943 p. 441.
Newall, C. (1990), *The Art of Lord Leighton* (Oxford).
Newton, C. (1880), *Essays in Art and Archaeology* (Oxford).
Nock, A. D. (1933), *Conversion* (Oxford).
—— (1947), 'Franz Valery Marie Cumont', *American Journal of Archaeology* pp. 432–3.
Nogara, B. (1935), 'Corrado Ricci', *In memoria di Corrado Ricci* (Rome) pp. 125–9.
—— (1943), 'Eugenia Strong', *Osservatore Romana* 19 September 1943.
Olin, M. (1992), *Forms of Representation in Alois Riegl's Theory of Art* (University Park, PA).
Old Master Drawings from Chatsworth (1969) (Meriden, Ct)
Ormond, L. (1969), *George Du Maurier* (Pittsburgh).
Ormond, R. et al., *Frederic, Lord Leighton: Eminent Victorian Artist* (New York).
Owen, S. G. (1926), 'John Percival Postgate 1853–1926', *Proceedings of the British Academy* 12 pp. 337–47.
Oxford and Asquith, Earl of (1928), *Memoirs and Reflections 1852–1927* (Toronto).

Bibliography

Palla, M. (1994), *Mussolini e il fascismo* (Florence).

Pallottino, M. (1937), 'La mostra augustea della romanità', *Capitolium* xii pp. 519–28.

Paribeni, R. (1935), 'Lo scopritore dei fori imperiali', *In memoria di Corrado Ricci* (Rome), pp. 119–24.

Parris, L. (1984), *The Pre-Raphaelites* (London).

Pater, W. (1959), *The Renaissance* (New York).

Payne, H. C. (1978), 'Modernizing the Ancients: The Reconstruction of Ritual Drama 1870–1920', *Proceedings of the American Philosophical Society* 122.3 pp. 182–92.

Peacock, S. (1988), *Jane Ellen Harrison* (New Haven).

Pearsall Smith, L. (1939), *Unforgotten Years* (Boston).

Pemble, J. (1996), *Venice Rediscovered* (Oxford).

Percy, C. and J. Ridley (1988), *The Letters of Edwin Lutyens to His Wife, Lady Emily* (London).

Peters, M. (1984), *Mrs Pat, The Life of Mrs Patrick Campbell* (New York).

Petricioli, M. (1990), *Archeologia e Mare Nostrum* (Rome).

Petter, H. (1992), *Lutyens in Italy* (Rome).

Piantoni, G. (ed.) (1980), *Roma 1911* (Rome).

Picard, C. (1938), 'L'exposition du Bimillenaire de la naissance d'August', *Revue Archeologique* pp. 335–7.

——— 'Ch.P' (1944), 'Eugénie Strong née Sellers (1860–1943)', *Revue Archéologique* p. 93.

Platner, S. B. and T. Ashby (1929), *A Topographical Dictionary of Ancient Rome* (London).

Pollak, L. (1929), 'In memoria di Giovanni Barracco, I dono di un museo a Roma (nel centenario della sua morte)', *Capitolium* 5 pp. 334–46.

——— (1994), *Römische Memoiren: Künstler, Kunstliebhaber, und Gelehrte 1893–1943* (Rome).

Pollock, F. (1933), *For My Grandson* (London).

Pollitt, J. J. (1965), *The Art of Greece 1400–31 BC* (Englewood Cliffs, NJ).

——— (1966), *The Art of Rome c.753 BC–337 AD* (Englewood Cliffs, NJ).

Ponsonby, A. (1943), *Henry Ponsonby: Queen Victoria's Private Secretary* (London).

Ponsonby, M. (ed.) (1927), *Mary Ponsonby: A Memoir, Some Letters, and a Journal* (London).

Pope, A. and T. S. Wragg (1963), *Old Master Drawings from Chatsworth* (Washington, DC).

Potter, T. (1979), *The Changing Landscape of South Etruria* (New York).

Pottier, E. ('E.P.') (1932), 'Salomon Reinach', *Revue archéologique* 5th ser., t. 36 pp. 136–54.

Potts, A. (1994), *Flesh and the Ideal* (New Haven).

Praz, M. (1952), 'La Signora Strong', *La Casa della Fama* (Milan) pp. 381–4.

——— (1979), *La Casa della Vita* (Milan).

Prettejohn, E. (1996), 'Recreating Rome in Victorian Painting: From History to Genre' in Liversidge and Edwards *Imagining Rome*, pp. 54–69.

——— 'Lawrence Alma-Tadema and the Modern City of Ancient Rome', *Art Bulletin* 84 pp. 115–129.

Quiggin, M. (1979), 'Students May Ride the Bicycle' in A. Phillips (ed.), *A Newnham Anthology* (Cambridge).

Raaflaub, K. and M. Toher (eds) (1990), *Between Republic and Empire* (Berkeley).

Ramage, N. (1993), '*Roman Sculpture* by Diana E. E. Kleiner', *American Journal of Archaeology* 97 p. 813.

Lord Reay (1905), 'Remarks', *The Memorial to Arthur Strong Unveiled 6 July 1905.* (London).

Reinach, S., (1906), 'Arthur Strong', *Nouvelles archéologique et correspondance.*

—— (1907), 'Adolf Furtwaengler', *Revue archéologique* pp. 326–7.

—— (1925), 'Depart de Mme Eugénie A. Strong', *Revue archéologique* p. 291.

—— (1931), 'Esquisse d'une histoire de l'archéologie de la Gaule des origines a 1895', *Amalthea* 3 pp. 407–44.

Rennell Rodd, G. (1922), *Social and Diplomatic Memories 1884–1893* (London).

—— (1925), *Social and Diplomatic Memories (Third Series) 1902–1919* (London).

Renfrew, C. (1994), 'Three Cambridge prehistorians' in R. Mason (ed.), *Cambridge Minds* (Cambridge) pp. 58–71.

Reynolds, J. M. (1991), 'Jocelyn Mary Catherine Toynbee 1897–1985', *Proceedings of the British Academy* 80 pp. 499–508.

Rhys Davis, T. W. (1903–4), 'Oriental Studies in England & Abroad', *Proceedings of the British Academy* 1 pp. 183–97.

Richard, E. (ed.) (1937), *The Earlier Letters of Gertrude Bell* (New York).

Richardson, L. (1992), *A New Topographical Dictionary of Ancient Rome* (Baltimore).

Richter, G. (1944), 'Obituary: Eugénie Sellers Strong' *American Journal of Archaeology* 48 pp. 79–80.

Richter, J. P. (1910), *The Mond Collection, An Appreciation* (London).

Ridley, R. (1986), 'Augusti Manes volitant per auras: the archaeology of Rome under the Fascists', *Xenia* 11 pp. 19–46.

Riegl, A. (1981), *Die spätrömische Kunstindustrie nach den Funden in Oesterreich-Ungarn* (Vienna).

Rizzo, G. E. (1926), *Ersilia Caetani Lovatelli* (Rome).

Robertson, M. (1989), 'Bernard Ashmole 1894–1988', *Proceedings of the British Academy* 75 pp. 313–28.

Rodenwaldt, G. (1927), 'Walther Amelung', *Mitteilungen des Deutsche Archäologischen Instituts, Römische Abteilung* 42 pp. v–xix.

Rosenhauer, A. (1993), 'Giovanni Morelli und Franz Wickhoff' in G. Agosti et al., *Giovanni Morelli e la cultura di conoscitori* (Bergamo) pp. 359–70.

Rostovtzeff, M. (1927), *Mystic Italy* (New York).

Rothblatt, S. (1968), *The Revolution of the Dons: Cambridge and Society in Victorian England* (London).

Rothenstein, W. (1923), *Men & Memories: Recollections of William Rothenstein 1900–1922* (London).

—— (1931), *Men & Memories* (New York).

—— (1940), *Since Fifty: Men and Memories 1922–1938* (New York).

Rowse, A. L. (1983), *Eminent Elizabethans* (Athens, GA), pp. 1–40.

—— (1983a), *London in My Time* (London).

Rushforth, G. McN. (1925), 'La scultura romana da Augusto a Costantino di Eugenia Strong', *Journal of Roman Studies* 15 pp. 281–3.

Russell, B. (1967), *The Autobiography of Bertrand Russell* (Boston).

Samuels, E. (1979), *Bernard Berenson: The Making of a Connoisseur* (Cambridge, Mass.).

———— (1987), *Bernard Berenson: The Making of a Legend* (Cambridge, Mass.).

St Clair, W. (1998), *Lord Elgin and the Marbles* (Oxford).

Santayana, G. (1945), *The Middle Span* (New York).

Scarrocchia, S. (1986), *Studi su Alois Riegl* (Aemilia Romagna).

Schlosser, J. von (1934), *Die Wiener Schule der Kunstgeschichte* (Innsbruck).

Schorske, C. (1980), *Fin-de-Siècle Vienna* (New York).

Schuchhardt, C. (1891), *(Schliemann's Excavations: An Archaeological and Historical Study* (translated by E. Sellers) (London).

———— (1944), *Aus Leben und Arbeit* (Berlin).

Schuchhardt, W-H. (1956), *Adolf Furtwängler* (Freiburg im Breisgau).

Scobie, A. (1990), *Hitler's State Architecture: The Impact of Classical Antiquity* (London).

Scott Thomson, G. (1949), *Mrs Arthur Strong: A Memoir* (London).

Scriba, F. (1995), 'Il mito di Roma; L'estetica e gli intellettuali negli anni del consenso: la Mostra Augustea della Romanita 1937–8', *Quaderni di storia* 41 pp. 67–84.

Sellar, E. M. (1907), *Recollections and Impressions* (Edinburgh).

Sellers, E. (1891), 'The Theatre at Megalopolis', *The Classical Review* 5 pp. 238–40.

———— (1891a), 'The Theatres of Megalopolis', *Athenaeum* 3323 4 July 1891.

———— (1891b), 'Review of E. Curtius' *Die Stadtgeschichte von Athen*', *The Classical Review* 5 pp. 486–7.

———— (1892a), 'Review of A. H. Smith's *A Catalogue of Sculpture in the Department of Greek and Roman Antiquities in the British Museum*', *The Classical Review* 6 pp. 368–71.

———— (1893), 'Three Attic Lekythoi from Eretria', *Journal of Hellenic Studies* 13 pp. 3–12.

———— (1893a), 'On Polykleitian Statues', *Athenaeum* 1 July 1893 pp. 38–40.

———— (1894), 'Greek Plastic Art', review of Furtwängler's *Meisterwerke der Griechischen Plastik, The Times* 3 March 1894 (unsigned).

———— (1894a), 'Review of Furtwängler's *Meisterwerke der Griechischen Plastik*', *The Classical Review* 8 pp. 169–75, pp. 219–25.

———— (1894b), 'Greek Head in the Possession of T. Humphry Ward Esq', *Journal of Hellenic Studies* pp. 198–205.

———— (1894c), 'Sir Charles Newton', *Revue Archéologique* 2 pp. 273–81.

———— (1895), 'The Art of Praxiteles and Skopas at the British Museum', *Nineteenth Century* 17 pp. 682–91.

———— (1895a), 'Review of S. Reinach's *Bronzes figures de la Gaule Romaine*', *The Classical Review* 9 pp. 138–9.

———— (1895b), 'Furtwängler's *Intermezzi* and *Über Statuenkopien im Alterthum*', *The Classical Review* 9 pp. 443–7.

———— (1896), *The Elder Pliny's Chapters on the History of Art: Commentary and Historical Introduction* (with translation by K. Jex-Blake, etc.).

211

────── (1896a), 'Review of Furtwängler's *Intermezzi* and *Uber Statuenkopien im Alterthum*', *The Classical Review* 10 pp. 443–7.

────── (1897), 'L'Hermes d'Olympie', *Gazette des Beaux Arts* 18 pp. 129–39.

────── (1897a), 'Review of Bornecque's edition of Cicero's *de Signis*', *The Classical Review* 11 p. 124.

────── (1898), 'Review of Furtwängler's *Catalogue of the Somzee Collection*', *The Classical Review* 12 pp. 326–8.

Seltman, C. (1952), 'Arthur Bernard Cook, 1868–1952', *Proceedings of the British Academy* 38 pp. 295–302.

'The Setting of a Greek Play' (1898), *Quarterly Review* 188 pp. 360–80.

Shand-Tucci, D. (1998), *The Art of Scandal* (New York).

Sharp, E. (1926), *Hertha Ayrton* (London).

Shaw, B. (1992), 'Under Russian Eyes', *Journal of Roman Studies* 82 pp. 216–28.

Shaw, J. (ed.), *Old Master Drawings from Chatsworth* (Meriden, Ct).

Shirakawa, S. H. (1992), *The Devil's Music Master* (New York).

Sidgwick, A & E. M. Sidgwick 'AS and EMS' (1906), *Henry Sidgwick: A Memoir* (London).

Simpson, C. (1987), *The Partnership* (London).

Smith, A. H. (1892–1904), *A Catalogue of Sculpture in the Department of Greek and Roman Antiquities, British Museum* (London).

────── 'A.H.S.' (1931), 'Thomas Ashby (1874–1931)', *Proceedings of the British Academy* 17 pp. 515–41.

Smith-Rosenberg, C. (1985), *Disorderly Conduct* (Oxford).

Smyth, E. (1919), *Impressions that Remained* (London).

────── (1936), 'Maurice Baring as Novelist', *Quarterly Review* 267 pp. 234–49.

────── (1938), *Maurice Baring* (London).

Sox, D. (1991), *Bachelors of Art* (London).

Spalding, F. (1999), *Roger Fry: Art and Life* (Norwich).

Speaight, R. (1957), *The Life of Hilaire Belloc* (New York).

Sprigge, S. (1960), *Berenson: A Biography* (Boston).

Stephen, B. N. (1927), *Emily Davies and Girton College* (London).

────── (1933), *Girton College 1869–1932* (Cambridge).

Stewart, J. (1959), *Jane Ellen Harrison: A Portrait from Letters* (London).

Stewart, Z. (ed.) (1972), *Essays on Religion and the Ancient World* (Oxford).

Stewart, Z. et al. (1964), 'Arthur Darby Nock', *Harvard Theological Review* 57.2 pp. 65–8.

Stokes, J. (1972), *Resistable Theatres* (London).

Stone, M. (1993), 'Staging Fascism: the exhibition of the Fascist revolution', *Journal of Contemporary History* 28 pp. 215–43.

────── (1999), 'A flexible Rome: Fascism and the cult of romanita' in C. Edwards (ed.), *Roman Presences* (Cambridge), pp. 205–20.

Stoneman, R. (1987), *Lands of Lost Gods* (Norman, Oklahoma).

Storrs, R. (1945), *Orientations* (London).

Strachey, B. and J. Samuels (eds) (1983), *The Story of the Pearsall Smith Family* (London).

────── (1983a), *Mary Berenson: A Self Portrait from her Letters & Diaries* (London).

Stray, C. (ed.) (1999), *Classics in 19th & 20th Century Cambridge: Curriculum, Culture & Community*, Proceedings of the Cambridge Phil., *Society* Supplement 24 (Cambridge).

Strong, Mrs A. (1898), 'Klein's *Praxiteles*' *The Times* 4 March 1898 (unsigned).

—— (1899), 'Furtwängler's Archaeological Papers 1898–1899', *The Classical Review* 13 pp. 278–81.

—— (1899a), 'Review of Petersen's *Dakische Kriege*', *The Classical Review* 13 pp. 371.

—— (1901a), 'The Dutuit Collection at the Petit Palace', *Times Literary Supplement* 20 February 1901 p. 57.

—— (1903), 'Three Attic Stelai in the Possession of Lord Newton at Lyme Park', *Journal Hellenic Society* 23 pp. 356–9.

—— (1904), *Catalogue of an Exhibition of Ancient Greek Art held at the Burlington Fine Arts Club in 1903*

—— (1904a), 'The proposed excavations at Herculaneum', *The Times* 23 April 1904 (signed 'Archaeologist').

—— (1906a), 'Letter to Mr John Burns, President of Local Govt Board (communicated by Mr Burns to the Court of Common Council on March 1st) on the impending demolition of Sir Christopher Wren's house in Fish Lane, London', *The Times* 2 March 1906.

—— (1906b), 'Statue of a Boy Leaning on a Pillar', *Journal of Hellenic Studies* 26 pp. 1–3.

—— (1907), 'Professor Strzygowski on the Throne of S. Maximian at Ravenna and on the Sidamara Sarcophagi', *Burlington Magazine* 50, May 1907 pp. 109–11.

—— (1908), *Roman Sculpture from Augustus to Constantine* (London).

—— (1908a), 'British Art Treasures and America', *The Times* 9 December 1908.

—— (1908b), 'Antiques in the Collection of Sir F. Cook, Bart. of Doughty House, Richmond', *Journal of Hellenic Studies* 28 pp. 1–45.

—— (1909), 'La tête Humphry Ward au Musée du Louvre', *Gazette des Beaux Arts* January 1909 pp. 51ff.

—— (1910), 'The Fanciulla d'Anzio', *The Times* 3 January 1910.

—— (1910a), 'The Fanciulla d'Anzio', *Burlington Magazine* November 1910.

—— (1911a), 'The Sculptures of the Temple of Aphaia in Aegina', *Transactions of the British and American Archaeological Society*.

—— (1912), 'Recollections of the late Duke of Devonshire' in B. Holland, *The Life of Spencer Compton, Eighth Duke of Devonshire* (London) Vol. 2, pp. 227–34.

—— (1913), 'The storied column of Mayence', *Revue Archeologique*.

—— (1913a), 'Six drawings from the Column of Trajan with the date 1467 and a note on the date of Giacomo Ripanda', *Papers of the British School at Rome* 6 pp. 174–183.

—— (1913b), 'Terra-cottas in Italian Museums', *The Times* 3 May 1913.

—— (1914), 'The Architectural Decoration in Terracotta from early Latin Temples in the Museo di Villa Giulia', *Journal of Roman Studies* 4 pp. 157–181.

—— (1914a), 'A note on Two Roman Sepulchral Reliefs', *Journal of Roman Studies* 4.

———— (1914b), 'The Juppiter Column at Mainz', *Burlington Magazine* 25, pp. 153–163.

———— (1914c), preface to *Religion and Art* by Alessandro della Seta, translated by Marion C. Harrison (New York).

———— (1914d), 'Forgotten Fragments of Ancient Wall Paintings in Rome: I, The Palatine', *Papers of the British School at Rome* 7 pp. 114–123.

———— (1915), *Apotheosis and After Life* (London).

———— (1916), 'Forgotten Fragments of Ancient Wall-Paintings in Rome: II, The House in the Via de' Cerchi', *Papers of the British School at Rome* 8 pp. 91–103.

———— (1916b), 'Bronze Bust of a Julio-Claudian Prince', *Journal of Roman Studies* 6 pp. 27–46.

———— (1917), 'The Approach to St Peter's', *Town Planning Review*.

———— (1917a), 'L'arte romana e l'arte mediovale nella Rumenia', *Emporium* Vol. 16, n. 274.

———— (1917b), 'Archaeological research in Italy', letter to *Times Literary Supplement*, 15–22 November 1917.

———— (1918), '"Victory" discovered on the Palatine', letter to *Time Literary Supplement* 14 March 1918.

———— (1918a), 'Archaeological research in Italy', letter to *Times Literary Supplement* 14–21 November 1918.

———— (1919a), 'The Late Teresio Rivoira', *Times Literary Supplement* 27 March 1919.

———— (1920a), 'Sepulchral Relief of a Priest of Bellona', *Papers of the British School at Rome* 9 pp. 205–213.

———— (1920b), 'Bronze Plaque in the Rosenheim Collection', *Papers of the British School at Rome* 9. pp. 214–224

———— (1920c), 'Copy of the *Responsiones* of R. Parsons', *Papers of the British School at Rome* 9 pp. 225–230.

———— (1920d), 'Bernini's Work at St Peter's Rome', *Builder* 24 December 1920 (letter).

———— (1922), 'Reputed portraits of S. Peter and S. Paul in the hypogaeum of the Viale Manzoni', letter to *The Times* 22 March 1922 (w. Dr T. Ashby).

———— (1922a), 'Note on the War Memorial, Stonyhurst College', *Stonyhurst Review* 16.

———— (1922b), 'The British School at Rome', *League of Empire Review* October 1922–January 1923.

———— (1923), *La scultura romana da Augusto a Costantino* (Rome)

———— (1923a), *La Chiesa Nuova (S. Maria in Valicella)*, with a preface by Piero Misciatelli (Rome).

———— (1923b), 'Rome's Strange Temple Underground', *Wonders of the Past* n. 24.

———— (1923c), 'The Basilica of Porta Maggiore', *The Times* 25 August 1923 (letter).

———— (1923d), 'English mural art' (suggested compilation of early English mural painting), *The Times* 2 October 1923.

———— (1925), 'A New Museum for Rome' (Museo Mussolini), *The Times* 4 December 1925.

———— (1925a), 'St Peter's, the Holy Year, and Bernini', *The Dublin Review*, Vol. 177.

—— (1925b), 'Di un recente volume sulle Chiese di Roma' *Roma* III, p. 9.

—— (1926), 'S. Francis in Rome' (No. 10 of *S. Francis of Assisi: Essays in Commemoration* (London).

—— (1926a), 'A Modern George Herbert' (review of André de Lujan's *Le Miroir Divin*) *Blackfriars* November 1926.

—— (1926b), 'Review of Lehmann-Hartleben's *Trajanssaule*', *Journal of Roman Studies* 17 pp. 261–263.

—— (1927a), 'Review of R. Eisler's *Orphisch-Dionysiche Mysteriengedanken in der Christlichen Antike, Journal of Roman Studies* 16 pp. 255–8.

—— (1927c), 'Rivoira's *Roman Architecture' Dublin Review* n. 362.

—— (1927d), 'The friendship of S. Francis of Assisi with Dame Jacopa di Settesole', *Downhill Training College Magazine* January 1927.

—— (1928b), *Bibliography of Eugénie Strong presented to Miss E.H. Major, MA, Mistress of Girton College, Cambridge* (Rome-Cambridge)

—— (1937), 'Temples of the Gods XXII: Rome's Strange Temple Underground' in J. A. Hammerton (ed.), *Wonders of the Past* (New York), pp. 1015–22.

Strong, D. (1976), *Roman Art* (Harmondsworth).

Strong, E. (1899), 'Furtwängler's Archaeological Papers 1898–1899', *The Classical Review* pp. 278–81.

—— (1899a), 'Helbig's Guide to the Antique Classical Collections in Rome', *The Classical Review* 13 pp. 328–9.

—— (1901), 'Some Recent Works on Classical Art' (notices of publications by E. Loewry, J. Lange. S. Reinach, H. Thiersch, E. Courband, etc.', *The Classical Review* 15 pp. 185–91.

—— (1906), 'An Official Registration of Private Arts Collections', *The Nineteenth Century* 348 pp. 239–54.

—— (1909), 'Gaulish Bas-Reliefs', *The Classical Review* 23 pp. 265–7

—— (1920), 'Greek Portraits in the British Museum', *Quarterly Review* 234 pp. 22–40.

—— (1922), 'Treasures from Vatican Rubbish: Rich "Finds" of Greek and Roman Sculpture', *ILN* 4351, 9 September 1922.

—— (1928), *Catalogue of the Greek and Roman Antiques in the Possession of Lord Melchett, PC, D.Sc., FRS at Melchett Court and 35 Lowndes Square* (Oxford).

—— (1928), 'La formazione delle accademie e scuole straniere di Roma', *Capitolium* 4, May 1928 pp. 94–111.

—— (1928a), *Art in Ancient Rome from Earliest Times to Justinian* (London).

—— (1930), 'Recent Criticism of Roman Art', *Formes* VIII, October 1930.

—— (1931), 'Un romano d'elezione', *Il Giornale d'Italia* 27 May 1931 p. 3.

—— (1935), 'Corrado Ricci, Personal Memories', *In Memoriam di Corrado Ricci* (Rome) pp. 131–4.

—— (1938), *Viaggio attraverso le stade della Britannia romana* (Le grandi strade del mondo romano VI) (Rome).

—— (1939), 'La legislazione sociale di Augusto ed i fregi del recinto dell'Ara Pacis', *Quaderni di Studi Romani* II pp. 2–24.

—— (1939a), '"Romanità" throughout the Ages', *Journal of Roman Studies* 29 pp. 137–66.

—— (nd) *Chapters from the Unfinished History of the Vatican Palace*, manuscript in Cambridge University Library.

Strong, E. and N. Joliffe (1924), 'The Stuccoes of the Underground Basilica near the Porta Maggiore', *Journal of Hellenic Studies* 44 pp. 65–111.

Strong, S. A. (1897), 'Pliny's History of Artists', *Guardian* 24 February 1897.

—— (1903), Introduction to *Reproductions of Drawings by Old Masters in the Collection of the Duke of Devonshire* (London).

—— (1905), *Critical Studies and Fragments* (London).

—— (1905a), 'A propos de Burke et de Warren Hastings', *L'Action Française* 7/152 pp. 110–12.

Strong, Mrs S. A. (1911), 'The Exhibition Illustrative of the Provinces of the Roman Empire at the Baths of Diocletian, Rome', *Journal of Roman Studies* 1 pp. 1–49.

Strzygowski, J. (1907), 'A Sarcophagus of the Sidamara Type in the Collection of Sir Frederick Cook, Bart, and the Influence of Stage Architecture upon the Art of Antioch' (translated by Mrs A. Strong), *Journal of Hellenic Studies* 27 pp. 99–122.

Stuart-Jones, H. A. (1905), 'Art under the Roman Empire', *Quarterly Review*, January 1909 pp. 111–37.

—— (1909), 'The Remains of Ancient Painting' *Quarterly Review* 210 pp. 419–454

—— (ed) (1912), *Catalogue of the Ancient Sculptures Preserved in the Municipal Collections of Rome* Vol.1 (Oxford).

—— (1915), '*Apotheosis and After Life* by Mrs S. Arthur Strong', *Journal of Roman Studies* 5 pp. 141–3.

Stubbings, F., 'Alan John Bayard Wace (1879–1957)', *Proceedings of the British Academy* 44 pp. 263–80.

Sturge Moore, T. (1905), 'Arthur Strong', *The Speaker* 17 June 1905.

Sutherland, G. (1994), 'Emily Davies, the Sidgwicks and the education of women in Cambridge' in R. Mason (ed.), *Cambridge Minds* pp. 34–47.

Sutherland, J. (1991), *Mrs Humphry Ward: Eminent Victorian, Pre-eminent Edwardian* (Oxford).

Sutton, D. (1972), *The Letters of Roger Fry* (London).

Swanson, V. G. (1977), *Sir Lawrence Alma-Tadema: The Victorian Vision of the Ancient World* (New York).

Symonds, R (1991), *Oxford and Empire*.

Taylor, R. (1997), *Berlin and Its Culture* (New Haven).

Tea, G. (1932), *Giacomo Boni* (Milan).

Thompson, E. M. (1903–4), 'Alexander Stuart Murray', *Proceedings of the British Academy* 1 pp. 321–3.

Thompson, F. (1951), *Chatsworth, A Short History* (London).

Thompson, F. M. L. (1988), *The Rise of Respectable Society* (London).

Thompson, R. D'Arcy (1958), *D'Arcy Wentworth Thompson. The Scholar Naturalist 1860–1948* (London). cf. Lewis Campbell.

Thwaite, A. (1984), *Edmund Gosse: A Literary Landscape 1849–1928* (London).

Todd, M. (1918), *The Life of Sophia Jex-Blake* (London).

Todd, P. (2001), *Pre-Raphaelites at Home* (New York).

Tollemache, L. (1984), *Gladstone's Boswell, Late Victorian Conversations* (New York).

Tomlinson, R. (1991), *The Athens of Alma-Tadema* (Stroud, Gloucestershire).

Toynbee, J. M. C. (1928), 'Ancient Art in Rome by Eugénie Strong', *Journal of Roman Studies* 18 pp 235–7.

—— (1943), 'Obituary Notice: Mrs Arthur Strong. Born 25th March 1860; died 16th September 1943', *Antiquaries Journal* 23 pp. 188–9.

—— (1949), 'Review of Scott Thompson', *Cambridge Journal* p. 122.

Traill, D. A. (1995), *Schliemann of Troy* (New York).

Traill, H. D. (1883), 'South Kensington Hellenism: A Dialogue', *Fortnightly* 34 pp. 111–119.

Traube, L. (1907), *Nomina sacra* (Munich).

—— (1988), *Ruckblick auf meine Lehrtatigkeit*, ed. G. Silagi (Munich).

Tree, H. B. (1917), *Herbert and I* (New York).

Treuherz, J. (1993), *Victorian Painting* (London).

Trevelyan, J. P. (1923), *The Life of Mrs Humphry Ward* (London).

Trevelyan, R. (1997), *Principi sotto il vulcano* (Milan).

Tullberg, R. (1998), *Women at Cambridge* (Cambridge).

Türks, P. (1996), *Filippo Neri: una goia contagiosa* (Rome).

Turner, F. M. (1981), *The Greek Heritage in Victorian Britain* (New Haven).

—— (1989), 'Why the Greeks and not the Romans in Victorian Britain' in G. W. Clarke (ed.), *Rediscovering Hellenism* (Cambridge) pp. 61–81.

—— (1993), *Contesting Cultural Authority* (Cambridge).

Lord Tweedsmuir (1940), *Pilgrim's Way* (Cambridge, Mass.).

Uhde-Bernays, H. (1947), *Im Licht der Freiheit, Erinneringen aus den Jahren 1880–1914* (Munich).

Valentine, L. and A. Valentine (1973), *The American Academy in Rome 1894–1969* (Charlottesville, VA).

Van Nuffel, R. (1995), *Léon Kochnitzky: Umanista belga, Italiano d'elezione 1892–1965*, Institut historique belge de Rome, Bibliotheque XXXV (Brussels/Rome).

Varès, D. (1955), *Ghosts of the Spanish Steps* (London).

Vicinus, M. (1985), *Independent Women* (Chicago).

Visser, R. (1992), 'Fascist Doctrine and the Cult of the Romanita', *Journal of Contemporary History* 27 pp. 5–22.

Wadleigh, H. R. (1910), *Munich: History, Monuments, and Art* (London).

Waldstein, C. (1904), 'Professor Furtwängler's Methods', *The Classical Review* 18 pp. 470–4.

Wallace-Hadrill, A. (2001), *The British School at Rome: One Hundred Years* (Rome).

Wallach, J. (1996), *Desert Queen* (New York).

Walpole, S. (1903–4), 'Mr Lecky', *Proceedings of the British Academy* 1 pp. 307–10.

Walton, A. (1908), 'Roman Sculpture from Augustus to Constantine by Mrs Arthur Strong', *CJ* pp. 291–2.

Ward, Mrs H. (1918), *A Writer's Recollections* (London).

Ward Fowler, W. ('W.W.F.') (1916), 'Review of *Apotheosis and Afterlife*', *The Classical Review* 30 pp. 117–19.

Warr, G. C. (1887), *Echoes of Hellas* (London).

Waterhouse, H. (1986), *The British School at Athens: The First Hundred Years* (Oxford).

Watkin, D. (1980), *The Rise of Architectural History* (London).

Weintraub, S. (1993), *Disraeli* (New York).

Weitzmann, K. (1994), *Sailing with Byzantium* (Munich).

Wellek, R. (1966), 'Vernon Lee, Bernard Berenson and Aesthetics' in V. Gabrieli, *Friendship's Garland* pp. 233–51.

Wes, M. A. (1990), *Michael Rostovtzeff, Historian in Exile: Russian Roots in an American Context* (Stuttgart).

Whyte, F. (1929), *William Heineman, A Memoir* (Garden City, NY).

Wickhoff, F. (1900), *Roman Art, Some of its Principles and their Application to Early Christian Painting*, translated and edited by Mrs S. Arthur Strong LL.D. (London).

Wilson, E. (1966), 'The Genie of the Via Giulia' in V. Gabrieli, *Friendship's Garland* pp. 5–17.

Wilson, D. (1987), *Gilbert Murray OM 1866–1957* (Oxford).

Winstone, H. V. F. (1978), *Gertrude Bell* (New York).

Wiseman, T. P. (1981), 'The First Director of the British School at Rome', *Proceedings of the British School at Rome* 49 pp. 144–63.

—— (1990), *A Short History of the British School at Rome* (London).

Woolf, V. (1945), *A Room of One's Own* (Harmondsworth).

Woodbury, L. (1985), 'Gentleman-Scholar: A Memoir of Gilbert Bagnani', unpublished memorial article.

Woods, M. L. (1920), 'Mrs Humphry Ward: A Sketch from Memory', *Quarterly Review* 234 pp. 147–60.

Wyke, M. (1999), 'Screening ancient Rome in the new Italy' in C. Edwards (ed.), *Roman Presences* (Cambridge) pp. 188–204.

Notes

Introduction

1. Scott Thomson 1949.
2. Haynes 1949. A more sympathetic review is Toynbee 1949.
3. Peacock 1988; Beard 2000.
4. Winstone 1978; Wallach 1996.
5. Berg 1996.
6. For Smith Bodichon cf. Hirsch 1998; For Mrs Ward cf. Sutherland 1990.
7. For Morrell cf. Darroch 1976; for Mary Berenson cf. Strachey & Samuels 1983; for Mrs Pat Campbell cf. Peters 1984.

Chapter 1

1. Scott Thomson 1949: 13–4.
2. Years later Eugénie was to meet her aged namesake when she was in exile in Britain, cf. Girton College Archives: Violet Hippioly/ES 1903.
3. Jolliffe 1943. The information on the Sellers family at Oporto was obtained from the genealogical archives of the Church of Latter Day Saints.
4. Trevelyan 1997: 40, 60, 110, 308.
5. *DNB 1941–1950* 848; Scott Thompson 1949: 14–16.
6. Scott Thomson 1949: 14–15.
7. Scott Thomson 1949: 15.
8. Girton College Archives: ES/Edmund Gosse 17 November 1925.
9. Girton College Archives: autobiographical notes.
10. Caracciolo 1993.
11. Colby College Archives: ES/Violet Paget 16 January 1886.
12. Girton College Archives: ES/D. S. MacColl 20 December 1920.
13. Ibid.
14. de Grummond 1996 672; Belli 1974; Girton College Archives: ES/S. Reinach 8 October 1931.
15. Scott Thomson 1949: 17.
16. Fowler 1982–3.
17. Colby College Archives: ES/Violet Paget 16 January 1886. Eugénie describes her return to England after earlier travels on the Continent as 'rather sudden', suggesting events connected with her father's death. I have not been able to determine the exact death date or circumstances for either her father or her mother.
18. Girton College Archives: D. S. McColl/*The Times* 22 September 1943.

19. L. Curtius 1943–6; Girton College Archives: Mary Costelloe/ES 4 November 1896: 'Berenson regards you as the most beautiful woman he has ever seen.'.

20. Praz 1952: 382.

21. Girton College Archives: W. Furtwängler/C. Leigh Smith 28 September 1953; Mosley 1996: 205–6. I owe the last reference to my University at Buffalo colleague Professor Frederick See.

22. Leedham-Green 1996.

Chapter 2

1. Girton College Archives: Postgate/ES 23 October 1889.

2. Hirsch 1998.

3. Russell 1967: 35.

4. *WWW 1897–1916* 670.

5. *Spectator* of 16 January 1869 as quoted in A. Sidgwick & E. M. Sidgwick 1906: 188–9. For the general issues related to women's higher education, cf. Brittain 1960; Vicinus 1985: 121–162.

6. Stephen 1927; Hirsch 1998: 135, 200–206, 222; G. Sutherland 1994; Peacock 1988: 32–3.

7. Vicinus 1985: 125; A.S. & E.M.S. 1906: 208–211.

8. Girton College Archives: John Postgate/ES 26 March 1889.

9. Vicinus 1985: 134.

10. As cited in Vicinus 1985: 134.

11. Bradbrook 1969: 58.

12. Colby College Archives: ES/Violet Paget 16 January 1886.

13. Girton College Archives: C. A. Hutton/ES 1 January 1927.

14. Fowler 1982–3; Breay 1999.

15. Faber 1957; Jenkyns 1980; Turner 1993: 322–361.

16. Cook 1931: 42; Jebb 1883; Waterhouse 1986: 5–8.

17. Crust & Colvin as cited in Waterhouse 1986: 6.

18. Hill 1937.

19. Browning 1910: 288; Cook 1931; Beard 1993: 9; Dyson 1998: 56–8.

20. Lucas 1928; Cook 1931: 46.

21. Lucas 1928: 28.

22. Ibid.: 29.

23. Girton College Archives: Elinor Ritchie/ES 14 August 1883.

24. Smith-Rosenberg 1985: 53–76.

25. Scott Thomson 1949: 19–20; Vicinus 1985: 168–70.

26. Vicinus 1985: 169.

27. Scott Thomson 1949: 20.

28. *WWW 1897–1916* 115–16.

29. Girton College Archives: Lewis Campbell/ES 30 November 1890.

Chapter 3

1. Girton College Archives: Blanche, Countess of Airlee/ES 17 October 1882.

2. Hirsch 1998: 278–96, 307–14.

3. Hirsch 1998.

4. Girton College Archives: Edwin Abbott/ES 15 January 1888.

5. Girton College Archives: Jan Jian/ES 11 April 1889.

6. For Humphry Ward, cf. J. Sutherland 1991. For Mrs Humphry Ward, cf. Woods 1920; J. Trevelyan 1923; J. Sutherland 1991.

7. Girton College Archives: J. Trevelyan/ES 23 September 1921.

8. Allingham and Radford 1907.

9. Stokes 1972: 53; Easterling 1999; Beard 2000: 37–53.

10. Stokes 1972: 51–4; Jenkyns 1991: 303–8.

11. Cited in Jenkyns 1991: 305.

12. Jenkyns 1991: 295, 304–6.

13. *WWW 1897–1916:* 743; Scott Thomson 1949: 21–3; Beard 2000: 38–41.

14. Beard 2000: 39–48.

15. Girton College Archives: S. Ray Lankester/ES 6 June 1883. For Gladstone's fixation on Helen of Troy, cf. Tollemache 1984: 29–30.

16. Tree 1917: 18–19.

17. Jenkyns 1980: 301–2; Treuherz 1993: 153; Beard 2000: 42–3.

18. As quoted in Peacock 1988: 63.

19. H. D. Traill 1883; Beard 2000: 44–5.

20. H. D. Traill 1883: 113–14.

21. Girton College Archives: G. Warr/ES 2 July 1883.

22. Peters 1984, esp. 80–100. Girton College Archives: ES's name is on the list of May 23, 1906 first-night patrons for 'The Whirlwind' by Henry Bernstein and 'Undine' by W. L. Courtey.

23. Acton 1970: 25–30.

24. Girton College Archives: Esther Rowland/ES 29 May 1914.

25. Rothenstein 1931: 277.

26. Hadley 1987: 414.

27. Girton College Archives: Newton/ES 11 May 1883.

28. Colby College Archives: ES/Violet Paget 16 January 1886.

29. Sellers 1894; Jebb 1895; Colvin 1921; Stoneman 1987: 218–25.

30. Jebb 1895: 82.

31. Ibid.; Evans 1954: 55, 97, 296, 309; Hilton 1985: 48–9, 76, 157.

32. Colvin 1921: 215–16.

33. Newton 1880: 1–38.

34. Colvin 1921: 213.

35. Girton College Archives: Newton/ES 3 October 1887.

36. Girton College Archives: Arthur Strong/ES 19 October 1892.

37. I Tatti Archives: ES/Bernard Berenson 6 April 1939.

38. P. Gardner 1933: 25.

39. Kenyon 1941: 394–5.

40. Jenkins 1992. A good example of this revived interest in the Elgin Marbles was Alma-Tadema's 1868 painting *Phidias and the Frieze of the Parthenon.* cf. Liversidge and Edwards 1996: 162, fig. 33.

41. Ormond 1969: 254–5.

42. Girton College Archives: A. R. Dryhurst/ES 14 January 1909.

43. J. Stewart 1959; Peacock 1988; Beard 2000.

44. Girton College Archives: autobiographical notes; Scott Thomson 1949: 24.

45. Colby College Archives: ES/Violet Paget 16 January 1896.

46. Ackerman 1991: 79; J. Stewart 1959: 19–22; Calder 1998; Beard 2000: 55–8.

47. J. Harrison 1882: xii–xiii; Ackerman 1991: 74–5.

48. J. Harrison 1882: vi–vii. The themes of Plato as the best route for understanding Pheidias was developed in Harrison 1892: 196–249.

49. J. Harrison 1892: 309–310.

50. Girton College Archives: autobiographical notes.

51. Quoted in Peacock 1988: 58. For an interesting view of this relationship seen from the Harrison side, cf. Beard 2000.

52. Beard 2000, esp. 85–97.

53. Gunn 1964; L. Ormond 1969: 249.

54. Gunn 1964: 33–46, 165, fig. 9.

55. Emanuel 1989: 175.

56. Praz 1952: 382.

57. Ibid.

58. Girton College Archives: F. Leighton/ES 1885. I have not been able to identify this portrait in Leighton's published works.

59. Jones 1996: 67. For Leighton and his work, cf. *Frederic, Lord Leighton* 1996; Ash 1997.

60. As quoted in Jenkyns 1991: 226.

61. Swanson 1977: 8–12.

62. Swanson 1977: 19–20; Jenkyns 1991: 233–45; Treuherz 1993: 170–3.

63. Fry 1913; Spalding 1999: 169.

64. Swanson 1977: 24, 31–5.

65. L. Curtius 1943–5.

66. Fitzgerald 1997.

67. Bailey 1945; Fitzgerald 1997: 214, 217–18.

68. Treuherz 1993: 75, 82, 95–6, 154.

69. Beard 2000: 99–105.

70. Girton College Archives: ES/F. Bell Jan. 7, 1900.

Chapter 4

1. Jenkins 1992.

2. Jenkyns 1980: 148–54, 274–5; Dowling 1994.

3. Jenkyns 1980: 173.

4. Hirsch 1998: 315–19.

5. Girton College Archives: Mary Costelloe/ES 23 October 1896.

6. Girton College Archives: Mary Lowndes/ES 21 March 1913.

7. de Grummond 1996: 372.

8. McDonald and Thomas 1990: 72–6, 84–6, 218–21; D. A. Traill 1995: 213, 215, 218–30.

9. Jebb 1878, 1883; Waterhouse 1986: 5–7.

Notes

10. Waterhouse 1986: 7–8.
11. Farnell 1934: 228–9.
12. Myres 1940.
13. Rennell Rodd 1922: 196.
14. *Annual Report of the British School at Athens* 1890–1; Sellers 1892–3.
15. D. Wilson 1987: 117; Beard 2000: 106.
16. As quoted in Ackerman 1991: 77.
17. Ashmole 1985.
18. D. A. Traill 1995: 211–12, 284–97, 315.
19. McDonald and Thomas 1990: 14.
20. Girton College Archives: B. Berenson/ES n.d.
21 de Grummond 1996: 1093; Dörpfeld 1896; Gardner et al. 1892; Waterhouse 1986: 10; Dyson 1998: 83; Beard 2000: 66–70.
22. E. Gardner et al. 1892; 'The Setting of a Greek Play' 1898.
23. Sellers 1891, 1891a.
24. Sellers 1891a.
25. Girton College Archives: L. Campbell/ES 20 June 1891: 'Even in matters of scholarship it requires watchful circumspection to make a career'.
26. Girton College Archives: W. Loring/ES 3 August 1899.
27. Girton College Archives: autobiographical notes.
28. Marsh and Nunn 1997: 131–5; For Stillman and archaeology, cf. Dyson 1998: 61–4.
29. Girton College Archives: autobiographical notes.
30. Ibid.
31. Chanler 1934: 274.
32. Ward 1918: 113–17; Chanler 1934: 275–6.
33. Rennell Rodd 1925: 9.
34. Ward 1918: 115.
35. Rizzo 1926: 10–11; Lister 1926: 92: Carcopino 1968: 210–11.
36. Rennell Rodd 1925: 9.
37. Pollak 1994: 91–2 n. 4.
38. Anstruther-Thomson 1969.
39. Girton College Archives: Violet Paget/ES 17 December 1905.
40. Wellek 1966: 239–244; Samuel 1979: 25, 47, 89, 152–3, 168, 174–5, 255–6.
41. Wellek 1966: 244; Samuels 1979: 283–91.
42. Samuels 1979: 270.
43. Ibid.: 259–60.
44. Strachey and Samuels 1983: 16–30.
45. Ibid.: 67.
46. Einstein 1968; Acton 1970: 305–6.
47. Santayana 1945: 224–30.
48. Samuels 1979: 234–6.
49. Santayana 1945: 225.
50. Pottier 1932; Samuels 1979: 191–2, 263, 331, 383; Borowitz and Borowitz 1991: 248 n.13.

51. Conway 1932.
52. Girton College Archives: Mary Costelloe/ES 18 May 1895.

Chapter 5

1. *Quarterly Review* 1893: 61.
2. de Grummond 1996: 202–3; Flasch 1902.
3. Potts 1994; Brilliant 2000.
4. L. Curtius 1943–6: 29–30.
5. Praz 1995: 353.
6. Strong 1909: 6, 253.
7. Girton College Archives: Lawrence Alma-Tadema/ES 7 December 1895.
8. Girton College Archives: A. S. Green/ES 5 February 1893.
9. *EHCA* 475–6; Lullies 1988: 110–11; 1988a: 47–8; Marchand 1996: 110–11, 143–5.
10. Church 1908: 64–5.
11. Reinach 1907: 327; Schuchardt 1956: 23; Marchand 1996: 337.
12. Furtwängler 1895: vii.
13. Whyte 1929: 989–94.
14. Shirakawa 1992.
15. Lindsay 1907: Mengarini 1907.
16. Girton College Archives: M. Costelloe/ES 29 November 1896.
17. L. Curtius 1943–6.
18. Wadleigh 1910: 91.
19. Editorial 1971: 344.
20. Isager 1991.
21. Pollitt 1965, 1966 provide a good introduction to the use of such materials to interpret ancient art.
22. Schoder in Jex-Blake and Sellers 1967: E.
23. Schoder in Jex-Blake and Sellers 1967: E–K. For recent re-evaluations of Pliny the Elder and his work, cf. Isager 1991, Beagon 1992.
24. Jex-Blake and Sellers 1967: ix.
25. Furtwängler and Urlichs 1914.
26. Bather 1897.
27. Girton College Archives: Logan Pearsall Smith/ES 19 May 1895.
28. I Tatti Archives: ES/Mary Costelloe 21 February 1896.
29. I Tatti Archives: ES/Mary Costelloe 17 November 1895.

Chapter 6

1. Girton College Archives: Mary Costelloe/ES 23 October 1896.
2. Ibid.
3. Griffin 1992: n.1.
4. Tribble 1984.
5. Beard 2000.
6. I Tatti Archives: ES/Mary Costelloe October 1896.

7. Girton College Archives: Mary Costelloe/ES 17 March 1897.
8. Girton College Archives: Arthur Strong/ES 26 October 1892.
9. Girton College Archives: Arthur Strong/ES 7 March 1893.
10. Samuels 1979; Simpson 1987.
11. Crowe 1895; Sutton 1972; 188–9.
12. Sutton 1972: 18.
13. Girton College Archives: Charles Loeser/ES 27 July 1903.
14. I Tatti Archives: ES/Mary Costelloe 1896.
15. Girton College Archives: Mary Costelloe/ES 9 December 1898; Strachey and Samuels 1983: 79.
16. Samuels 1979: 2, 4–5,12–6, 39–40, 69–70.
17. Balcarres 1905: 7.
18. Baring 1922: 185.
19. Chapman 1972: 177; Ellmann 1988: 529–30. Rowland Strong was at a dinner with Esterhazy and Oscar Wilde, where Esterhazy supposedly confessed his involvement.
20. Dimier 1905.
21. Balcarres 1905. It is worth noting that on at least one occasion the Strongs invited the Zionist Israel Zangwell to dinner. Girton College Archives: Zangwill/ES 2 February 1902.
22. Lowndes 1905: 119.
23. Baring 1922: 185.
24. Girton College Archives: Letter of Recommendation by S. Reinach for A. Strong 23 November 1890.
25. *DNB 1941–1950:* 849–50; Anson 1949; Masterman 1975: 85–6, 128–9.
26. Girton College Archives: Letter of Recommendation by S. Schechter for A. Strong 14 November 1890.
27. Girton College Archives: Gertrude Bell/ES n.d.
28. Barry 1905; Chadbourne 1957.
29. Lang 1887.
30. Girton College Archives: Violet Markham/ES 5 May 1909.
31. *Journal of the Royal Asiatic Society* April 1904.
32. Ibid.
33. Sturge Moore 1905.
34. *DNB* supplement 2: 443. For Disraeli and the Young England Movement, cf. Weintraub 1993: 205–12.
35. Blennerhassett 1905: 632.
36. Santayana 1945: 36–7.
37. *The Times* 14 December 1897.
38. Girton College Archives: Lawrence Alma-Tadema/ES 15 August 1897.
39. Girton College Archives: S. Reinach/ES 2 August 1897.
40. Girton College Archives: Mary Costelloe/ES 29 October 1897. For the reaction of Vernon Lee, cf. Girton College Archives: V. Lee/ES 19 October 1897.
41. I Tatti Archives: ES/Mary Costelloe 17 April 1898.
42. Santayana 1945: 36.
43. A. Ponsonby 1943; Kuhn 2002.

44. E. Marsh 1939: 78.

45. Hazeltine 1949; Fifoot 1971.

46. Howe 1942: v. I, 22.

47. Auchmuty 1945.

48. Girton College Archives: daybook for 2 January 1895.

49. Thwaite 1984: 1–241.

50. Ibid.: 416–23; Girton College Archives: J. Badely/ES 29 November 1907. 'No, you will not meet me at the table of Gosse … for he has never forgiven me for telling him he ought to be more in the Library and less in the House.'

51. Beinecke Archives: Maurice Baring/ES 24 April 1925.

52. Courtney 1931: 91–104; Winstone 1978: 2–3, 6–11, 41–4.

53 Girton College Archives: S. Reinach/ES 1905.

54. Girton College Archives: Gertrude Bell/ES 30 September 1913; Winstone 1978: 53–65.

55. Girton College Archives: S. Reinach/ES 20 October 1907; ES/Florence Bell 8 July 1927.

56. Gathorne-Hardy 1963.

57. Munro and Stirton 1998; Girton College Archives: ES diary 11 February 1899.

Chapter 7

1. Fitzroy 1923: 6–7.

2. F. Thompson 1951: 12–19; Rowse 1983.

3. F. Thompson 1951: 19–28; Arnold 1994.

4. Bessborough 1955; Foreman 1998.

5. F. Thompson 1951: 29–31; Cannadine 1994: 167–81.

6. Hutchinson 1920; Magnus 1964: 270, 274, 316, 388.

7. Hutchinson 1920: 25.

8. Michaelis 1882: 276–7; Fürtwangler 1896, 1901; Sprigge 1960: 177.

9. Strong 1899: 328–9.

10. de Grummond 1996 576–8; Guarducci 1980; Moltesen 1987.

11. de Grummond 40–1; Rodenwaldt 1927.

12. Brendel 1979: 15–24; Potts 1994: 11–46.

13. Beckwith 1979: 127–36. Eugénie read with interest Wickhoff's volume soon after it was published. I Tatti Archives: ES/Mary Costelloe 21 February 1896.

14. Wickhoff 1900: 114.

15. Brendel 1979: 28.

16. *EHCA* 1192–3; Bianchi Bandinelli 1981: 242–6; Rosenhauer 1993: 363–4.

17. Brendel 1979: 28–35.

18. Schorske 1980: 234–6.

19. P. Gardner 1901; Boardman 1985: 49–50.

20. P. Gardner 1901.

21. de Grummond 1996: 958–9; Scarrocchia 1986: 25–6.

22. Brendel 1979: 25–6; Riegl 1981: 1; Bianchi Bandinelli 1996: 110–15.

23. de Grummond 1996 1061–2; Morey et al. 1942.

24. Morey et al. 1942: 460.
25. Ibid.: 461.
26. Clark 1974: 142.
27. BSR Archives: ES/Arthur Darby Nock 25 January 1924.
28. Strzygowski 1907.
29. H. Stuart-Jones 1905.
30. Girton College Archives: letter of agreement between Duckworth and Arthur Strong 18 February 1902.
31. Girton College Archives: Martin Hume/ES 15 May 1904.
32. Girton College Archives: Maude Cantwell/ES 23 November 1906.
33. Kleiner 1992.
34. Strong 1907: viii.
35. Girton College Archives: Adolf Furtwängler/ES 9 March 1907.
36. A. M. Daniel 1908.
37. Walton 1908.
38. Girton College Archives: R. Langton Douglas/ES 16 January 1907.
39. Girton College Archives: C. Loeser/ES 6 September 1907.
40. Girton College Archives: G. F. Hill/ES 31 May 1907.
41. Muirhead 1933: 39; Haskell 2000: 93–7.
42. Girton College Archives: A. Higgins/ES 5 April 1903.
43. Strong 1904: xv.
44. Haskell 2000: 94. For E. P. Warren as collector, cf. Sox 1991; Dyson 1998: 135–9.
45. Girton College Archives: Gilbert Murray/ES 18 July 1903.
46. Girton College Archives: Resolution of 26 May 1903.
47. Strong 1904: xiii.
48. Girton College Archives: Addy Furtwängler/ES 13 March 1903.
49. Cunningham 1927: 254–5.
50. *Journal of the Royal Asiatic Society* 1904; *The Times* 19 January 1904.
51. For Gleichen cf. *DNB 1922–1930:* 341–2. For the dedication, cf. Girton College Archives: Jack Badely/ES 11 July 1905.
52. Girton College Archives: *The Memorial to Arthur Strong, unveiled July 6, 1905.*
53. Ibid.
54. Balcarres 1905.
55. Girton College Archives: C. G. Hamilton/ES 21 April 1904, 14 November 1904.
56. Browning 1923; 158.
57. Bolitho 1933: 1–39.
58. J. P. Richter 1910; Bolitho 1933: 56–8, 75.
59. *DNB 1922–1930:* 602–05; Bolitho 1933: 56–8, 354–77.
60. Richter 1910; Bolitho 1923: 75–84; Pollak 1994: 53–7, 199–201.
61. Bolitho 1933: 166.
62. E. Strong 1928: v–vi; Ashmole 1994: 35.
63. F. Thompson 1951.
64. Sutton 1972: 710; Girton College Archives: Herbert Cook/ES 29 February 1907.
65. J. P. Richter 1910: 2.

66. E. Strong 1906: 254.
67. Girton College Archives: ES/? 1906.
68. Girton College Archives: Betty Lewis/ES 28 February 1906.
69. P. Gardner 1907: 251; Girton College Archives: A. R. Dryhurst/ES 15 October 1907.
70. Girton College Archives: V. Markham/ES 25 April 1908.
71. Percy and Ridley 1988: 157 n.4.
72. Girton College Archives: Violet Markham/ES 19 May 1909.

Chapter 8

1. Wiseman 1989: 4–5; Wallace-Hadrill 2001: 20–2.
2. Wiseman 1981: 146–50; Wallace-Hadrill 2001: 22–7.
3. Wiseman 1981: 159; 1989: 6.
4. Smith 1931: 518–19; Wallace-Hadrill 2001: 28–34.
5. Lugli 1931: 518–19.
6. de Grummond 1996: 658–9; Smith 1931: 516; Hodges 2000: 22–5, 100–102.
7. Smith 1931: 517; Hodges 2000: 22–30. On Haverfield cf. Craster 1920; Hingley 2000.
8. Rennell Rodd: letter to *The Times* 20 May 1931.
9. Girton College Archives: Salomon Reinach/ES 7 July 1909.
10. Ashby 1927; Barker et al. 1986.
11. *EHCA* 1182–3; Blegen 1958: 164; Wiseman 1989: 6–7; Wallace-Hadrill 2001: 28.
12. Myres 1940: 471.
13. Browning 1923: 157–8.
14. *EHCA* 171–2; Tea 1932; Barbanera 1998: 82–6.
15. The Girton College Archives contain several letters from Boni's biographer E. Tea asking for personal reminiscences of the archaeologist: E. Tea/ES 14 May 1929, 19 June 1928, 21 November 1928, 13 June 1929.
16. Girton College Archives: Violet Markham/ES 22 December 1909.
17. Lister 1926: 85–6.
18. Girton College Archives: K. Jex-Blake/ES 19 November 1910.
19. Ibid.: M. Ponsonby/ES 3 December 1910.
20. Ibid.: Maude Stanley/ES 14 December 1910.
21. Gathorne-Hardy 1963: 249.
22. Macioti 1995.
23. Piantoni 1980; Caracciolo 1993: 291–2.
24. Strong 1911: 49.
25. Petricioli 1990: 91–148; Barbanera 1998: 97–106.
26. Lanciani 1894, 1897, 1988; Barbanera 1998: 86–90.
27. Girton College Archives: Robert Bosanquet/ES 8 October 1909.
28. E. Sellers 1895a.
29. Mrs A. Strong 1912.
30. Lutyens 1991: 101–2; Piantoni 1980: 270–3; Percy and Ridley 1988: 149, 211; Petter 1992.

31. Wiseman 1990: 10.
32. Petter 1992: 26–7; Hodges 2000: 45–6, 85–6.
33. A. Campbell 1988; Wallace-Hadrill 2001: 39.
34. Girton College Archives: William Hubbard/ES 12 July 1891.
35. BSR Archives: ES/E. Shaw 11 May 1914; Hodges 2000: 52–7; Wallace-Hadrill 2001: 41–50.
36. Dyson 1998: 50–1.
37. Girton College Archives: ES/Mitchell Carroll 17 May 1913.
38. Ibid.: press clipping file from AIA tour.
39. Ibid.: Louise Randolph/ES 11 January 1912.
40. Ibid.: Harold Parsons/ES 16 February 1914.
41. Hadley 1987: 503, letter of 30 September 1913.
42. Girton College Archives: Thomas Ashby/ES 14 November 1913.
43. Ibid.: ES/Mary Berenson 4 November 1913.
44. Wiseman 1990: 13; Wallace-Hadrill 2001: 53.
45. Girton College Archives: William Miller/ES 7 July 1914.
46. Ibid.: Robert Gardner/ES 3 September 1914.
47. Ibid.: Gilbert Ledward/ES 28 December 1916; Crawford 2001: 147.
48. Ibid.: Colin Gill/ES 6 January 1918; Crawford 2001: 147.
49. Ibid.: H. Bradshaw/ES 20 December 1916; Wallace-Hadrill 2001: 52–3, 59–61.
50. Ibid.: M. Hindenberg/ES 22 February 1915.
51. Ibid.: unpublished obituary of Emmanuel Loewy.
52. Ibid.: Azra Hincks/ES 14 July 1915.
53. Ferro 1973: 201–2; Bolton 1970: 177–85.
54. BSR Archives: ES/E. Shaw 13 December 1916.
55. Percy and Ridley 1988: 312.
56. BSR Archives: ES/E. Shaw 11 April 1917; Percy and Ridley 1988: 'Mrs Strong is in a very querulous and yah yah mood'.

Chapter 9

1. Mrs A. Strong 1915: v–vi.
2. Girton College Archives: biographical notes on Christian Mallet by Eugénie Strong.
3. BSR Archives: Lutyens/ES n.d.
4. Girton College Archives: F. Wyndham/ES 4 January 1914.
5. BSR Archives: Eugénie Strong postcard collection.
6. Girton College Archives: M. Berenson/ES 14 December 1913.
7. Ibid.: 'Etapes et Cambet', narrative on Christian Mallet; Robert Gardner/ES 3 September 1914.
8. Ibid.: Betty Montgomery/ES 12 October 1919.
9. Ibid.: Thomas Ashby/ES: 10 August 1920.
10. BSR Archives: Eugénie Strong postcard collection.
11. Girton College Archives: ES/Crum 6 August 1920.
12. Ibid.: Arthur del Care of the British Delegation in Vienna/ES 1 April 1920.

13. Sprigge 1960: 178.

14. Nogara 1943; Bolton 1970: 166.

15. *DNB 1922–1930:* 330–2.

16. Girton College Archives: Denis Sheil/Eugénie Strong correspondence. Typical of Father Sheil's approach was his advice after her first communion: 'It is perfectly natural that you should feel overwrought, but gradually you will learn to take everything quite simply and calmly. Religion is quite a humdrum affair very often.' D. Sheil/ES 17 February 1917.

17. Girton College Archives: ES/F. Gasquet 5 September 1918.

18. Ibid.: Robin Holloway/ES July 1918.

19. Ibid.: F. Gasquet/ES 6 June 1923.

20. Mitford 1968: 165.

21. Russell 1967: 37.

22. Mitford 1968: xii–xiii.

23. Speaight 1957: 159–60.

24. DeLuca 1949.

25. Curtius 1943–6: 32.

26. Türk 1996.

27. Girton College Archives: Betty Montgomery/ES 15 November 1919.

28. Ibid.: M. Berenson/ES 25 February 1917.

29. Ibid.: Florence Bell/ES 2 November 1926.

30. *DBI* 476–81; *Osservatore Romana* 17 June 1945; Barbanera 1998: 112–16, 131–6, 221–3.

31. Mrs A. Strong 1913: 5–15.

32. Mrs A. Strong 1915: 21–2.

33. Ibid.: 175–9, 222–8; Bianchi-Bandinelli 1988: 59–81.

34. Mrs A. Strong 1915: 205–13; Beard 2000: 28–9, 98–9.

35. Mrs A. Strong 1915: 231–2.

36. Warde Fowler 1916.

37. Stuart-Jones 1915.

38. *Journal of Hellenic Studies* 1916: 408.

39. Cumont 1922: xi; Lion 1927: 421.

40. Harrison 1918: 89–93.

41. Richardson 1992: 57; Coarelli 1995: 235–8.

42. Cumont 1918.

43. Strong and Joliffe 1924.

44. de Grummond 1996: 340; De Ruyt 1947; Nock 1947.

45. Mrs A. Strong 1915: 182.

46. *Religious Studies* 1973: 392; MacMullen 1981: 116, 122–3, 200 n.11.

47. Dodds and Chadwick 1963; Z. Stewart et al. 1964; Z. Stewart 1972.

48. Z. Stewart et al. 1964.

49. Girton College Archives: Arthur Darby Nock/ES 16 May 1937.

50. Carcopino 1968.

51. Carcopino 1926.

52. Carcopino 1944: 148–74.

53. Rostovtzeff 1927; Wes 1990; Shaw 1992; Dyson 1998: 196–9.

54. Watkin 1980: 118–20; Girton College Archives: Gerald Wellesley/ES 12 April 1927: 'I am afraid that the English are hopeless baraccophobes.'
55. Browning 1923: 205.
56. BSR Archives: Text of Eugénie Strong's British Academy Lecture on Bernini.
57. Girton College Archives: Leo Ward/ES 9 July 1920.
58. Ibid.: Fr Bede Jarrett/ES 1 January 1921.
59. Mrs A. Strong 1923: 5, 138–9; Girton College Archives: ES/Rev. Father 11 May 1923.
60. Barbieri et al. 1995.
61. Goldsmith 1984: 124.
62. Leach 1988; Clarke 1991; Ling 1999.

Chapter 10

1. Goldsmith 1984: 273.
2. Boethius 1943.
3. Petter 1992.
4. BSR Archives: ES/E. Shaw 17 June 1924.
5. Hodges 2000: 70–1.
6. Hodges 2000: 71–6; Wallace-Hadrill 2001: 61–4.
7. BSR Archives: ES/E. Shaw 5 June 1924 and 17 June 1924.
8. BSR Archives: Memo of ES to E. Shaw and T. Ashby 22 September 1922.
9. BSR Archives: Undated memo of ES to E. Shaw and T. Ashby; ES/E. Shaw 11 August 1922.
10. BSR Archives: E. Shaw/ES 31 October 1922.
11. BSR Archives: clipping from 12 June 1924 issue of *La Tribuna*.
12. BSR Archives: E. Shaw/ES 15 October 1919.
13. E. Sellers 1892a; I Tatti Archives: ES/B. Berenson 6 April 1939.
14. Girton College Archives: Violet Mond/ES 18 July 1924; Wallace-Hadrill 2001: 64–6.
15. BSR Archives: Rennell Rodd/E. Shaw 25 October 1924.
16. Ibid.: minutes of the subcommittee 4 June 1924.
17. Ibid.; Hodges 2000: 76.
18. BSR Archives: E. Shaw/ES 12 June 1924.
19. Ibid.: E. Shaw/ES 25 June 1924.
20. *DNB 1922–1930:* 106–9; Esher 1923, 1938; Wiseman 1989: 12; Wallace-Hadrill 2001: 38.
21. BSR Archives: Blomfield/E. Shaw 16 October 1924.
22. Ibid.: Smith, 'Summary of Points Raised and Comments on Memo of Sr Reginald Blomfield'.
23. Ibid.: Rennell Rodd/E. Shaw 8 November 1924.
24. Ibid.: E. Shaw/Esher 1 November 1924.
25. Girton College Archives: H. K. Mann/ES 7 October 1924; D. J. Cameron/ES 4 August 1924.
26. Girton College Archives: E. Howard/ES 12 May 1920.
27. Girton College Archives: ES/S. Reinach 23 September 1925. In later corre-

spondence Shaw placed varying degrees of blame on Strong. Hodges 2000: 81–2.

28. BSR Archives: E. Shaw/A. H. Smith 5 August 1931; Hodges 2000: 90–3.

29. BSR Archives: I. A. Richmond/E. Shaw 8 June 1931.

30. BSR Archives: E. Shaw/A. H. Smith 5 August 1931.

31. Girton College Archives: G. Wyndham/ES 11 February 1926.

32. Ibid.: autobiographical notes.

33. Ibid.: A. Mond/ES n.d.

34. Ibid.: ES/S. Reinach 23 September 1925. The identity of the lady is not given. It is almost certainly not Mrs Ashby, since she did not have influence in such powerful circles.

35. Ibid.: ES/E. Maclagan 24 September 1925.

36. Ibid.: ES/Thomas Strong 19 June 1925.

37. Ashby 1927; Lugli 1931: 289; Hodges 2000: 83–6.

38. Smith 1931: 517; I. A. Richmond in Ashby 1935; Hodges 2000: 84–5.

39. Girton College Archives: ES/Stuart-Jones 27 August 1926: 'Don't you think the university or his college can be induced to do something for Ashby. It is not in the least that he is in financial difficulty, far from it. But for the honour of England, this great scholar should fill some sort of post.'

40. *The Times* 21 May 1931; Hodges 2000: 1–2.

41. Girton College Archives: Tisserant/ES 28 October 1935.

42. Potter 1979: 1–18.

43. Ashmole 1994: 36–9; Wallace-Hadrill 2001: 72–7.

44. BSR Archives: minutes of Executive Committee 4 December 1924.

45. Girton College Archives: ES/Bernard Ashmole 22 December 1926. In the end her judgment of Ashmole was very negative. In a letter to Bernard Berenson (I Tatti Archives: ES/B. Berenson 6 April 1939) she observed of his new appointment at the British Museum, after a scandal associated with the 'cleaning' of the Elgin Marbles, 'I should admire the talent of a man, who like the new keeper, sees an occasion for his own advancement in the troubles and misfortunes of others. He played this game successfully at the BSR in 1925.'

46. Girton College Archives: Tenney Frank/ES 20 July 1939.

47. Pollak 1994: 107.

48. Lion 1927: 414.

49. Wiseman 1989: 16; Hodges 2000: 92.

50. Girton College Archives: ES/S. Reinach 14 January 1929.

51. Wiseman 1989: 17; Hodges 2000: 92; Wallace-Hadrill 2001: 80–6.

52. Wiseman 1989: 17–18; Wallace-Hadrill 2001: 87–91.

53. Wiseman 1989: 18; Wallace-Hadrill 2001: 91–6.

Chapter 11

1. Lago and Beckson 1975: 111–12; Wallace-Hadrill 2001: 65–6.

2. Girton College Archives: article from *Daily News* 1 January 1927.

3. Oxford and Asquith 1928: 274–5.

4. Girton College Archives: ES/Thomas Strong 19 June 1925.

5. Ibid.: David Evan/ES 17 March 1927; Wallace-Hadrill 2001: 65.

6. Ibid.: ES/David Evans 25 March 1927; Harvard University Houghton Library: ES/William Rothenstein 15 April 1926.

7. L. Curtius 1943–6: 32.

8. Girton College Archives: Robert de Bonneville/ES 17 December 1932.

9. J. Y. Marsh 1929.

10. Ibid.

11. Boethius 1943.

12. Smith-Rosenberg 1985: 53–76.

13. Scott Thomson 1949: 100; Girton College Archives: Rennell Rodd/ES 7 January 1927, 29 December 1935.

14. Las Vergnas 1938: 88–133; Horgan 1970: 1–52.

15. Girton College Archives: Mary Lowndes/ES n.d.

16. Speaight 1957: 490.

17. E. Marsh 1939: 65.

18. Beinecke Archives: Maurice Baring/ES 1900.

19. Ibid.: 8 April 1939.

20. Hadley 1987: 329.

21. Ibid.: 330.

22. Mariano 1966: 42, 120, 244.

23. Girton College Archives: B. Berenson/ES 1937.

24. Sprigge 1960: 177.

25. Berenson 1954.

26. Mariano 1966: 296–320.

27. Goldsmith 1984: 136, 190.

28. Girton College Archives: ES/D. S. MacColl 20 December 1920.

29. Ibid.: D. S. MacColl/ES 18 January 1891.

30. Ibid.: 15 December 1920.

31. Ibid.: ES/D. S. MacColl 20 December 1920.

32. de Grummond 1996: 342.

33. R. Faber 1995; Marchand 1996: 196–7, 275–6, 335–6, 355–6.

34. Evans 1970: 85–145.

35. Ibid.: 112–24; Marchand 1996: 313–14, 361–2.

36. Ashmole 1994: 42–3; Wallace-Hadrill 2001: 73–4.

37. Dyson 1998: 145–50.

38. Richter was to write Strong's obituary for the *American Journal of Archaeology*.

39. Pollak 1994: 15–33.

40. Magi 1955–6.

41. Girton College Archives: Stanley Casson/ES 1 August 1922.

42. Reynolds 1991.

43. She published the results of that research in *The Hadrianic School* (1934).

44. Berg 1996.

45. Woodbury 1985.

46. Gabrieli 1966; E. Wilson 1966.

47. Praz 1979.

48. Girton College Archives: ES/Israel Gollancz November 1922.

49. Van Nuffel 1995: 39–58.

50. Ibid.: 9–18.

51. Ibid.: 151. The essay was published in Kochnitzky 1983.

52. Girton College Archives: ES/E. Curtius 3 July 1929.

53. Mrs A. Strong 1928b.

54. J. Y. Marsh 1929.

55. E. Strong 1928: ix.

56. Ibid.

57. Toynbee 1928: 236.

58. E. Strong 1928: viii.

59. Girton College Archives: ES/F. Poulsen n.d.

60. Ibid.: M. Wheeler/ES 6 September 1935. On the excavations at Maiden Castle, cf. Hawkes 1982: 162–77.

61. Drower 1985: 199–230, 375.

62. Girton College Archives: ES/F. Petrie 2 February 1928.

63. Kleiner 1992.

64. Girton College Archives: ES/Methuen n.d.

Chapter 12

1. Berenson and Marghieri 1989: 172–3.

2. Cannistraro and Sullivan 1993.

3. Girton College Archives: ES/Henry Furst 23 September 1925.

4. Ibid.: ES/Aline Lion 29 December 1926.

5. Ibid.: Josephine Ward/ES 26 October 1926; Scott Thomson 1949: 102.

6. For a general study of the appeal of Fascism in Europe, cf Hamilton 1971. For Fascism and America, cf. Diggins 1975.

7. Rennell Rodd 1925: 249–50.

8. Praz 1952: 381.

9. Hamilton 1971: 257–90.

10. Wiseman 1989: 19; Girton College Archives: Rennell Rodd/ES 25 June 1936.

11. Munoz 1934; Paribeni 1935.

12. de Grummond 1996: 502.

13. Giglioli 1928.

14. Girton College Archives: ES/Sylvia Sturre 23 December 1934, Lowndes/ES n.d.; Berenson and Marghieri 1989: 17, 134–5; Barbanera 1998: 143–4, 150.

15. MacDonald 1982; Manacorda and Tamassia 1985; Gentile 1994: 146–54.

16. Cederna 1981: 1–103; Manacorda and Tamassia 1985.

17. Girton College Archives: ES/C. Hudson 31 March 1926.

18. Stone 1999: 214–20.

19. Tweedsmuir 1940.

20. Buchan 1937: 7–9; Tweedsmuir 1940: 198–9.

21. Scott Thomson 1949: 102; Girton College Archives: ES/Arnold Wilson 21 January 1938, M. Lowndes/ES 14 February 1940. Buchan's interpretation of Augustus was one of the reference points for her last article on Augustan art. E. Strong 1938.

22. Girton College Archives: R. Syme/ES n.d.; E. Strong 1938: 138 n.2a.
23. Raaflaub and Toher 1990; Alfoldy 1993; Bowersock 1994.
24. I Tatti Archives: ES/M. Berenson 23 June 1938.
25. Girton College Archives: R. Collingwood/ES 15 May 1934.
26. M. V. Taylor quoted in *Capitolium* 1937: 57.
27. Pallottino 1937: 519; Barbanera 1998: 146–7.
28. Pallottino 1937: 519.
29. E. Strong 1939.
30. *The Tablet* 28 October 1938, 5 November 1938, 10 December 1938, 31 December 1938.
31. Girton College Archives: ES/S. Jans 27 August 1926.
32. Scott Thomson 1949: 112; Girton College Archives: F. J. Kenyon/ES 30 May 1938.
33. Manacorda and Tamassia 1985: 196–205.
34. E. Strong 1938: 1.
35. Nogara 1943.
36. Pollak 1994: 56.
37. Girton College Archives: L. Pollak/ES 10 June 1938.
38. Bianchi-Bandinelli 1996: 112–30; Barbanera 2003: 149–53.
39. Acton 1970: 24–5, 68–80.
40. For Van Buren, cf. Valentine and Valentine 1973: 100, 105–6. For Berenson during the war, cf. Mariano 1966: 268–95.
41. Girton College Archives: M. Lowndes/ES 9 May 1941, 22 July 1941.
42. Ibid.: 18 September 1940.
43. Lehmann 1945; Brilliant 2000: 9–10.
44. Girton College Archives: Mary Lowndes/ES 12 October 1939, 28 July 1940.
45. L. Curtius 1943–6.
46. Strong n.d.: 7 n.1.
47. Strong n.d.: 29.
48. Girton College Archives: Mother Mary Amadeus/C. Leigh Smith.
49. Ibid.: 16 October 1943 provides a list of the most regular visitors.
50. Ibid.: Axel Boëthius/C. Leigh Smith 10 October 1943.
51. Ibid.: ES/Conte Calza Bini n.d.; Praz 1952: 383–4.
52. Praz 1952: 383–4.
53. Boëthius 1943.
54. Pollak 1994: 18.
55. Praz 1952: 384.
56. Girton College Archives: Mother Mary Amadeus/C. Leigh Smith 16 October 1943.
57. Masson 1965: 317; *Touring Club Italiana: Roma* 1993: 292.
58. Pollak 1994: 10, 106 n.21.
59. *The Times* 21 September 1943.
60. *Star* 21 September 1943.
61. Girton College Archives: letter of D. S. MacColl to *The Times* 22 September 1943.
62. Ibid.: news clipping from an unidentified Italian newspaper.

63. *41st Annual Report, BSR, Faculty of Archaeology, History and Letters 1945–6.*

64. Picard 1944.

65. Jolliffe 1943; Toynbee 1943; Richter 1944.

Afterword

1. Dyson 1998: 223–8.

Index

237